# CREATING THE
# ADVERTISING MESSAGE

# CREATING THE ADVERTISING MESSAGE

Jim Albright
*University of North Texas*

**Mayfield Publishing Company**
Mountain View, California
London • Toronto

Library of Congress Cataloging-in-Publication Data

Albright, Jim.
  Creating the advertising message / Jim Albright
      p.      cm.
  Includes index.
  ISBN 0-87484-884-9
  1. Advertising copy.  2. Advertising campaigns.  I. Title.
  HF5825.A43   1991
  659.1—dc20                                             91-14088
                                                         CIP


Manufactured in the United States of America

10 9 8 7 6 5 4 3 2 1

Mayfield Publishing Company
1240 Villa Street
Mountain View, California 94041

Sponsoring editor, C. Lansing Hays; managing editor, Linda Toy; production editor,
Carol Zafiropoulos; manuscript editor, Joan Pendleton; text and cover design, Vargas/
Williams/Design. This text was set in 10½/12 Janson by Thompson Type and printed
on 50# Finch by R.R. Donnelley and Sons Company.

Cover illustration: The Image Bank/West/Matt Zumbo © 1991

Text and photo credits appear on a continuation of the copyright page, p. 286.

# C O N T E N T S

CHAPTER 6   **WRITING FOR TV   93**

In a perfect world, the copywriter who writes least, writes best. Hours devoted to researching the target market, the client's service or product, and the competition *should* lead to a creative strategy that is stronger than garlic. The creative strategy should birth copy that writes itself.

It's *not* a perfect world. Is anything harder to teach than creative strategy? Most working copywriters seem to hit upon strategy instinctively, though beneath that instinct lies an unconscious formal structure. Teaching strategy is like asking a movie star how to be appealing; it's like shoveling smoke.

This book on copywriting is the result of eight years of college teaching added to 25 years as a copywriter and creative director on local, regional and national advertising for major and non-major agencies. Its purpose is to translate instinctive smoke into hard methodology. I started teaching with the typical professional's overconfidence, slowly becoming aware that things need to be spelled out for students. I've emerged humbled and dedicated to writing down what seems impossible — the teaching of strategy. Compared to strategy, teaching actual execution — the copy for print and broadcast — seems like a piece of cake.

This book goes into the actual writing of copy and the format to showcase that copy, true. But my experience also reflects what most copywriting teachers know — that once a strong strategy is created, the copy could in fact write itself. Perhaps the writing is so easy because most students taking copywriting in an advertising sequence, either as a required or elective course, already have good writing skills. On the other hand, a beautiful piece of copy aimed at faulty strategy is not a beautiful piece of copy at all. That's the premise of this book: Find a good strategy, and good copy and execution will inevitably tumble into place.

Furthermore, I think a copywriter's experience in education and just plain living are part of his or her craft. To that end, the book attempts to cover the major day-to-day situations facing a copywriter and the social, educational and philosophical realities of copywriting. I believe the copywriter — corporate or agency — is a Renaissance person. On any account, the copywriter is the one who should know all: all about the product or service or cause, all about the advertising category, all about the competition, both real and ancillary, all about the target market and all about life. How else can a 25-year-old copywriter convince a client to agree to a budget based on that copywriter's vision?

The first chapter makes the point that copywriting is actually copy thinking and informs the student that whatever is brought to copywriting will count for success in writing advertising. The chapter is meant to show the student that a liberal education and knowledge of current affairs is as necessary to good copywriting as knowing how to structure a TV script.

The second chapter dives into creative strategy, stressing the Creative Work Plan and the thinking that goes into formulating that document. I've known good college copywriting teachers — fine copywriters in a prior life — who say strategy is too tough for basic students. I hope I am not tilting at windmills in introducing the concept of strategy to basic students; to teach copywriting without teaching strategy is to teach a temporary skill in a vacuum.

The third chapter covers campaigns in general, what they are and why we talk about them. Students who don't have the concept of a campaign down at the start might be only making ads rather than planning a long-term effort.

The fourth chapter introduces writing concepts that are similar in all advertising media, so the student will realize that an ad is an ad is an ad and that only the formats change according to medium.

The fifth chapter begins with print advertising because print still determines who is a great copywriter. Someone who can persuade — grammatically — on paper should have no trouble graduating to broadcast or outdoor; the opposite may not be true.

Chapters 6 through 9 concentrate on TV, radio, collateral materials and outdoor. Included in the TV and radio chapters are segments on production and jingle writing.

Print production is covered generally in the tenth chapter, along with exploration of the very real and necessary relationship between copywriter and art director.

Because presentation is a daily affair in the advertising business, agency or corporate, creative or noncreative, the eleventh chapter is devoted to that subject.

Chapter 12 is a matter of priorities: in the 3- to 5-hour courses I have taught, there has been less room for intense examination of the admittedly important areas of PR, newspaper and transportation advertising, promotion, business-to-business, specialty advertising, Yellow Pages, etc. than full chapter coverage allows.

The thirteenth chapter is our secret, because it explores the area most likely to revive the accusations of "Trade School" — getting a job and the sample book. We've gone this far, why not go all the way?

## Acknowledgments

These efforts have been midwifed for three years by a sensitive, intelligent crew of reviewers who have gently steered a new textbook writer into what I hope is a good apprenticeship, to wit: Lee Bartlett, Brigham Young University; Lawrence Bowen, University of Washington; Tom Duncan, Ball State University; Tom Jordan, San Jose State University; Ann Keding, University of Oregon; Walter Lubars, Boston University; Deborah Morrison, University of Texas at Austin; Barbara Mueller, San Diego State University; Joseph R. Pisani, University of Florida; Tommy Smith, Texas Tech University; Donald H. Stoffels, University of Wisconsin; Lee Wenthe, University of Georgia; Willis L. Winter, University of Oregon; Eric J. Zanot, University of Maryland; and Fred Zandpour, California State University at Fullerton. I am very grateful for their invaluable suggestions.

I wish to acknowledge the contributions of a diverse lot of people who made this book possible. Although the book was written without reference to any sources, obviously something or somebody along the way filled my brain with what was necessary to the writing.

That something is the advertising business, client-side and agency-side, which is the platform for all I know. It is a respectable, well-intentioned business, full of interesting and ethical people.

Some of those people include my bosses: Al Wilson at the Toledo Trust Company, Toledo; Frank Phillips at Phillips Associates Agency, Toledo; Bob Bloom and Bill Hill at Bloom Advertising, Dallas; Morris Hite at Tracy-Locke, Dallas; and Jim Heatherly at McCann-Erickson, Houston.

Some of those people were owners or managers of production houses, corporations and small businesses and friends with connections who gave me work during a long free-lance career. One in particular, Herb Stott of Spung-buggy, accelerated my career and helped me in some bad days.

Some of those people were art directors and copywriters with whom I worked: Betty Dunagan, Bob Boatman, Jack Ciaccio, Peter Rosler, Polly Bohmfalk, Howard Karp, Jesse Caesar, Joe Kilgore, Ken Sutherland, Ed Kennard, Ben Carter, and many others.

The most important people were the people of America, the most receptive people on Earth to a good advertising idea, and the most discriminating when exposed to bad ideas.

*To*    Krispen, who took a chance on me in marriage and on this book in her classes

Jimmy, Becca, Rachel, Naida, Kate, Adam and Lucky, who patiently suffered lack of attention because of this book

My dad, Harold Albright, for all the right reasons

Henry Hager, Missouri professor and friend, who first edited the manuscript for this book

Ron McQuien, art director, who taught me to think like a copywriter

Lansing Hays, editor and guide through a most unusual four-year trip

Former and present students, whose questions led to this book and who inspire me to be a better teacher

# CHAPTER 1

# COPYWRITING, AN OVERVIEW

Some copywriters might think that *Creating the Advertising Message* is a dumb title for this book. It's so pretentious: "creating" should be left to God, and "advertising message" sounds so vague.

But the word **copywriting** is unduly restrictive in describing what copywriters do. They don't *write* all that much. They *think* a lot; and when they finally have something to say, they write it—usually on one page and usually without taking too much time, unless they're writing a business film, an annual report, a brochure or something else of great length. In fact, some copywriters think it a great achievement to write a TV commercial with no words at all, except for a slogan, plus music and pictures. Others are proud of a magazine ad with no words, only a great picture, dreamed up by the copywriter. The Nike catalog page shown in Figure 1.1 is a good example.

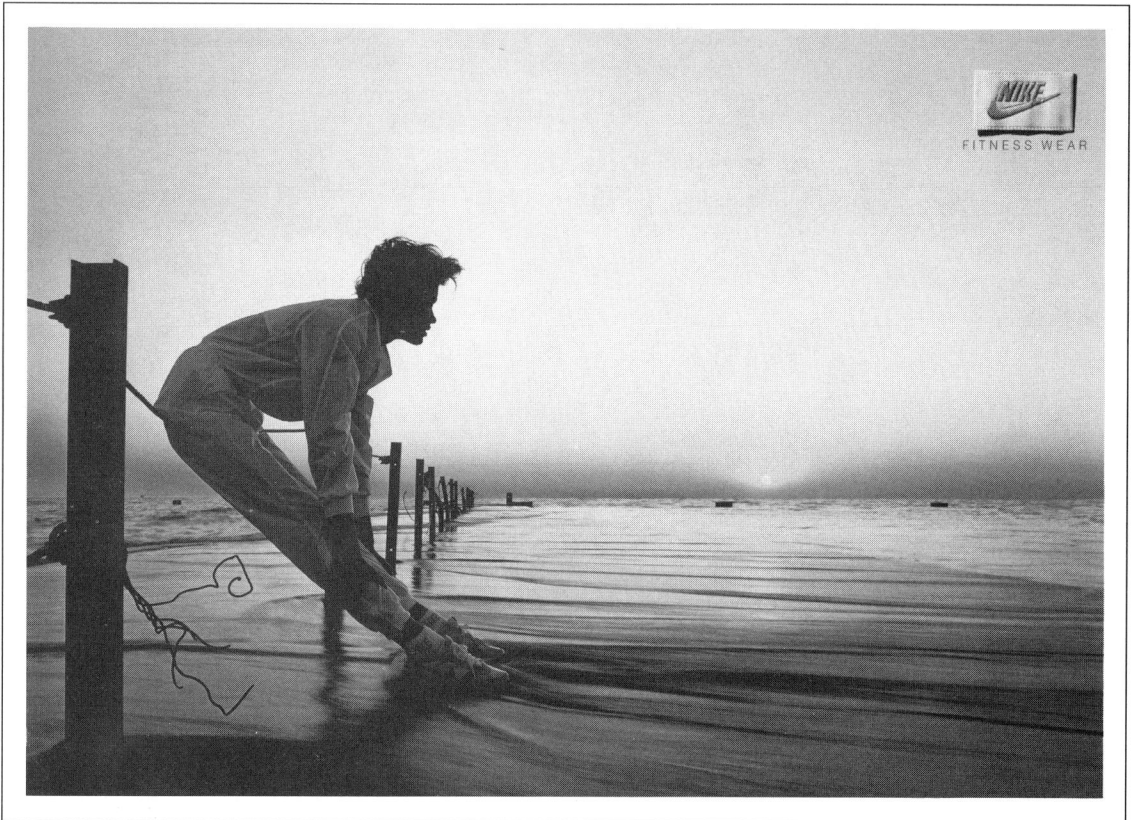

1.1 *Though a catalog page, this Nike advertising is similar to the wordless advertising Nike has presented on outdoor boards.*

Obviously, if a copywriter can come up with a print ad that doesn't have words, the ad wasn't "written" in the standard sense of writing, but "created." Hence: Creating.

Moving on to the rest of the title, someone might ask you, "What do you create?" You don't want to have to say, "I create TV and radio commercials, magazine and newspaper ads, **outdoor** advertising, bus bench ads, subway posters, direct mail materials, brochures and other collateral materials, shelf liners, short and long video presentations, point-of-purchase displays, skywriting and a bunch of other stuff."

## GENERAL ATTITUDES TOWARD ADVERTISING

Consumers might say they've had it with advertising. By some estimates, it invades their eyes and ears and noses (in scented ads) 1,500 or more times a day. You would think that the last thing consumers would want is somebody teaching you to write *more* advertising.

Curiously, consumers seem to enjoy certain advertising—witness their logo-covered clothing, listen to them talk about their favorite TV spots. You can read the lives of some consumers by the advertising on their cars, from vanity license plates that reveal personality (Ima Doc), to signs and bumper stickers that proclaim political views on candidates, gun laws, nuclear weapons and other issues. Some people want to tell you where they've been as tourists, what organizations they belong to, what their sense of humor is like (Bumper sticker: "I'm not a cowboy. I just found this hat"). If asked, many of these same consumers would say they don't like advertising and are not affected by it.

Most consumers seem to appreciate good advertising. The goal of the copywriter should be to write that small percentage of advertising that not only sells but also is popular with the consumers who buy the products and services advertised and with the clients who pay for the advertising. Such advertising is popular with consumers because it provides needed information in an intelligent, interesting way. It is popular with the client because it creates profits by stimulating demand for the client's product or service. Unfortunately, much advertising can be, and is, written by amateurs—amateurs who own their own businesses or amateurs in the advertising business. Although consumers often appear to know the difference between the good stuff and the bad stuff, they may judge our craft by the bad.

Advertising professionals, many of them—maybe still a majority of them—entered the business without a degree in advertising. They learned advertising on the job. That's not bad. The same kind of on-the-job training was once also true of bankers, stockbrokers and journalists—for lawyers as recently as the turn of the century. Even movie actors have been known to learn political science on the job. That advertising is a relatively recent academic discipline doesn't make it less worthwhile than banking, hotel management, engineering or any other recognized vocation. More and more advertising professionals, regardless of background, are beginning to appreciate the advertising degree, if the number of graduates who find jobs in their chosen craft every year is any indication.

In fact, advertising is not all that recent as an academic discipline, except as a major. Walter Williams, founder of the world's first school of journalism at the University of Missouri in 1908, insisted that advertising courses be part of the journalism curriculum. Today, advertising is a respectable degree program at many universities. The advertising degree program is heavy in liberal arts—maybe heavier and more diverse than an English degree—with a maximum of only 25 percent of total college coursework allowed to be taken in advertising or journalism. Even so, many advertising professionals may not appreciate the edge in skill an advertising degree can give to entry-level ad people. Advertising as an academic discipline is still a curiosity to many advertising professionals.

Advertising is the art and science of selling, one step removed from face-to-face selling. It's half business and half show business, both stressful and fun, but its bottom line is persuading people to buy products, services or ideas. It's possible that your friends and relatives, along with many other

Americans, consider advertising practitioners to be on a status level with used-car salespersons and lawyers, who have traditionally low rankings. But some lawyers become judges and some salespersons buy dealerships and run for mayor. Then they gain status. In the minds of many people, however, a successful advertising person, because of the selling orientation, is especially manipulative, cunning and devious. When friends and relatives realize that advertising is a part of marketing, which is a part of business, your chosen craft may seem more respectable to them. But have no doubt that the image of advertising needs much improvement before the craft earns the respect it deserves.

## HELPING ADVERTISING'S IMAGE

David McHam, a well-known journalism professor at SMU, advises new professors of any subject that "Before you can be a good professor, you have to be a good person." That's easy for *him* to say—he's a good person. When you think about it, the same thing is as true for copywriters as it is for professors. Perhaps it's more so, because although professors, through teaching, research and publishing, may influence thousands of minds a year, some copywriters influence millions of minds a week. If you're not a good person, you can do much damage.

What McHam is talking about is a matter of ethics. Many occupations, including advertising, have published standards of ethics. But advertising is so pervasive and so often created by non-advertising persons that the ethical practitioners are often blamed for unethical advertising. The criticism is disturbing to the teachers, practitioners and students of advertising.

So if you translate "being a good person" to holding to ethical behavior in advertising copywriting, you can do your part to help advertising's image. It's a matter of attitude—not only the obvious attitudes on matters of racism, sexism and social stereotyping, but more subtle attitudes as well. Your attitude toward life in general is important, for instance, because a bitter, cynical copywriter couldn't write "The Color of Life" or "The Color of Kids" for Kodak (Figure 1.2). It takes an open heart to see into the exuberant character of people and families as reflected in Kodak advertising.

There are many other examples. GE's "We Bring Good Things to Life" campaign is all heart, all instinct about humans, all insight into the finer parts of the human condition. GE advertising, too, explores the better parts of our nature by showing people and family scenes that ring true. There is a sensitivity in these, as in McDonald's and many other advertisers', that persuade you that a mighty fine person must have written the copy. You're also convinced that someone admirable approved it on the advertiser side. Your attitude determines whether your copy makes people feel good, brings a tear to the eye or a laugh, or does *something* to move us in some direction, such as buying a worthwhile product or service from a worthwhile company.

Your attitude toward the consumers matters because you can't sell to people you dislike or have no respect for. You have to be able to love them and

# KODAK FILM

## "THE COLOR OF LIFE" :60

ANNCR: (VO) Introducing Kodacolor VR-G. Now there's a film so real and alive

it can capture the color of life.

SINGERS: WE'RE ALL MOVIN' TO A DIFFERENT RHYTHM.

OUR HEARTS ARE BEATIN' TO A DIFFERENT DRUM.

THAT'S WHAT KEEPS THE WHOLE WORLD SPINNIN'

AND THAT'S WHAT MAKES THE WHOLE WORLD FUN.

DON'T YOU KNOW WE'RE ALL PART OF THE COLOR OF LIFE.

YOU MAKE IT SHINE SO BRIGHT.

DON'T YOU KNOW WE'RE ALL PART OF THE COLOR OF LIFE.

YOU MAKE IT FEEL SO RIGHT.

YOU'RE THE HEART.

YOU'RE THE SOUL.

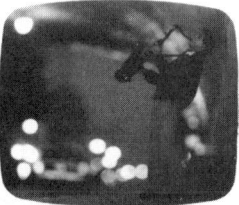

YOU'RE WHAT MAKES THE WORLD ROCK N' ROLL.

ANNCR: (VO) The most accurate,

realistic color in print film is here.

New Kodacolor VR-G. SINGERS: THE COLOR OF LIFE.

**1.2**   *It's hard to imagine a mean, insensitive person writing advertising that celebrates life the way these Kodak ads do. (Continues.)*

# KODACOLOR VR-G FILM
## "THE COLOR OF KIDS" :30

ANNCR: (VO) Introducing Kodacolor VR-G film.

SINGERS: WE'RE ALL MOVING TO A DIFFERENT RHYTHM

OUR HEARTS ARE BEATING TO A DIFFERENT DRUM

WE'RE WHAT MAKES THE WHOLE WORLD SPARKLE

WE'RE WHAT MAKES THE WHOLE WORLD FUN

DON'T YOU KNOW WE'RE ALL PART OF THE COLOR OF LIFE.

ANNCR: (VO) The most accurate, realistic color

in print film is here.

New Kodacolor VR-G.
SINGERS: THE COLOR OF LIFE.

their foibles so that you can effectively and gently persuade them to part with a few of their dollars for the product or service or cause for which you write.

Your attitude toward the product or service you're selling matters because you must find a reason why the product or service is worthwhile or else get off the account or out of that advertising agency or corporate ad department. Advertising people are often accused of taking money for selling anything that comes along. You will be glad to know, as a student and future advertising practitioner, that those you aspire to work for and with do not want to sell products, services or causes that have no ethical or rational basis. For one thing, it's unprofitable and a waste of time, in the long run, to sell inferior products. For another, all humans want to be associated with good things. Of course, many times the creators of advertising are naive about defects in products and are tarred with the brush of inferiority by association. Perhaps in the case of Exxon, the creators of its advertising were appalled by the 1989 oil spill in Alaska and wondered if it was worthwhile sticking with that account.

Your attitude toward learning matters because intellectual curiosity is a must for advertising copywriters. The best are truly Renaissance persons, interested in Beethoven and modern music alike, in formal, classic study as well as up-to-date pop culture. The mind of the informed and effective copywriter is attuned to art, music, film, football, opera, hiking, the evening news, nutrition, standup comics, Sunday comics, TV sitcoms, PBS and more, in equal measure — as many facets of American and earthly life as possible.

Your attitude toward writing, not only copywriting but also writing in general, matters — letters, books, plays, the whole range of writing. It should be an obsession, your all-consuming passion, to write. You should want to write when you're happy, when you're sad, when your other writing work is done and you're looking for a good time. A writer is a person who writes. It's that simple.

Your attitude toward advertising matters because a copywriter is a person who ghostwrites for products and services and ideas. Unlike novelists or magazine writers, who often start a project before making a deal for payment, copywriters know they will be paid. There is nothing to write until a **client** asks the advertising **agency** or advertising department for advertising. Furthermore, although there are restrictions on all kinds of writers and artists — even Michelangelo had creative restrictions laid down by the pope — the copywriter is loaded with must-do's: space and time restrictions; copy points to be included; deadlines; color and music to be used; budget problems; competitive advertising; opinions of your creative partner the **art director;** opinions of the copy chief, **creative director, account executive,** agency or company president and other managers, the client, the public and yourself. It's your job to mold all these factors into a cohesive, interesting advertisement. Advertising is the mouthpiece of business, a tool of capitalism. The combination of the love of writing and respect for capitalism makes a copywriter good at the job and a happy person.

All these attitudes help make the copywriter a good person who can be trusted not to take liberties with the consuming public. If you have these attitudes, the public's respect for your advertising cannot help but follow.

## WHAT ABOUT TALENT?

A little talent for creating and writing can't hurt; but some students, especially those who transfer from business school after making good grades there, cop out, saying "I'm not creative." They have made good grades in subjects that require learning what is already known, whereas copywriting depends on creating what has never been known. Even if you borrow from old movies or songs, the result is something new, something unique. But many students have said they were not creative and then become creative in half a semester, which would lead us to believe that learning experiences largely determine whether we can act creatively or can create for a living.

Yes, some people have an apparently natural aptitude for creating — and for using words — and some people don't. But there are people without that natural aptitude who do go on to create, and those with natural aptitude who fail because they lack the passion to create or because they don't behave ethically.

## CHECKLIST OF STEPS TO AN ADVERTISING MESSAGE

The copywriter normally goes through a checklist of steps to an advertising message when taking on a new copywriting problem or, as more optimistic people say, "a copywriting opportunity."

If a copywriter has been in an advertising agency or corporate ad department writing copy for some time, the following steps will be followed more instinctually than formally. But be assured that whether the checklist is in the head or on paper, it will be followed, because these steps are necessary to the kind of thinking that leads to persuasive advertising copy.

### Analysis of the Advertising Assignment

Perhaps the best way to start working on an advertising assignment is to ask, "Why does the client want to run this ad (or commercial)?" The obvious answers are "To help sell a product or service or cause" and "To make more money." All true. Ultimately, most ads (including radio and TV commercials, which are often called **spots** rather than ads) are run to make money for the client.

Some ads, such as ads for preventing forest fires or ads to discourage smoking and littering, are not necessarily run to make a profit. These are efforts, often contributed by advertising people without charge, that all advertising people can be proud of (Figure 1.3). Yet even some of these ads may ask for a contribution of money to help support a cause, and the ultimate effect on the consumer is similar to the hoped-for effect of ads run for profit. Of course, economic considerations are important even with "cause" ads, given the costs of fire fighting, medical insurance and state clean-up crews (in the case of the ads mentioned) to individuals and society as a whole. Still other ads may aim to improve the image of a corporation, influence legislators, or perform a public service, as in the case of a liquor company ad that asks people

# Words hit as hard as a fist.

"You're pathetic. You can't do anything right!"

"You disgust me! Just shut up!"

"Hey stupid! Don't you know how to listen."

"Get outta here! I'm sick of looking at your face."

"You're more trouble than you're worth."

"Why don't you go find some other place to live!"

"I wish you were never born."

Children believe what their parents tell them. Next time, stop and listen to what you're saying. You might not believe your ears.

**Take time out. Don't take it out on your kid.**

Write: National Committee for Prevention of Child Abuse. Box 2866E, Chicago, Illinois 60690

**1.3**

*This Ad Council ad is but one of many contributed by the advertising industry every year.*

to drink in moderation (Figure 1.4). Some may argue that successful ads of this nature will still make money for the client in the long run, and that is true in many cases.

But most of the time you will face a more traditional commercial opportunity on the part of a client who directly, or indirectly through your bosses,

# WHAT TO GET FOR THE PERSON WHO'S HAD EVERYTHING.

Having too much to drink is never a good idea. But if this happens to one of your guests, present him with a cab ride home. You'll be giving a gift that will insure many happy returns.

**1.4**

## The House of Seagram

*An ad for a cause, which is selling moderation, may be an image or public relations effort rather than an ad for profit.*

will ask you to write an ad or spot. And though the reason for writing the ad is generally to make money for the client, there is normally a more specific reason for the request for that particular ad or ad campaign. You need to know the reason before you go on to the next link of the advertising chain.

This is not the time to put paper in the typewriter or fire up the computer or put pen to legal pad — whatever your style — and start writing copy. This is the time to analyze exactly why an ad has been requested at this particular moment. And if you've been asked to write a TV spot, then you might ask why TV instead of a magazine or newspaper ad. To analyze the situation you may have to ask a lot of questions that might seem rude: "Is the client doing well in business? Are sales up? Is there a problem with this product? Is there a merger or a buy-out behind this? Is there a secret reason to run this ad — for instance, to influence legislators — that I should know about?" These certainly sound like impertinent questions from a copywriter, who may be right out of college; but a copywriter who doesn't know the answer can't create and write an ad that will go to the heart of the advertising problem or opportunity.

Your analysis of the advertising assignment should reveal to you in no uncertain terms why the client is going to the expense of paying you to write and paying others to produce materials — print or broadcast — and paying still others the costs to appear in TV, radio, newspapers, magazines, billboards or whatever. Here are some specific reasons why a client might want to run an ad:

- A restaurant has great breakfast and lunch business but wants to improve supper business.
- A university wishes to convince minority students that the university has the proper environment for minority needs.
- An American car company wants to reflect an increased concern with and improvement in quality (see Figure 1.5).
- A fast food hamburger chain wants to show specific nutritional information the public might not be aware of (Figure 1.6).

Once you know why the ad is to be written, you will understand the goal of the ad or ad campaign. If the goal turns out to be as vague as "We just want to keep our name in front of the public," then it might give you the opportunity to define a goal on your own that is more specific and productive (and maybe get you a raise for your clear thinking!). Such guidance from a copywriter is not uncommon. Your job may very well be to analyze and identify important things about your client that the client hasn't determined. You would do this along with other specialists in your agency or corporate advertising department, people who specialize in market research, media or account service.

Often the analysis of the situation will come to you all figured out and written out from the marketing director of your corporation or the account executive in an advertising agency, and you need only read and absorb the information — and question it if you feel the necessity to do so. Sometimes, if not directly, then indirectly through your account executive in an agency or your marketing director in a corporation, you will have to dig out the information from a client who knows advertising is needed but doesn't really know why or about what or to whom.

Whatever methods you choose to analyze your advertising situation are likely to involve some research, the next step.

**Reliability:**

Profile in quality #5. *For the 7th year in a row owners of Ford Motor Company cars and trucks have reported fewer problems, on average, than owners of any other vehicles designed and built in North America.* And this reliability is backed by Ford with a 6 year/60,000 mile powertrain warranty on all Ford, Mercury and Lincoln cars and Ford light trucks.*\*

FORD
MERCURY
LINCOLN

**One more reason
Ford Motor Company
has designed and built
the highest quality
American cars and trucks
for 7 years running.**

*Ford*

**Quality is Job 1.**

FORD · LINCOLN · MERCURY · FORD TRUCKS · FORD TRACTORS

*Based on an average of owner-reported problems in a series of surveys of '81-'87 models designed and built in North America.
**Restrictions and deductible apply. Ask your dealer for a copy of this limited warranty. **Buckle up—Together we can save lives.**

**1.5**

*Because the public may perceive foreign cars as higher quality, Ford faces that issue, an example of a specific reason for running an ad or an ad campaign.*

## Research

Most advertising research can be broken down to primary research and secondary research. **Primary research** may be as simple as eating a client's candy bar or as complicated as wiring sensors to an audience viewing TV spots to get an electronic readout of audience reaction to a commercial. **Secondary**

We shop where you shop.

Sara Lee

McDonald's

IT'S A GOOD TIME FOR THE GREAT TASTE.

For real.

McDonald's

IT'S A GOOD TIME FOR THE GREAT TASTE.

**1.6**   *McDonald's answer to public criticism of the quality of fast food. This is not only an advertising solution, but also a product improvement solution.*

**research** means searching out and absorbing material that already exists. An advertising problem may not require both kinds of research, but there is some research in every advertising assignment.

**Consumer Research**   What are the demographics (age, education, income, and so forth) of the prospective consumers—the **target market?** What are their buying patterns, their needs, their motives? Or, in the words of a popular research model called VALS, which goes beyond dry demographics, what are their values and lifestyles?

**Product Research**   What are the benefits of the product or service to the target market? What is the history of the product or service? Does the consumer know what it is and how to use it? Is it a new product that needs to be described in detail? Or an old one that needs reintroduction? These are questions you need to ask at a minimum. You will have more questions as you delve deep into the subject. The point is, you really should try to know more about the product than the client, though that may be an impossible goal because a successful client usually knows all there is to know about the organization's product or service. You can't know more than the engineers and the people on the front line, of course, but you can know more than the **marketing director** or the client representative. Yes, it's truly possible for you to get so involved in the product or service or cause that you know more than the specific person who hires you or your agency, more than the person who is calling upon your advertising department in a corporation for help.

But to be so aware, you have to do your research. A tour of toy and candy factories is not unenjoyable research, and you can learn a lot on such a research trip. Where you will have to be at your best, however, is on a tour of a brick plant. Let nothing you see go without full understanding of what is happening, and why. Then later, after you figure out your advertising approach, you will know more than enough to write the advertising without notes.

**Competitor Research**   Who are the competition? What do they do in their advertising? How is their product the same? Different? Better? Worse? Why should the target market buy your client's product rather than the competitors'? The answer to this question, of course, comes close to being your advertising campaign, but the answer might not be very clear when you first consider the question.

Sometimes you will be handed a pile of research along with the request for the ad you are to write. Sometimes you will get nothing, and will have to figure out what research you need. But research will always be a part of creating the advertising message.

## Creative Work Plan (CWP)

Although analysis and research are built-in first steps to solving the advertising assignment, this book formally starts (in Chapter 2) with the creative work plan. Whole courses are devoted to research, and much of the analysis we speak of here is covered in courses on marketing or advertising management. What is important is that you know to ask why advertising has been requested, and ask for any research that will help you understand the product, market, competition, and so forth.

It's likely in a copywriting course that your professor will explain the why's of the advertising assignment and the relevant research for any assignments you are given, just as your bosses or clients will explain such things to you when you receive an assignment on the job. If you are assigned the exercises in this book, much of the research will be up to you.

The **Creative Work Plan (CWP),** as you will see in the next chapter, includes a condensation of the relevant research and analysis. Sometimes alone, but usually in concert with your art director, your creative director and marketing people, including the client, you will be involved in assembling a CWP. The CWP functions as a short blueprint of what you need to know to attack the advertising assignment. It is valuable as a document that you, the client and your bosses can all agree upon, particularly the **creative strategy** part of the document — creative strategy being the overall theme or "way to sell," as opposed to the **creative execution,** the words and pictures on each ad. For example, the creative strategy behind Bud Light is to tell consumers to ask for light beer by name. The execution of Bud Light is a bizarre set of things that happen if you don't ask for a Bud Light by name.

With agreement on why the client is running the ad, on who the target market is, and on the creative strategy, you as a copywriter are ready to attack the actual copy you are going to write. But wait! Before you start writing down words, you and an art director will probably kick around some ideas so that you both agree on the general direction of the copy and the visuals.

## Preparation of Creative Work

As a student, you will not have an art director to consult with before you actually start writing the copy. But like most students, you will probably discuss your advertising problem with your roommate or friends, just as they discuss their term papers with you. That process will be similar to the give-and-take of creating an advertising execution with an art director. After you and your art director (or you and your roommate or you alone) decide what approach you are going to take, you will at last start writing the words in a script for TV or radio or in an appropriate form for print copy.

The way you write these words down — the **format** of your copy — is different for various media. Getting your words down in the proper format means you are approaching the end of the advertising chain, at least for the copywriter. After you and your art director, or you and your roommate, or you alone decide that the words you wrote are ready to be exposed to the world, you will have to expose them to your bosses and then your clients (or your professor) for approval. You will do so in a presentation, which could be as informal as a meeting over lunch or as formal as a meeting in a big room filled with people. Or, in a course, you'd simply turn in an assignment.

To put your words in proper context with visuals, you as a copywriter will have drawn little sketches called **thumbnails,** which will be very simple, even stick figures. If you have an art director, there might be comprehensive layouts for print or storyboards for TV to help your bosses and clients understand what the ads or spots will look like.

When this is all done, and all approvals have been secured, there is one last step.

## Production

If your ads are outdoor boards, after type is set and art is created or photography employed, somebody has to paint the outdoor bulletins or print the posters to go up on the outdoor boards. If you've created a TV spot, somebody has to shoot and record that spot. If it's a radio spot, somebody has to record it. If you've written a newspaper or magazine ad, somebody has to design the ad and order type and paste it down and get the camera-ready art to the proper place. Bus benches, bus signs, subway posters, direct mail, shelf liners in grocery stores, point-of-purchase displays — you name it, all advertising you write must eventually be produced.

Production of advertising materials — even jingles — will be covered in this book, but more superficially than analysis of an advertising problem, development of creative strategy and writing effective advertising.

## IN CONCLUSION

Copywriting as an occupation does not exist only in large and small advertising agencies or corporate advertising departments in banking or other industries. There are also jobs for copywriters in retail businesses such as department stores and in the media. Radio and TV stations may have "continuity" writers, who write (and often produce) scripts for clients without an agency. As a sales representative in newspaper or magazine sales, you might also find yourself writing copy for clients who have no advertising agency.

These four areas where you might practice copywriting — agency, corporation, retail store, or media — are different. But the job of copywriting in each area is not. The principles enunciated in the next chapters apply equally to all four areas, though on occasion we'll pay attention to some interesting and specific nuance of working in one of these areas.

*Creating the Advertising Message* has to do not with writing, strictly speaking, but with persuasion by any means. In the checklist of steps to an advertising message, note that only "Preparation of creative work" includes the writing. Art, design and many other jobs in this category are not writing jobs. This *is* a book about copywriting, but our intent is to show the incredible scope of knowledge and the amount of time spent on matters other than writing that is necessary before the proportionally small amount of time spent in the actual *act of writing* is taken.

Chapter 2 covers one of the most important links in the advertising chain: developing a CWP with a creative strategy that is "stronger than garlic," as some wordsmiths like to put it. Chapter 2 will concentrate on the creative work plan; the rest of the book will deal mostly with preparing creative work and production.

# GETTING THE CREATIVE STRATEGY

In Chapter 1 you learned that the first step to solving an advertising assignment is to analyze the problem, to start by asking the client (or account executive or marketing VP), "Why has this advertising been requested?" The more sophisticated ways to prepare a situational analysis, in an advertising plan prepared by an account executive or corporate marketing person, are beyond the scope of this book. For a copywriter intent upon creating an advertising message, this question is a solid first step in the preparation of a creative work plan.

The second step is research, a logical second step because once you know why advertising is to be created, you then have to educate yourself about the market, the product, the service, the competitors, and so forth, through either formal or informal research methods.

The third step is the writing of the Creative Work Plan (CWP), a big part of this chapter. The CWP has several parts,

17

the most important part being the creative strategy. Once you nail down a creative strategy and your client and fellow workers on the project approve that strategy, you are ready for creative execution and production of advertising materials (the fourth and fifth steps in the checklist of steps to an advertising message). These last two steps constitute the remainder of this book, for the most part.

Before we jump into preparation of a CWP, let's consider the implications of the words *creative strategy*.

## CREATIVE STRATEGY

Copywriters and art directors use a variety of words to describe the creative strategy, which is the main idea behind an advertising campaign. Words such as *idea* itself ("What's the idea behind this campaign?") or *hook, thrust, strategy* alone and very often the word *theme* will be heard in place of the words *creative strategy*. Account service and marketing people will often refer to "creative strategy" when talking to the creative people (copywriters, art directors, producers), who among themselves might be using one of the other words just mentioned. For clarity in this most difficult of advertising concepts, in this book the words *creative strategy* or *strategy* will be used.

Creative strategy is a plan for action, a statement of the one overall thought about a product or service to be left with the consumer. It's the idea that the ads and commercials and other advertising materials (the creative executions) explain. The difference between creative strategy and creative execution is important to keep in mind because you don't want to write a creative execution when it's a creative strategy that's wanted. For instance, the creative strategy of the California Raisin campaign is to position raisins as an alternative to other snacks. The creative execution of that strategy is to have the raisins posture and dance to the tune of "I Heard It Through the Grapevine."

To differentiate strategy from execution, think about football. A coaching staff would create a certain strategy (a game plan) for playing a team with a great passer and poor runners and a different strategy for a team with good runners and a poor passing game. So, against the team with the good passer, when an extra tackler is moved up to the line to rush the passer, that's strategy. When the tackler tackles the passer, that's execution. Obviously, the tackler is in no position to tackle the passer unless there is first a strategy to put him into position. Similarly, the copywriter is in no position to write (execute) advertising copy without knowing what the creative strategy calls for. The creative execution of the creative strategy is commonly thought of as copywriting, but it is only half of copywriting; developing a creative strategy is the other half.

Creative strategy leaves it wide open for the copywriter to create the execution in many ways. The strategy doesn't demand the use of humor or animation or any other kind of execution. It is a direction. It tells the copywriter what the overall plan is and leaves it up to the copywriter to find a way to execute the plan, even as the tackler has several options on how he penetrates the backfield to tackle the passer.

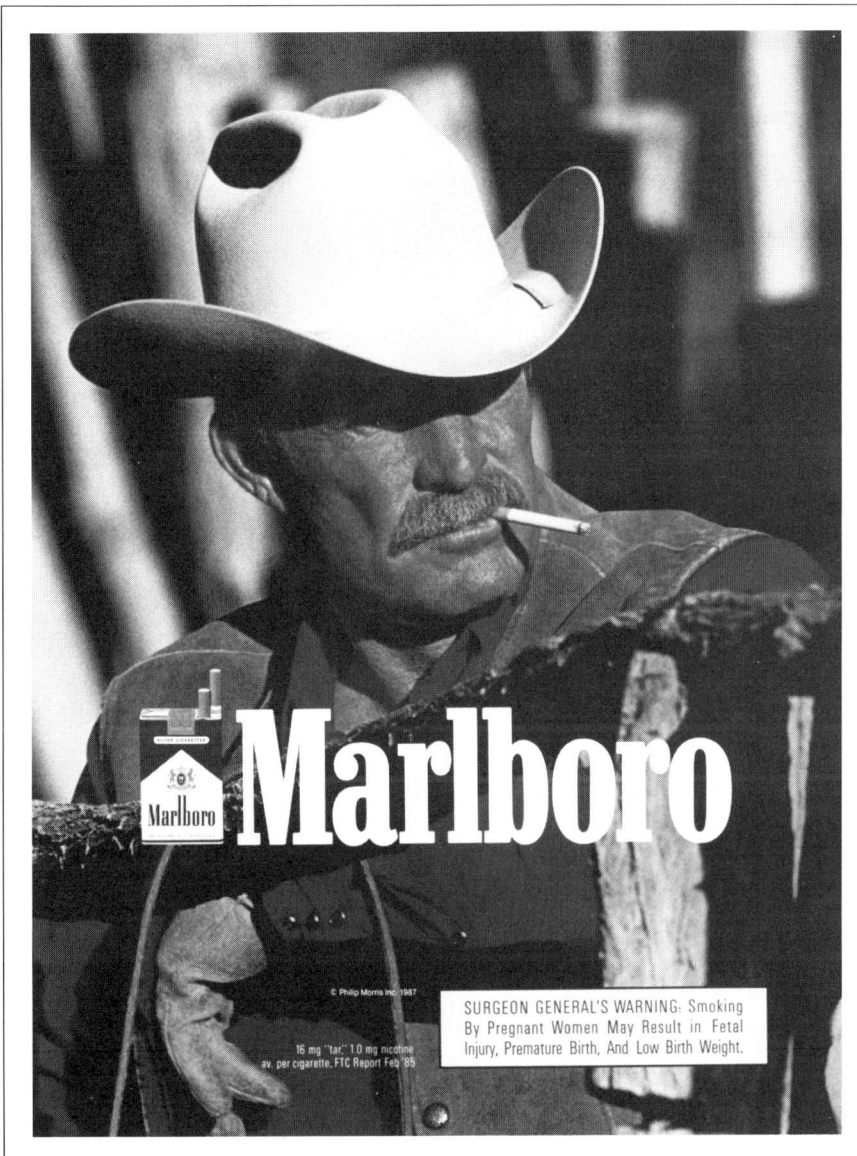

© Philip Morris Inc. 1987

16 mg "tar," 1.0 mg nicotine
av. per cigarette. FTC Report Feb '85

SURGEON GENERAL'S WARNING: Smoking
By Pregnant Women May Result in Fetal
Injury, Premature Birth, And Low Birth Weight.

**2.1**

*With a strategy of masculinity, the words and visuals will be similar in all the ads in the Marlboro campaign; there's not much for a writer to do except think up a new situation in a new locale.*

Although the copywriter should have a hand in formulating the strategy, sometimes the strategy is already set when the copywriter gets the call to write some advertising. Either you have been assigned to execute some new advertising for a campaign already running, or your account team in conjunction with your creative director and the client has formulated a creative strategy before you came aboard the account.

For instance, if you were the new copywriter for Marlboro cigarettes, you would already know the strategy: masculinity (Figure 2.1). You wouldn't have to develop a strategy. You wouldn't have to write copy, either, because

"Come to Marlboro Country" is usually the copy. What would you have to do?

Your job as the copywriter would be to dream up a new scene and situation: sitting around a campfire or crossing a river, for instance. (This situation illustrates how poor a job description is the word *copywriting*.) In such a case, the art director will probably dominate the creation process, given that new Marlboro ads contain mostly visual changes. Yet copywriters come up with good visuals and art directors come up with good headlines and copy approaches every day, so it would not be unusual for a copywriter to work on a new Marlboro visual. But nothing will be created at all without a strong creative strategy at first.

Marlboro advertising is shown and discussed here because it is a classic and clear example of a simple but powerful strategy, one that changed a cigarette with a feminine image in the early 1950s to a best-selling cigarette with a masculine image. Before the cowboy became the execution for this strategy, the ads used men with tattoos on their hands to carry the notion of masculinity, strange as that seems now. As to the ethical considerations behind using a cigarette ad in this book, I am not interested in foisting political or social theories on you; the book does discuss, later on, what to do if you are assigned to a project and you have objections.

## THE CREATIVE WORK PLAN (CWP)

Whether you help figure out the CWP for a particular product or not, as a copywriter you will have to follow a creative strategy as embodied in some version of the Creative Work Plan. Many agencies and companies have their own style of CWP. The one you are about to see is basically a CWP created by Young & Rubicam advertising agency, massaged a bit by Bozell advertising agency and tweaked by several professors into what you see here.

Some plans have more elements, some less. They're also called Copy Platforms. Some people consider the entire plan the creative strategy because it details target market profiles and other items that all contribute to the creative strategy. Some take a narrower view and consider the item marked *creative strategy* (number 7 in our example) to be the actual creative strategy. I take that narrower view, feeling that the overall effort is a work plan that includes number 7, creative strategy, with the other information supporting it. Number 7 will also be called the *consumer promise* in some other work plans.

Regardless of the variations in Creative Work Plans, they all serve the same purpose: they are a plan for action for creative, media, research and account personnel in an advertising campaign. By the time you finish this chapter, you should have a good idea of how to put together a CWP and how to come up with a creative strategy. Again, you may be handed a CWP containing a strategy, and you will move on to steps 4 and 5, writing and production. But for the many times you will have to work out the creative strategy, if not the entire CWP, here are nine items you will want to consider before beginning.

1. The correct name of the product or service or cause and why it's being advertised
2. What it's like to have tried the product or service
3. The history and philosophy of the client
4. The history, philosophy and advertising of the competitors
5. The history and philosophy of the industry involved (advertising categories like beer, banks or bras)
6. Whether the art director, copy chief and creative director feel positive or negative about advertising for this client
7. Whether agency management, including the account executives and account supervisors, on the account feel positive or negative about advertising for this client (You may be writing copy for a department store or a TV station or a magazine; in that case the titles of the management personnel will be different.)
8. Who your target market is, by demographics, psychographics and lifestyles
9. How you feel about this effort, because if you're not enthusiastic about what you're doing, you can't create your best work

As you will see, the answers to these thoughts will, when considered, be the basis for the rather formal structure of the CWP. Its bare bones can be listed as follows:

1. Client
2. Key fact
3. Consumer problem to overcome
4. Advertising goal
5. Principal competition
6. Target market
7. Creative strategy
8. Reason why
9. Mandatories

The following sections describe what is required for each step of the CWP.

## Client

When client name and the product, service or cause are synonymous, write only that, as in:

Avis
Chase Manhattan Bank
Mothers Against Drunk Driving

When the client has several brands under its corporate name, be specific, as in:

Ford, Mustang

ABC, television network

American Cancer Society, anti-smoking

If the product, service or cause is unfamiliar, explain how it works or what it is, as in:

American Brick Company, AMBRICO (partial and inexpensive brick siding)

Sweet Roll Delivery (a weekend breakfast delivery service)

Solidarity (a labor and political movement in Poland)

## Key Fact

The key fact is the *one* fact most relevant to the advertising of a given brand at a given time. It may relate to product performance or improvement or to consumer perceptions, attitudes or patterns of usage. The key fact may relate to competitive activity, marketing situations or economic trends; it may represent an opportunity or an obstacle. The following are examples of key facts:

Most people do not want to think about death, so it is hard to interest them in *funeral home* advertising.

People question the honesty of *car dealers*.

People perceive *malt liquor* as being stronger than beer in alcohol content.

Many people go to the *circus* at least once.

People like the music format and on-air personalities of a leading *rock radio station*.

The *typewriter* business is in the process of disappearing.

Buyers are confused by conflicting claims about *business computers* (Figure 2.2).

The key fact can often be determined by using common sense, depending on your knowledge of advertising and various advertising categories. If you know nothing about underwear or tools or whatever category the client is selling in, then you may have to research the consumers, the product, the competitors and the general marketing environment for the product, service or cause to come up with an accurate key fact.

## Consumer Problem to Overcome

The consumer problem is simply a key fact stated from the consumer's point of view; it is what keeps the consumer from buying or trying the product. A key fact may or may not describe a consumer problem; often it doesn't. The

**2.2** *Part of Apple's success in the business computer market may be due to copy as easy to read as the product is to use.*

consumer problem describes what the *consumer* needs, as opposed to a general key fact about the client or the client's advertising category.

For example, if the key fact on Sanka coffee (which is decaffeinated) is that the brand (and *all* decaffeinated brands) is healthier to drink, the consumer problem might be that people don't believe that Sanka tastes as good as regular coffee. Or, if the key fact is that the University of Whatever is in a convenient location, the consumer problem may be that students think the school is too big, too expensive, and so forth. Sometimes the problem is hard to identify, because the product is well-known and selling well. Campbell's soup had an unusual problem some years ago, when it discovered that people kept their shelves stocked with soup, but were not eating it. Campbell came up with a strategy to encourage eating more product, which seems obvious. Usually you ask people to buy the product and, if they do, you expect them to eat it. But Campbell had to go one step farther to move reserves of soup off America's shelves so that more soup would be bought. The slogan used in the campaign was "Reach for the Campbell's. It's Right on Your Shelf."

## Advertising Goal

As mentioned in Chapter 1, the copywriter's first question on a new assignment asks why the advertising is to be written. The CWP formalizes that question; if you're lucky, you'll be handed a CWP with the question answered, saving you some research.

The advertising goal should be obvious once you have asked "why" you are advertising and once you know the key fact and the consumer problem to overcome. If the key fact suggests a consumer problem and the consumer problem section confirms that suggestion, the advertising goal will be to act upon and overcome that problem. If the key fact shows consumer acceptance of the client, the advertising goal may be to urge the consumer to use the product in new ways or more often. (Arm & Hammer baking soda, for instance, ran a campaign that encouraged a new way to use the product — by putting an open box of baking soda in the refrigerator to reduce odors.)

Other advertising goals include getting the consumer to change ideas (perceptions), switch brands, try a new product, trade up, change a habit, add a brand to the shopping list, or simply try or become aware of a product. The advertising goal may be as simple as reassuring consumers they did the right thing in buying the client's product or service in the first place — for example, telling consumers that their high-priced automobile is a world leader. The key fact section and the consumer problem section should lead you directly to the advertising goal. Some examples follow:

Make customers more comfortable with their views on death, so they will be more comfortable with the service *funeral homes* are selling.

Expose the public to proof of a *car dealer's* honesty.

Maintain the public's perception of *malt liquor* as being stronger than beer (Figure 2.3).

Put forward the idea that the *circus* is a great once-a-year event for the whole family.

Communicate a *rock radio station's* leadership status.

Encourage trial of a *new toothpaste*.

Promote awareness of an established but seldom-advertised *restaurant*. (Hey folks, we're still here.)

## Principal Competition

You need not just a list of direct competitors (though you want to know their names) but also knowledge of what they are doing to take away business. Or, in reverse, you need to know what they are doing wrong that is bringing your client business. Discussion of competition should be broad enough to list economic, sociological or other external factors that could be competition. For example, if the product is a typewriter, the competition would most likely be word processors rather than other typewriters. In selling computers, the

**B&B**  BARTON & BOWLES
449 THIRD AVENUE
NEW YORK, N.Y.
(212) 754-6200

CLIENT: SCHLITZ
PRODUCT: MALT LIQUOR
TITLE: "BACHELOR PARTY/FP"
COMM'L NO.: SZML 0108
LENGTH: 30 SECONDS

(MUSIC UNDER)
FOUR TOPS SING: Tonight you're still a
bachelor, tomorrow's almost here.

So while you're still a free man, let's
bring on the beer . . .

KOOL AND THE GANG: Bull!

FOUR TOPS: Bull???

KOOL AND THE GANG SING: On this
night to remember, it's so clear.

You deserve to celebrate with more taste
than beer.

The bull's got a taste so big, so bold,
so smooth.

Let's all party with the Schlitz Malt
Liquor Bull.
ALL SING: Don't say beer, say Bull.

BACHELOR: Hey Gang how about
another Bull?

(SFX: CRASH)

(SFX: CRASH)

ALL SING: No one does it like the Bull!

**2.3**

*A bull breaking
through the walls of
a bar is the creative
execution of a creative
strategy that seeks to
reinforce a consumer
perception of malt
liquor as being stronger
than beer.*

competition might be fear of the unknown. In a campaign for Mothers Against Drunk Driving, the competition could be public apathy or even the belief that a lax justice system releases drunk drivers too soon. In a campaign for a TV station, the competition could be radio, movies, reading, VCRs, cable, and so on. The principal competition, then, is what keeps people from buying your client's product, service or cause, and it may not be a direct competitor as much as these other factors.

## Target Market

Who are the prime prospects for the product or service? What are their ages, their education, their income? What are their lifestyles, their prejudices? Where do they live? What media do they see? As a copywriter, you should imagine the face of someone in the target market hovering over your typewriter or computer. You must know that person extremely well, through personal experience or through research. Only then can you define the target market for the CWP. Knowing age, education and income is seldom enough. The target market's attitudes about life may well be much more important.

Think about exactly whom you'll be addressing. In the case of the funeral home, you're probably talking about people over 45. In the case of typewriters, you might be describing a very narrow bunch of consumers, people who resist new technology. In the case of the circus, just about anyone is a prospect. In the case of MADD, you could be talking to alcoholics, drug addicts, or so-called respectable people with disdain for law and/or little self-control. Or you might be talking to the non-drinking and driving part of the populace to influence them to vote for laws to take drunk drivers off the road. The target market depends, in part, on the advertising goal.

Your understanding of, and empathy for, the target market may be one of the most important aspects of copywriting. If you can put yourself in the potential consumer's shoes and head, you have a big head start when you start writing, because you know that person's hopes, dreams and aspirations. Your pitch should reflect that knowledge.

## Creative Strategy

Creative strategy is the "idea" behind the advertising campaign. Once you develop a creative strategy, you still don't know what the creative execution will be — the headlines, visuals and copy — but you have the essential first step to creative execution, because creative strategy gives direction to those efforts. The creative strategy is a spinal cord of continuity for an ad campaign. It's a blueprint for selling a particular product or service at a particular time. It's the answer to "You should buy this because. . . ." If your creative partners, your bosses and your clients don't agree on the creative strategy, *you have nowhere to go*.

The creative strategy is the promise to the consumer of the *unique* benefits of the product or service that set it apart from competing products and services in the marketplace. The creative execution is the way you bring to life the creative strategy. In the case of Schlitz, the execution is a bull blowing through the wall, a demonstration of power. Examples of creative strategy follow:

For Schlitz Malt Liquor: We will reflect power.

For Smith Funeral Homes: Death will be dealt with in a matter-of-fact way.

For Jones Typewriters: Identify with the consumer's dislike of new technology.

For MADD: You will be safer if alcoholic beverage advertising is banned.

Note that these four strategies leave plenty of room for the development of a creative execution, but still dictate a certain direction.

## Reason Why

The formal presentation you make to a client is like a lawyer's arguments in a legal case. Your advertising case should reveal the creative strategy and answer beforehand the client's question, "What reason(s) do you have for choosing this particular strategy?"

In your presentation you will take time to explain research about consumer attitudes toward the product or service in general and the consumer attitudes toward your client and the competition specifically. The reason why is a concise recapitulation of that elaborate presentation explaining why you have chosen a particular strategy.

For the four creative strategies listed, the reasons why might read as follows:

*Schlitz strategy:* We will reflect power.

*Reason why:* The consumer, right or wrong, perceives the words *malt liquor* to mean a product with higher alcoholic content, and many malt liquor buyers purchase the product with that expectation. Our creative strategy plays on that perception.

*Smith strategy:* Death will be dealt with in a matter-of-fact way.

*Reason why:* Death is the greatest fear of most humans, leading to many religious and other philosophies to overcome the fear of death. It is not a subject most people want to talk about, though they know that death is inevitable. And they certainly don't want to hear much talk about preparing for their own death, even though deep down they know they should do so. For that reason, our strategy tries to treat death without all the solemnity and finality and seriousness normally found in funeral home advertising, but with a more matter-of-fact approach that we hope will sound sensible.

*Jones strategy:* Identify with the consumer's dislike of new technology.

*Reason why:* Research shows that word processors are the biggest reason for a declining market in typewriters and that most of the new typewriter buyers are set in their ways, preferring not to learn a new technology to accomplish what they already do every day on a typewriter. Jones needs to grab a bigger slice of a smaller pie. Our strategy lets consumers know *we know* how they feel; by seeing that we understand their feelings, they may have a more memorable reason for choosing our brand.

*MADD strategy:* You will be safer if alcoholic beverage advertising is banned.

*Reason why:* Though many non-drinkers would be expected to vote to ban alcohol advertising, a certain percentage of them will not agree because of First Amendment or other arguments. We need to explain to non-drinkers and drinkers alike that children who are exposed to alcohol through advertising virtually from birth accept it as part of the American lifestyle. If we ban such advertising, these children may not be tempted to go crazy with alcohol when they reach drinking age — or even before. This is important, because the group of drivers ages 18–24 represent a significant percentage of driving and drinking accidents. Therefore, a strategy that says both non-drinkers and drinkers alike will be safer may encourage a vote for the client's proposal.

The preceding reasons why are longer than others might be. If your client has the only bath soap that floats, your reason why may be as simple as "Our product is the only one that floats, which makes this product truly unique. We should adopt the strategy 'It Floats' for that reason."

## Mandatories

The last part of the CWP, mandatories, consists of points that must be mentioned in the ad or spot, though they have nothing to do with the actual sell at the moment. The points might deal with legalisms like "subsidiary of," corporate tone, or a statement of "no blonds" in a commercial, depending on the client. There might be a directive to use a certain union mark or other graphic. Very often, there are no mandatories.

Credit cards accepted, maps and phone numbers are not mandatories, because they are part of the "sell" of the ad. Remember, what you label a mandatory must be something completely unnecessary to sell the product or service, something added to the advertising message for other reasons.

## Sample Creative Work Plan

1. *Client:* University Barbershop.
2. *Key fact:* The campus barbershop more often than not finds its customers are men older than college age, including faculty or mothers who bring in young children.
3. *Consumer problem to overcome:* College men don't perceive barbershops as places that understand current hairstyles.
4. *Advertising goal:* To change male college students' perception of University Barbershop as old-fashioned and unstylish.
5. *Principal competition:* Local and chain unisex hair salons. Apathy about getting a haircut, stylish or not.
6. *Target market:* College men who go to unisex salons for what they see as "stylish" hair care, college men who put off haircuts (stylish or not), and

adventurous college women who want style, convenience and a lower price for hair care.

7. *Creative strategy:* The target market should come to University Barbershop because it specializes in campus hair fashions.

8. *Reason why:* University Barbershop can claim to specialize in campus hair fashions because it has invested in two women barber/stylists who are experts in campus hair fashions, while still offering male haircutting service for the older men. The women barber/stylists should reassure the college males who usually have their hair done by female hairdressers in unisex salons (often at a higher price), and the women barber/stylists could attract more adventurous college women who would like the convenience and price of University Barbershop.

9. *Mandatories:* None.

This sample CWP represents a rather simple plan to advertise a simple business that is part of your experience. Note that it doesn't take much research to figure out all the sections as they are filled in, except perhaps for the creative strategy, which is discussed in more detail next.

Don't be fooled by the simplicity of this plan. In an advertising agency or corporate situation where you are dealing with a large metropolitan, regional or national account, you may have to do much reading and thinking to determine the key fact, the consumer problem, and so forth. A foot-high pile of materials may be dumped on your desk, for you to analyze and reduce to a CWP. Or, you might get no background information, and alone or in concert with a research person, will be forced to dig out information from available sources or even conduct original research. Or, best of all, you might receive a CWP with everything filled in but number 7; and after absorbing all the other information, you'll go to work on the creative strategy.

## GETTING THE CREATIVE STRATEGY — COMING UP WITH NUMBER 7

### Getting Started

Although getting the creative strategy is the hardest part of copywriting, it can also be the most fun. Time spent in a relaxing environment developing a strong strategy can save you hours of writing time later. Copywriting, as we've noted, is really "copythinking" that leads to a strategy followed by an execution. There are some things you can do to aid you in getting the creative strategy, although no two creative people work alike. But generally, some tested techniques for getting started include:

• Know the nine points listed on page 21. If you have been working as a copywriter, most of this research will be instinctive or already done. You'll know how the client feels, what the product is about, how your bosses think and so forth before you get the assignment. Then you can concentrate on the creative strategy without notes. Many new copywriters think they should refer to a pile of notes while working. Not so. It's most important to have absorbed all information gathered through analysis and research. Then you can sit anywhere — in your car, in a canoe — and focus on a creative strategy.

• Make quiet time. If you intend to be a creative person for a living, remember that quiet time is not a luxury, but a necessity. Plan your life to have large chunks of time reserved for unstructured thinking.

• Write a list of possible strategies willy-nilly. Use anything that comes to mind. Don't be tense about it, just let it flow out, no matter how silly or weird or off the subject. This technique works well for the person who can't sit still and feels the need to do something.

• See a movie. Read. Watch TV. If you have absorbed the information and reserved quiet time to focus on a creative strategy, these activities will allow your subconscious to work while your mind is relaxing. It's surprising how often a thought will strike you in the middle of a football game or tense drama.

• As you work on the creative strategy, don't ask: "What's a good headline?" Work on that later. Don't ask: "What's good copy?" You write that later. Ask: "What's the promise? What's the big idea? What's unique about this product or service?"

## Finding the Unique

Uniqueness of your product, service or cause is *the key* to the creative strategy. If you're selling a video camera, you don't need to make a case for videotape vis-à-vis film; you have to make a case for your particular video camera as opposed to the competition. Your client's camera may have a unique feature, such as a more powerful zoom lens. Or, in the case of soap or antacid medicines, a chemical ingredient might make your product unique. These creative strategies are easy to come by, because a unique feature or ingredient is often all the consumer needs to hear about to be influenced.

But if you're talking about beer, banking or gasoline — products and services often perceived by consumers as basically alike — the uniqueness you seek may be more elusive. In the case of beer, the uniqueness may be no more than the advertising. This is a hard concept for some hard-sell, ingredient-oriented marketing people to accept, but the advertising itself can reassure consumers that they have done the right thing. If you are a macho person, you will tend to drink beer that reflects a macho image. If you're a person who appreciates humor or dancing or beach scenes, you might want the advertising for your beer to reflect those qualities. In banking, because money is money, the uniqueness may be in location, friendly people, or willingness to listen to loan requests — services rather than products. In gasoline, location might again be a key as could the variety of items available at the convenience stores associated with self-serve stations or the multiplicity of credit cards accepted. Technically, this claim to be unique has nothing to do with what is being sold — gasoline — but acceptance of your claim in these areas might indeed result in more gasoline being sold.

The uniqueness may be the company itself. When you talk about Borden, RCA, Ford, Westinghouse, Sears and others, you're talking about many of the greatest names in American commercial history. Playing off the stature of a company may be a way to say something unique. After all, only Ford is Ford.

## Magic

After you receive a copywriting assignment, you enter a never-never land of research, introspection, intuition, hard work and an indefinable flash of understanding that leads to the creative strategy. This is the moment of magic that cannot be reduced to simple rules on a page in a textbook. Cry as you might for a formula of creation, none exists. Simple as it sounds, the best advice for getting the creative strategy lies in the call to find uniqueness in the product or service or cause you are to sell. Your greatest asset will be your realization that you need a strong creative strategy before you write the creative execution.

For other help, there lies before you a world of advertising that you can study every day. If you will pay attention to the radio and TV commercials and the newspaper and magazine advertising, the outdoor boards, the direct mail that comes to your mailbox, the supplements and inserts in the Sunday paper, the signs in supermarkets and windows of gas stations, the messages on matchbooks, the wording of menus — really pay attention — you will soon begin to see who has a strategy and who doesn't, who is successful and who isn't. In such simple observation of what is happening around you, will you find the education and, yes, your own formula for coming up with a creative strategy.

## SUCCESSFUL CREATIVE STRATEGIES

Three of the strategies to follow — Doritos, Curtis Mathes and Mexene Chili — are based on the author's experience with those accounts. The other strategies are based on conversations with their creators or guesswork, but the lessons are the same.

## Seagram's Wine Cooler (TV)

*Creative strategy:* To impart a certain sense of "cool" to the product.

*Creative execution:* TV/film personality Bruce Willis in bar situations with women, giving him an opportunity to display his talent for the fast quip and bon vivant style (Figure 2.4).

*Slogan:* It's Wet and It's Dry.

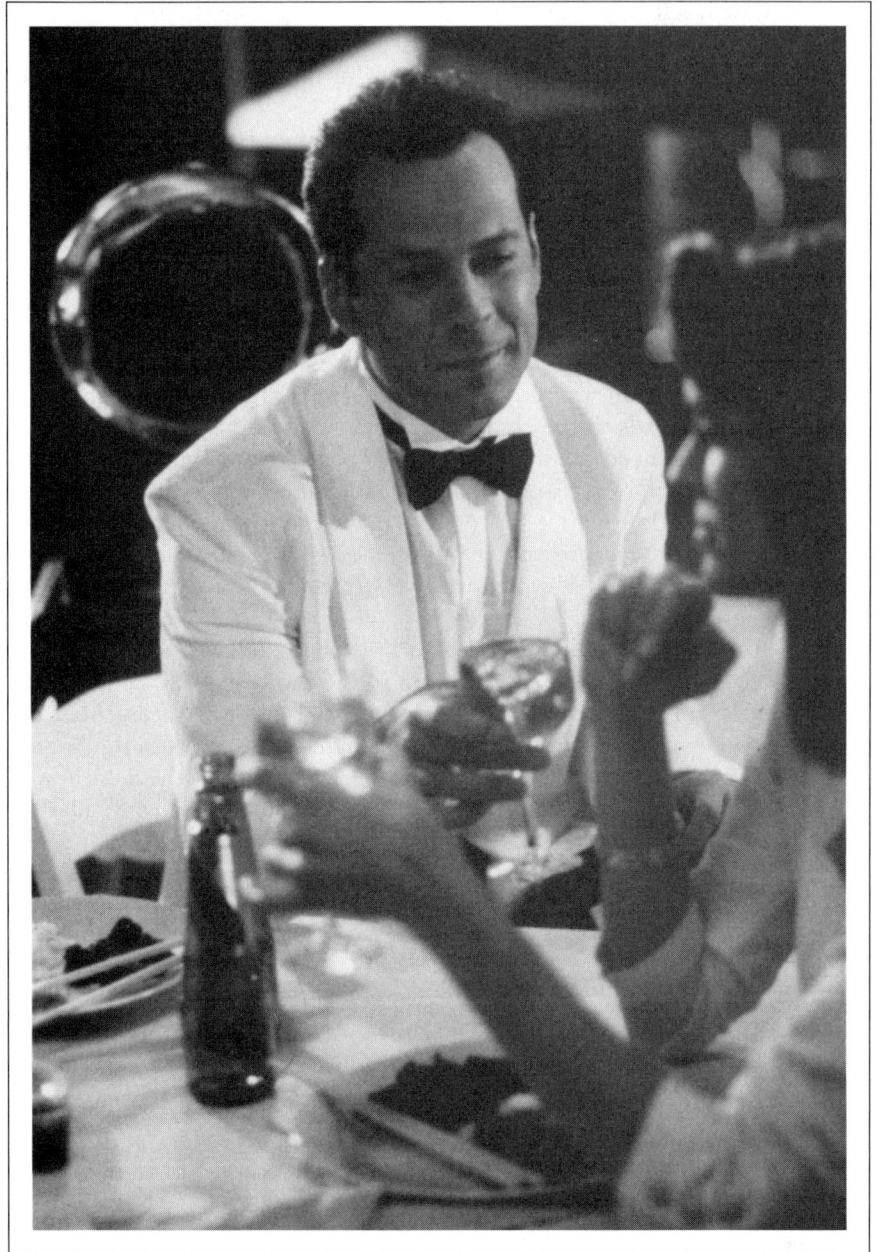

*A fast-talking smarty — Bruce Willis — brought his own brand of cool to the screen while integrating Seagram's Wine Cooler into the scenario.*

WE'RE FIGHTING FOR
YOUR LIFE

**American Heart
Association**

*AHA's long-lasting
slogan was created by
Dallas writer Lynn
Zanville in the mid-
1970s, when she was
the AHA's marketing
director. It describes the
organization's strategy
perfectly, a message of
helpfulness.*

## American Heart Association

*Creative strategy:* To reflect a sense of dedication to helping consumers
live longer.

*Creative execution:* Various ads and commercials about healthy lifestyles
(Figure 2.5).

*Slogan:* We're Fighting for Your Life.

## Curtis Mathes

*Creative strategy:* To say: "You get what you pay for."

*Creative execution:* Discussion by a spokesperson of the client's four-year
warranty, the longest warranty in the industry (Figure 2.6).

*Slogan:* The Most Expensive TV Set in the World, and Darned Well
Worth It!

## Doritos (TV)

*Creative strategy:* To equate crunchiness of the snack with freshness, which
consumers perceive as flavor.

*Creative execution:* A fat guy with a moustache has something funny happen to him every time somebody bites into a Dorito, because the crunch
is so loud (Figure 2.7).

*Slogan:* Taste As Good As They Crunch.

## Mexene Canned Chili (TV)

*Creative strategy:* To combat the perception that good chili doesn't come
in a can.

*Creative execution:* Animated "chili experts" ridicule canned chili. An entire can is shoved down their throats by another animated man who says,

## If TV sales are so bad, why is this man smiling?

Because he's Ray Harvey, National Sales Manager for Curtis Mathes. And while the big boys are having a tough time right now, Curtis Mathes sales are booming.

Naturally, most Curtis Mathes dealers are up, as well. And with an average gross profit margin of 33%, they're smiling, too.

Some people *are* buying TV sets now. And they're looking for quality. So, when you offer the only four year warranty in the industry – this tells them something.

For 1976, we're planning to add a few new dealers in selected areas. If you're interested in taking on a line of color TV and audio products that will give you profit instead of promises, get in touch with Ray. You can call him at (214) 675-2294 or write him at Curtis Mathes Company, P.O. Box 151, Athens, Texas 75751. Maybe he can put a smile on your face, too.

## Curtis Mathes
The most expensive TV sets in America
And the most profitable.

**2.6**    *The Curtis Mathes four-year warranty made it unique among TV sets, a unique selling proposition only this brand could make. This Curtis Mathes trade ad plays to that uniqueness.*

"Try it." The chili expert then says, "I just ate a great can of chili."

*Slogan:* It's Uncanny.

### *Wall Street Journal* Trade Advertising (Print)

*Creative strategy:* To demonstrate *Wall Street Journal*'s writing style with information that is instructive to the target market.

*Creative execution:* Advertising leaders of today are profiled and quoted on advertising theories, ending with a comment about the value of the *Wall Street Journal* (Figure 2.8).

*Slogan: The Wall Street Journal.* It Works.

## TIPS ON DEVELOPING A CREATIVE STRATEGY

- When you get a copywriting assignment, don't start writing advertising until you have a Creative Work Plan that includes a creative strategy.

Taste as good as they crunch

**2.7**

*Though the "crunch" strategy may be a cliche, Frito-Lay's marketing weight and the humor in the execution made this approach unique to the client's product.*

- If you don't have a CWP, prepare one in cooperation with all parties involved in requesting and delivering the advertising.

- To prepare a CWP, research everything pertinent to the assignment. See page 21.

- Save the creative strategy section of the CWP for last.

- Find quiet time to focus on and absorb all information.

- Consider everything that is unique about the product or service under study.

- If you can't find something unique about ingredients, durability, variety, availability, size, service, ownership, status or history of client, consider a creative strategy that will represent a unique advertising approach in the advertising category under consideration. It's risky to make the advertising (creative execution) itself the creative strategy. It has been, is and will be done, but it's rare for the creative strategy to be the advertising itself. (Bugle Boy jeans advertising comes to mind.) To offer such a creative strategy risks criticism that you have not done your homework and have not focused carefully on possible unique aspects of the product, service or cause.

- When you have worked out a creative strategy, phrase it in keeping with the tone of the CWP, submit it to all interested parties, secure approval of the creative strategy and get ready to start writing.

# Jay's Way.

*Jay Chiat. Co-founder and leader of Chiat/Day, California-based agency that's become a formidable competitor in the East. A New Yorker by birth, he came home to establish a Manhattan office for the L.A. agency—and quickly proved creative prowess works on both coasts. Here, from a recent conversation, are a few of the directions that have pointed Jay's way to success.*

**On beginnings:**

I was born in the Bronx but grew up in Fort Lee, New Jersey. In those days, Fort Lee wasn't suburban but rural. Safe. Comfortable. A good place for kids. After Rutgers and a degree in education, I got my first job as an NBC guide at $37 a week. A year later, the Air Force took me west to Mather Air Force Base in Sacramento. When my tour ended, I wanted to stay in California. That led to a job as a technical recruiter—and my start in advertising, doing recruitment ads. Then a media rep told me a small Orange County agency was looking for a young writer. I moved south and, after four years, started my own agency with $4,000. I figured if it didn't work out, I could always get another job. We survived for four years with real estate and technical accounts; then moved into L.A. where I got together with Guy Day to form Chiat/Day.

**On risk-taking:**

I'm uncomfortable when I'm comfortable. I have to start something new—in the agency, or in my personal life—every two years or so. Taking risks gives me energy. I can't help it, it's my personality. I'd like to think it's not really a compulsion toward high risks, but the spirit of the entrepreneur. This *is* the age of the entrepreneur, isn't it?

**On the big loss and the bigger win:**

Our first major client was Honda. We did terrific work, but got caught in the middle of a battle between sales and advertising. The experience was traumatic—but, in retrospect, it was the best thing that could have happened to us. It forced us to recognize the need for sophisticated account handling. Until then, we hadn't had enough respect for account management.

**On New York:**

Being in New York has given the agency new purpose, new energy. The myth is that New York is a tough place to crack. Well, it is—but it isn't. There's so much business, so many opportunities, that you have far more chances. So that makes it easy. But it *is* tough to change your perspective and your life style.

**On building a campaign:**

Our best work has always begun with a marketing solution, not a creative solution. The ads flowed from the strategy, not the strategy from the ads. Then we found a way to do it with consistency.

We introduced a third discipline, account planning to represent the consumer in the agency, alongside account management and creative.

**On the system:**

Every account has a team of equals—account planner, account manager, writer and art director. Together, they develop the strategy based on knowledge of the target audience. Creative people are involved from the start so they buy into it. Once the strategy is well defined, the client has to approve it before creative work is done. There are fewer delays, fewer disasters. We feel it leads to better creative. It isn't foolproof—but what is?

**On bringing the client into the act:**

Halfway through the process, we bring the client in. It's a shirt-sleeves session. No effort to slick up the ads, just felt tip roughs. We don't talk about techniques, only about ideas. We don't even try to sell. It's just a matter of telling the client, "Here's where we stand; here's how we got where we are." That gets the client involved—and at a point where the client can contribute and also have a sense of *ownership* in the campaign.

**On self-perception:**

I'm in charge of quality control. If the work's not up to standard, I call the creative team or even the client, and tell them. Clients appreciate that—who wants to waste time looking at work the agency doesn't like? My other job is to keep the agency simple. As you grow bigger it's easy to grow complicated. So I do things like eliminate memo writing. Memos aren't communication; they're a corporate disease.

**On new people:**

One of our toughest problems is assimilating new people. They come with a lot of mental baggage, and it takes time before they understand *their* baggage isn't *our* baggage. Our only interest is the quality of the work. And we won't compromise.

**On failure:**

If you see a bad ad coming out of Chiat/Day, blame it on us. We can't fall back on the excuse that the client made us do it. We just don't have those kinds of clients. They come to us for the kind of work we do. If we fail, it's our failure, not theirs.

**On print:**

We were *weaned* on print. In the early years, 99.97% of our business was print. And, on top of that, this is an agency started by two writers. So you can see where we've always been concerned about doing great print advertising. I think there's going to be an explosion of print. Just think of all of the magazines that have been launched in the past few years. There *must* be a lot of people reading.

**On finding good account people:**

We look for account people who understand advertising. It's amazing how few do. All account people are interviewed by creative people. Anyone who's just entranced with the *structure* of advertising won't be comfortable with us. It's tougher hiring account people than creative people. After all, you can look at a creative person's portfolio. Maybe we ought to have account people tear out twenty ads they like, and tell us why. In any area, I look for energy, for a *passion* about the business.

**On good writers:**

Good writers come in all sizes, shapes and ages. What they all seem to have in common is the ability to hear, to listen, to understand—and to distill what they hear and learn into something that's human and persuasive.

**On office organization:**

We don't have geographical departments. Instead, we cluster the people who work on a set of accounts together. When an agency is organized by functions, there's empire-building and departmental loyalties. I think our way helps make people responsive to the client, not to the department head—and that's the way it should be.

**On The Wall Street Journal:**

No matter what you sell, if the price tag is high, The Journal's audience is right. They have the means, and you can instill the will. The Journal offers what no other publication can match: an incredible immediacy. You run the ad, the ad generates the business. I used to teach an advertising class at the University of Southern California. My students had to subscribe to two major trade magazines—and to The Wall Street Journal. I find there's something in The Journal every day that I can use in our agency. I'm not looking for it, but there it is—a piece of news or information that *helps*. If you're in sales, or marketing, or advertising, there's no other way to stay current. After all, this is a business that moves very, very fast—and you can't stay on top of it without The Journal!

## The Wall Street Journal.
## It works.

---

**2.8**

*These in-depth articles about well-known adpersons are very interesting and useful. Because the ads are about credible people, that credibility must then rub off on the* Wall Street Journal *as an advertising medium.*

# IN CONCLUSION

Strategy is to copywriting as a thought is to action. Henry Ford's thought was to eliminate the horse as a means of personal locomotion; his action was the car. Edison's thought was to have light without gas or kerosene; his action was the light bulb. Fulton's thought was to propel a boat without a sail; his action was the steamboat.

It must be obvious to you in your work as a copywriter that the great thought, or strategy, must come first and then the writing of the ad or commercial that brings the strategy to life. There is one big difference between copywriters and Ford, Edison and Fulton. We can, *on occasion*, write an ad or commercial and go back afterward and find a great thought to support it. It's a dangerous way to create advertising, but it happens sometimes.

Your next activity is what is normally considered copywriting—writing print ads, broadcast spots for all media, or **collateral materials.** (Collateral materials are, generally, all advertising created and produced to appear not in newspaper, magazine, radio, TV, outdoor or transit formats, but rather in familiar areas like direct mail, brochures, **point-of-purchase** displays, match book covers and so forth. See Chapter 8 for explanation of and creation of collateral materials.)

Before you leave this chapter, be sure you understand one point: if you have a strong creative strategy—something you can come up with while showering or fishing or watching a baseball game—the copy could almost write itself and *you have much less work to do.* For the busy college student, that should be a bonus. For the professional copywriter, it's the secret to success and the reason why there's time to play ball with the kids and go to movies with the spouse.

### EXERCISES

1. Prepare a Creative Work Plan for:
   a. A **retail** account (local businesses, department store, food store, etc.)
   b. A **durable goods** account (high-ticket items that last over three years—cars, appliances, electronic products, cameras, etc.)
   c. A **packaged goods** account (most grocery items)
   d. A **service advertising** account (rental cars, banking, professional services, a charity, etc.)

2. Watch, listen to and read the advertising for ten or more different products or services, and then finish this statement:

   "People should buy this (product/service) because _____."

   Example: "People should buy a Mercedes because it is engineered better than other cars."

# CAMPAIGNS

The five steps to an advertising message — analysis, research, CWP, execution and production — can lead to either a one-time advertisement or a campaign. The steps don't change, but knowing what form the message will take can influence your thinking as you go through the process.

You find one-time advertising in local advertisements for retail stores selling an item, TV stations asking you to watch a specific program, or holiday promotions by local, regional and national advertisers. In addition, short-term promotions that constitute one-time advertising are created and run all year long by local, regional and national advertisers. A Yellow Pages ad may be a one-time ad; so, too, are ads and commercials for an event like a play or a marathon. Many advertising messages are created to run only once for a short time or created once to run for a long time, such as a local hardware store ad that has run for 20 years.

As a new copywriter for an advertising agency, retail business or corporate advertising department, you may find yourself using the checklist of steps to an advertising message to create one-time advertising as your full-time job. Equally possible, however, is that your first job may be as a copywriter for clients who run advertising campaigns. Eventually, as a typical copywriter, you will do both. In the long run, your fame and fortune as a copywriter will depend more on your creation of a long-running campaign than on creation of one-time ads. One way you can move into that rarefied company of copywriters who have written great campaigns is to work just as hard on the one-time ad as you would on the more glamorous campaign. The highly innovative "Mac Tonight" TV commercials by McDonald's, for instance, were intended as a one-time promotional effort in Southern California. But so well thought out was the promotion and the creative execution that "Mac Tonight" went on to become a national campaign, earning plaudits for its creator. It's that word *campaign* we explore in this chapter.

## WHAT IS AN ADVERTISING CAMPAIGN?

The answer to this question explains why this chapter is not only in this book, but also at this point in the book. You should have an overview of the meaning of a campaign before you write one. There are certain differences between writing the one-time ad and the campaign, the most basic being the need for continuity in the various materials in a campaign as opposed to a different kind of continuity or no continuity at all in a one-time effort.

Definitions of the word *campaign* would include: (1) a series of military actions with a particular objective in war and (2) a series of organized, planned actions for a particular purpose, as for electing a candidate. *Series* is the key word that defines a campaign, for your advertising campaign includes a series of maneuvers designed to strike again and again—not at an enemy, but at your best friends, the consumers. If there is an enemy in advertising, it is the competition from other products and services or the negative perceptions of your product or service by the target market. Rather than military strategy (the big idea about a way to outwit the enemy), in advertising we have marketing strategy, media strategy and creative strategy (the big idea about a way to sell). Instead of military tactics (arranging forces before the enemy), we have media tactics (the placement of our advertising messages on radio, TV and outdoor locations or in print and collateral materials). The individual media are the heavy artillery, delivering the ammunition contained in the creative execution—copy and pictures and music. Because a campaign is a series of planned actions, we may also wage individual little skirmishes with collateral materials on the front lines—**shelf liners** in supermarkets, for instance, or point-of-purchase displays.

Through it all, our flag is flying to show who we are—with our **signature** (name) or **logo** (name with distinctive graphic look). And we have our advertising **slogans** to compete with the great slogans of the past, like "Don't Tread on Me" (Revolutionary War), "Remember the Alamo" and "A

Slip of the Lip May Sink a Ship" (World War II). Everything is controlled by the commanding officers (the agency owners, account directors and creative directors; the client owners and marketing directors), with us, the creative people, as the majors (pun intended). We have specialists: the account executives (AEs), production people, media people, research people and hundreds of outside suppliers of talent and material needed for a total effort. The only difference is that in a war the strategy is a painful way to win, and in advertising the strategy is a way to sell and win the target market over to a product or service.

## Campaigning Is Not a Difficult Concept

Campaigning means a combination of media attacks. Even a one-medium campaign, such as radio only, is still a campaign because you use a combination of stations and messages. Campaigning means you are able to think in terms broader than you do for only one ad. As a general sends out four different probes against the enemy, you will send out various pieces of advertising to do battle. Those that don't work will be buried or sent to the hospital for rehabilitation, and those that do work will be sent out again.

The only thing the advertising general has in mind is winning the overall battle of sales. In some parts of the country or city, as in war, the competition may win an isolated sales battle, and the product may slip to number two or three in sales. That would force a surprise counterattack with a price-off promotion or other advertising tactic to help regain the former position in the market (or advertising battlefield). It's all part of a campaign.

Even though many advertising curricula have capstone courses called Campaigns that frighten students to contemplate, a campaign is no more than putting together all the advertising skills you have learned in a concentrated, multi-pronged approach, based on the single creative strategy you developed.

## Think "Campaign" Even in a One-Time Ad

When you are given a one-time ad to do, you should still treat it like a possible campaign because someone may come to you and say, "Ace, that was a great print ad on the Razzle Dazzle account. We're dropping our old strategy and adopting yours. Can your idea work for a whole campaign?" In fact, this has happened often enough that you should think of everything you create in terms of a campaign, regardless of an advertising request for a one-time ad. When you get such a request, there are only two possibilities.

First, there is a look and a sound and a slogan already established for the branded product or service you are working on. In such a case, your job will be to make sure your "one-time ad" fits the previously established look and sound and slogan. If the assignment is to announce that your client, Hometown Bank, is sponsoring a marathon, with proceeds going to heart disease research, start your thinking with the brand name. The information you want to convey about the marathon is important and the immediate reason for the ad. But the long-term reason for the ad, if you think campaigning, is to register

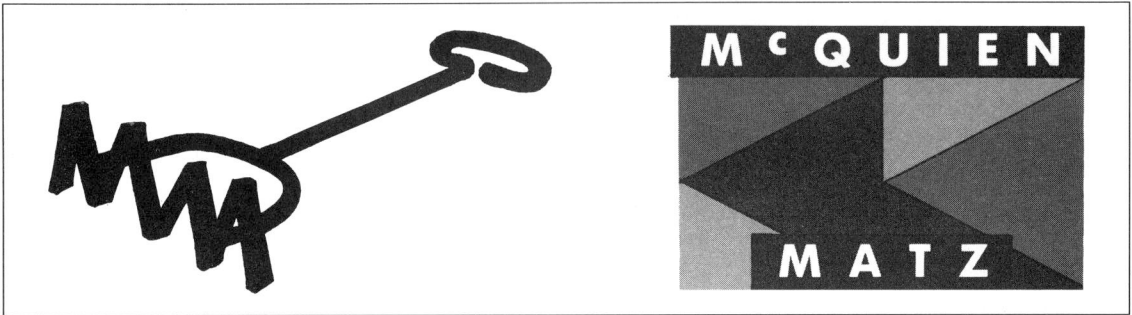

*A cattle brand and a modern corporate logo for an advertising creative service called McQuien Matz; the idea is the same for both.*

the brand name of the client yet one more time, to fit this ad into the continuum of the bank's advertising. If you think campaigning, you start out not by asking, "What's a great headline for this marathon?" but by asking, "How can I make the brand name dominate?"

Let's look at an example. Assume Hometown Bank's long-running slogan is: "Small Enough to Know You, Big Enough to Serve You." One-time ad thinking would give you a headline like:

RUN FOR YOUR LIFE,
AND THE LIVES OF OTHERS

Campaign thinking would give you a headline like:

HOMETOWN BANK'S MARATHON:
SMALL ENOUGH FOR FUN,
BIG ENOUGH TO DO SOME GOOD

You have still promoted the marathon, but under the umbrella of the brand name.

Second, if there has been no continuity in advertising efforts for this brand name before now, here's your chance to start that continuity. Though the ad is designed to encourage participants and spectators for a marathon and though you can earn your money just by drawing a record crowd to the marathon, if you don't take the opportunity to establish the brand name of the bank while you are doing all that, you haven't done your job. And you haven't sown the seeds for a future campaign. Again, one-time ad thinking might result in this headline:

RUN FOR YOUR LIFE,
AND THE LIVES OF OTHERS

But campaign thinking will allow you to plant the seeds of a future campaign while still announcing the marathon:

HOMETOWN BANK HAS
YOUR INTEREST AT HEART

**3.2** *Two frames from one of the most famous one-time ads of all time, the Apple "1984" commercial, which ran during the Super Bowl in January 1984.*

What makes the expense of a consistent advertising campaign worthwhile is the constant pounding away at the brand name of the product or service in every medium from TV to calendars. Never get so caught up in the immediate reason for an ad or commercial or collateral piece that you forget that copywriters exist to perpetuate the brand name (Figure 3.1).

One of the most famous one-time ads was the "1984" commercial for Apple's Macintosh computer. The cost of the spot was estimated at $500,000, and the cost for air time on the Super Bowl (always a great advertising showcase) in January 1984 was the same (Figure 3.2). A million dollars to run once! It was an extraordinary spot that had ad-watchers buzzing, and many are those people who believe they saw it more than once. Did the creators of that ad have a *campaign* in mind? After all, not only was it the only spot created for the product, but it was also only going to run once.

The answer, in a most subtle way, is yes. That commercial, though not repeated, established a *tone* for the company. You can be sure that the copywriter, though faced with writing what may theoretically be defined as a one-time ad, still thought "campaign" as applied to the future of Apple advertising. There was no ongoing slogan, the definitive symbol of a campaign, and the graphic look (throwing a hammer through the Big Brother TV set) was certainly not repeated. But there was a production value there and an aggressive advertising posture for the company that is unmistakable and continues to this day.

The bottom line here is that the ambitious copywriter will see even a one-time ad as a chance to (1) enhance a current campaign or (2) create a campaign look. Just make sure that your creative strategy for even a one-time ad is extendible, which means that your strategy and slogan will work in every medium—that it will even be singable or look good on T-shirts—and be capable of many creative executions for years and years.

## TAKE LOUSY LUCY HOME TO MEET YOUR MOTHER.

Lucy is a real little charmer. She loves to curl up and adorn windowsills with her trailing pale green foliage and buxom pink flowers. However, she is a heavy drinker. Outside that, she's a perfect lady.

### STEMWARE FLORISTS
603 Munger Ave., Suite 120, 871-9888

## DO YOU HAVE YOUR LITTLE PASSION FLOWER CLIMBING THE WALLS?

If her name is Passiflora Caerulea, she should be. These vigorous vines love to climb. And they don't demand a lot of attention. So if you're ready for a meaningful relationship, let us introduce you to a Little Passion Flower.

### STEMWARE FLORISTS
603 Munger Ave., Suite 120, 871-9888

## FIX UP YOUR MOTHER-IN-LAW WITH A ROVING SAILOR.

Roving Sailors are beautiful trailing plants. But they're real basket cases. And they need a lot of tender loving care. So if your mother-in-law is ready to make a commitment, drop by and we'll help you fix her up with a nice Roving Sailor.

### STEMWARE FLORISTS
603 Munger Ave., Suite 120, 871-9888

## DOES YOUR WIFE KNOW ABOUT BUSY LIZZIE?

This hot little number has a vibrant personality. She's an easy plant to raise indoors. And her richly colored flowers are always a welcome sight. If your wife hasn't already met this flirtatious charmer, introduce them soon.

### STEMWARE FLORISTS
603 Munger Ave., Suite 120, 871-9888

**3.3**

*Award-winning Dallas creative director/writer Ben Vergati came up with this campaign. You can just smell the "campaign-ness" of all these ads; there's a family feeling.*

# REPETITION

It is often said that repetition is the secret to advertising, but that doesn't mean frequent repetition of the same creative execution (or plot) in various media, although that's done all the time. What this saying means is that repetition of the creative strategy, in many different and interesting ways and often in different media, is vital to an outstanding campaign. For example, say your creative strategy for a chain of convenience stores (6-12) is a price structure midway between other convenience stores (high prices) and grocery stores (low prices). And say that in your first TV commercial under this strategy you show a person who cries with gratitude because he gets back more change for a bag of ice than he expected. Many excellent agencies, clients and advertising professors feel comfortable showing the same man, with the same tears, getting the same change, in magazine and newspaper ads, and on billboards. Even on radio, the man's sobs of gratitude carry through the plot of the TV spot.

Although this may be an effective and traditional method of advertising, in today's world of 20-second newsbites on TV and generally short attention spans, it's better to vary the plots of the creative execution. The strategy of pricing is broad enough to allow other plots for other media, rather than repetition of the same plot. The consumers who see this advertising will be disappointed if what was once a compelling minidrama is repeated everywhere. To those who say it's always been done this way or that a little irritation is known to help sales — well, those seem like poor answers. How many times can you listen to a joke after you've heard it or watch the same dramatic movie? It gets old very fast, and so does the same plot executed in various media.

# EXTENDIBILITY

Life is a balance, and never more so than when you knock yourself out to make sure your campaign has **extendibility;** you experience the thrill of selling the campaign, only to find yourself faced with the agony of creating extensions (more creative executions of the same strategy) all by yourself or with your art director (Figure 3.3). Many are the fine copywriters and art directors who create and sell to their agency and to the client, and eventually to the public, a fine campaign made up of a pool of three TV spots, six radio spots and three magazine ads, whatever the initial campaign consisted of. Then, as they are basking in the glory of acclaim for their creation and the higher sales that resulted, along comes a request for three more TV spots, six more radio spots, and so on.

During the original presentation to the client the copywriter and art director were asked if the campaign was "extendible." Infinitely so, they answered. Such a broad creative strategy here, they said, that we'll never run out of executions. Now we find these two optimists tearing their hair out after a week of trying to come up with three more TV spots as fresh and wonderful as the first three, and they begin to wonder if infinity is shorter than suspected. If they are good, they'll eventually find a way to go that moves the plots into new directions, though still under the same creative strategy—much as Bud Light commercials finally left the bar and went to people's homes and even to Russia.

## Examples of Extendibility

Consider the Miller Lite commercials. Applause must go to the creative people who have come up with so many variations on the same strategy (a lighter beer with the same taste as "regular" beer), drawing upon a repertory company of retired athletes for the creative execution. Infusion of new characters (Bob Uecker, Joe Piscopo, a Russian comedian, newly retired athletes and others) and situations outside of bars kept that campaign going longer than would be expected.

The classic Volkswagen campaign of the 1960s filled American streets with VW Beetles. And though advertising can't take all the credit for what may have been a marketing situation—disenchantment with the Detroit gas-guzzlers—advertising took advantage of that situation with an absurdly simple idea: reverse snobbery. VW made it chic to "Think small." Under such a strong yet broad strategy, additional executions, situations—extensions, if you will—appeared to come tumbling out of the innovative Doyle Dane Bernbach agency easily. Though modern thinking has it that a campaign's continuity is tied to repetition of a slogan and graphic look that reflects the creative strategy, there really was no slogan to the VW campaign, only a striking graphic look coupled with a rather off-handed copy approach that was consistent, thus insuring continuity. The creative strategy that said "small is good" was so strong that the strategy provided the continuity in the campaign without help from a slogan, and certainly without repeating the same plot in various media.

Though the Miller Lite and Bud Light campaigns were extended mostly on TV, VW was able to extend its campaign in both TV and print. You may be familiar with other campaigns that extend their basic strategies with different executions in both broadcast and print, including outdoor advertisements, among them the Peanuts characters for Met Life ("Get Met. It Pays."). Spuds McKenzie, the Bud Light dog, appears on TV, in print and posters in new situations, usually involving a bevy of beautiful semi-clad women around him.

Chevy's "Heartbeat of America" slogan has been running for several years and probably reflects a strategy that seeks to make Chevy *the* American car, as reflected years ago in the "Baseball, Hot Dogs, Apple Pie and Chevrolet" campaign. The "Heartbeat" campaign runs on TV, radio and in print. Apple's "The Power to Be Your Best" runs in broadcast and print, as does AT&T's "The Right Choice." The U.S. Army's "Be All That You Can Be" also runs in multiple media.

All of these and many more advertisements you've seen with a consistent slogan running for years call on art directors and copywriters to stay fresh in their search for new situations; extendibility in a campaign is a great asset for the client, but holds the problem of burnout for the creative people in many situations.

Extendibility is less of a problem if a client has many different services to offer, such as a bank that may sell savings, checking, safe deposits, vacation loans, home loans, CDs—maybe 20 different items. In a case like this, the creators have an easy time staying with the original strategy and slogan and have plenty of new copy points to play with. The real burnout problem comes with a campaign like Frito-Lay's "Bet Ya Can't Eat Just One," a one copy-point campaign.

## Believability Can Clash with Extendibility

After the first four or five Doritos commercials were a hit with the public and created a large jump in sales, my art director and I were faced with the problems of *extendibility*. The challenge to client and creator alike is to come up with another spot that says the same thing, but says it in a fresh new way. Songwriters, film directors or singers face the same problem. People respond to the work of these artists because of some indefinable quality in their work and want the same thing from them every time, albeit in a fresh, new way. It's quite a challenge.

We faced the challenge with a TV spot that we thought beautifully captured the whole campaign. We had the fat guy shaving around his moustache. When the crunch of the Dorito inevitably interrupts him, he shaves off half his moustache. We were working within the formula of having the talent be busy at doing something, then being interrupted by the crunch of a Dorito and finally having something comical happening after the crunch.

"Unbelievable," said the client, when we presented the storyboard to him.

"No more so than having him rip a pool table or knock the head off a sculpture when he hears a crunch," we retorted. (Those were two former plots that had been successful.)

The client shook his head. "No, it's unbelievable a guy would cut off his moustache. I don't know why, but it is."

Who were we to argue? This was the same guy who approved the campaign in the first place, showing some good taste, we thought.

In literature, "suspension of disbelief" is often discussed as vital to getting a reader into a story, particularly in sci-fi or fantasy stories. What the client was saying was that people will suspend their disbelief about a man ripping a pool table or knocking the head off a sculpture when surprised by the crunch of a Dorito, but will not go so far as to suspend their disbelief about shaving off a moustache.

Maybe the client was right. We'll never know. But I still think it would have been a great spot. The actor wore fake moustaches anyway, so it wouldn't have inconvenienced him.

As a student copywriter, your job is to think big, to understand that creating an advertising campaign is not a fearsome thing, but a way to stitch together all the various elements of advertising under the creative strategy you have settled upon. Advertising is, after all, a game for grown men and women.

"PAPER AIRPLANES"
30-Second Film

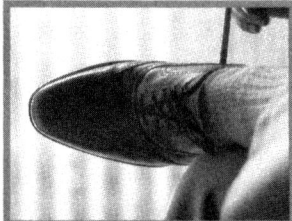

1

2

3

5

6

7

8

9

10

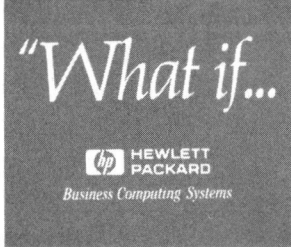

"What if...

hp HEWLETT
PACKARD

*Business Computing Systems*

11

**ANNOUNCER:**
Here at Hewlett-Packard, we believe that the best way to solve your business computing problem is to make it *our* problem. Because we know that whatever system we design for your company, we're going to live with it too. We never stop asking, "what if..."

**WOMAN:**
Wait a minute... they have this incredible backlog of data requests...

**GUY:**
You're right... what if... (FADE UNDER) we used the 3000 with HP Access to link up their workstations to the mainframe...

(CONTINUE FADE UNDER)

*This approach made the company, and hence the product, seem innovative.*

It's competition. And your creative strategy can make the difference between winning and losing sales for the client. Or, in more practical terms, it could be the difference between keeping or losing your job. The copywriter is paid to understand and create strategy first and to provide persuasive writing second.

Some advertising professors have said that along with the creative strategy, the concept of campaigning is the hardest thing for students to pick up on. Without a strong foundation in the understanding of these two concepts, the further study of creative execution will be built on quicksand. The other aspects of creating the advertising message — situation analysis, the CWP, writing, format, production, presentation — might be learned in an academic setting with a minimum of trouble. But the concepts of creative strategy and campaigning require original thinking of a nature many people are never called upon to exercise in making a living.

On the plus side, hard as it is to be original for a living, this craft allows you to come up with answers while driving a car, fishing or pursuing your favorite hobby. Hewlett-Packard's "What If?" campaign demonstrates that point, showing Hewlett-Packard employees creating in out-of-office situations and then calling the office from some wilderness location (Figure 3.4). There's some compensation in having a job that can make you a hero for solving problems while shaving your face or legs.

## TIPS ON CAMPAIGNING

- A campaign is a series of planned actions. Think big about a wide, multi-pronged attack on the marketplace.
- When assigned to write a one-time ad, check to see if the client has an ongoing look and sound and slogan. If so, make the point of the ad under the umbrella of the ongoing look, sound and slogan.
- If the client has no continuity in its advertising, write the one-time ad so that it could be extended into a campaign, if necessary.
- When writing an advertising campaign, don't repeat the same plot in different media. Repeat the creative strategy with different executions.
- Think extendibility from the beginning. Sometimes a strategy is so narrow that only one or two good commercials or ads can be written under that strategy. Think ahead to all the different ways you can execute advertising under your creative strategy. You may have to write a song or have T-shirts printed.

## IN CONCLUSION

Although a copywriter is often called upon to write a one-time ad for a one-time event (a marathon race for charity, a rock concert, and so on), most of the time the copywriter should think of creating an advertising campaign.

From the client's point of view, a campaign is a more effective, more profitable and more stable situation for establishing his or her brand name. From a purely selfish point of view, a long-running campaign becomes well-known, giving a copywriter credibility and clout when it's time to look for a new job or when pitching a free-lance account, because the prospective employer will have heard of the campaign and be impressed.

Chapter 4 deals with writing copy as a singular activity regardless of medium. As you will see in the chapters after that, there are certain format rules for each medium and collateral piece you write.

### EXERCISES

1. Take three ads from a magazine and write a short paragraph on each explaining how you would extend that ad into a campaign. Indicate what general visuals and copy you would suggest to maintain continuity with the creative strategy, as you define it, in future ads.

2. Do the same with radio, TV and newspaper advertisements you have seen or heard.

# GENERAL WRITING GUIDELINES

This chapter is meant to be a gentle buffer between analysis, research and creation of the CWP and the actual writing of advertising copy. In Chapters 5, 6, 7 and 8, we will emphasize the format and style differences between print, broadcast and collateral advertising; in this chapter we will emphasize the similarities in copywriting for all media.

Before you touch a keyboard or put pen to paper, you think about the ad or commercial (spot) you're going to write. You think about the target market, about finding the drama in an ad and telling a story. You think about grammar and mandatories and telephone numbers, problems common to writing advertising for all media. Before you craft a line of copy, you spend time thinking what the overall ad or spot will be about. And when you're ready to put down your first words, you need to know enough about the rules and mechanics of writing that you'll know which rules you can break.

## START WITH THE TARGET MARKET

You already know something about the target market from preparing the CWP. This is the time to concentrate even harder on that elusive face floating over your word processor. What does he or she look like? Think like? Act like? Dress like? Act like? Personalize this person (not these people) to whom you write, this person you're asking to spend money for a product or service.

If you're persuading people to quit smoking, don't show black lungs. Smokers already know about the health risks they take and will avoid reading your ad or watching your spot. You must figure out what will make them listen to your message. If you're persuading alcoholics to get help, don't tell them alcohol is bad for them. They know that. And you should know that they know that and yet drink anyway. So think of another way to get their interest long enough to hear your message.

In both cases, come in the back door with a unique way to reach your target market. For example:

> (DIALOGUE FOR AN ANTI-SMOKING COMMERCIAL. MAN IS ROWING A BOAT.) Oh how I miss smoking! I enjoyed every single cigarette I ever smoked. Trouble is, when I smoked, I couldn't do what I'm doing now. I'd get too winded. So, there are compensations for not smoking that I appreciate. (MAN NODS AT FRONT OF BOAT. REVEAL 8-YEAR-OLD BOY.) So does he.

> (DIALOGUE FOR AN ANTI-DRINKING COMMERCIAL. WOMAN SIPPING FROM A GLASS OF LEMONADE AND EATING A NECTARINE.) Never thought I'd sit around eating fruit and sipping lemonade and like it. Never was hungry when I was drinking. And I thought fools drank lemonade. Call me a fool. Turns out food is good, and I really only needed something to sip on. Didn't have to be alcohol . . .

The same principles apply to all target markets, whether you're selling shoes or skis. Try to understand what would motivate your target market to buy your product or service; and if you can't figure it out, go do some additional research until you do know what your potential buyer thinks and feels. Otherwise, you're scattering your message like buckshot, hoping some pellets will fall on your target market by accident.

## FIND THE DRAMA IN THE PRODUCT

Every product and service has a dramatic side if you look for it. What kind of drama can you find in razor blades? In one commercial, Gillette is singing about a little boy watching his daddy shave and talking about generations of users.

If you talk to the clients, or their engineers or research people long enough, you'll begin to hear the pride with which they developed this or that product or service. They'll tell you what's dramatic about the product, without even meaning to. It's up to you to pick up on it.

If a backyard chainsaw is as tough as the one the client makes for lumberjacks, there's the drama. If a retired man takes a job in a fast food restaurant, there's the drama. Long-distance calls between brothers, camping trips by beer drinkers, laundry room talk about detergent by two single people, the dream of a young chemical worker to increase food production, pantyhose for the larger woman, a station wagon for a family on the go, bread for a growing person — all are fraught with drama.

## TELL A STORY

Dramatic situations lead to stories. People love stories. Kids ask for the same story to be read night after night. And it's not just kids. Adults watch essentially the same plots unravel in soap operas and movies and TV sitcoms time after time. When those same kids and adults talk about their favorite ads and spots, listen to how often they recite the story contained within the ad — a story that ends with a reason for buying a product or service.

All advertising copy should tell a story, if possible, based on your creative strategy. No matter how short the copy is, it should have a beginning, a middle and an end. Even an outdoor board can tell a story through the visual just as the paintings in museums tell a story. Telling a story should be your goal every time you sit down to think through what you're going to write in an ad or commercial.

In the words of one country-western song, everybody likes a tale of somebody's dream coming true. Pepsi demonstrated that very well in a TV spot a few years ago. The spot opens with a 6- to 8-year-old girl practicing with her baton, throwing it high in the air and missing it when it comes down. She's wearing a cute costume. Quick cuts to various family members — Dad, Mom, Sis — confirm their concern that the little girl's going to make a fool of herself by trying her baton trick in public. The family members shake their heads and look apprehensive as they watch their baby practicing.

Cut to a parade headed into camera, led by you-know-who. The little girl is marching with élan, brandishing her baton, as the family members are shown watching the parade. The parade stops, and the little girl, to the horror of her family, tosses the baton high in the air. In slow motion we watch its path up, up, up, and then the turn downward toward the little girl's outstretched little hand.

Now the scene cuts to family waiting for the worst: the embarrassment of their baby. The scene moves back to regular speed. Pow! The baton smacks into the little girl's hand and a joyous smile of pride cracks her face. Now the scene cuts to wet-eyed and wildly applauding family members as the music soars and lyrics remind us of the Pepsi Generation. There's not a dry eye in the house. It's great copy. In this case, four somebodies' dreams came true.

Such copy is easy to write for Pepsi. How do you have similar success with, say, an electrical appliance manufacturer? You mean GE's "We Bring Good Things to Life"? All right, how about a film manufacturer? You mean Kodak's "True Colors" and "We're Gonna Get Ya with a Kodak Disk"? Right. How about a softener for dryers? You mean the Bounce campaign, with slow-motion pictures of people flying through the air? Cars? How about the man who played Mr. Whipple in Charmin spots (Dick Wilson), saying goodbye to his old car in a Buick spot, caressing it like a favorite horse, before he trades it in (to the swelling sounds of "Auld Lang Syne")?

It's said that every person's life is a potentially good story, if it were just written well. The same thing is true of products and services. Tell a story.

## HINTS ON WRITING ADVERTISING

So you've got a lock on the target market, you see drama in the product or service, and you have an idea for a story that makes a hero of the product and supports the creative strategy. Before you start the actual writing of the copy, keep in mind the following general hints on copywriting.

### The Writing Part

Every good writer knows that the rules can be broken. The important thing is to know the rules well so that you know when it's okay and even preferable to break them. And, remember, you don't learn the rules just by studying grammar books; you learn them when you read good writing.

**Grammar and Style**   You have to be an excellent golfer to be a trick-shot expert. You have to dive very well to be a comedy diver. And you have to know grammar very well to break its rules. If you know your grammar, and you shouldn't be a copywriter if you don't, understand this: you can sometimes break the rules of syntax all to smithereens, but you can't violate the basics — spelling, punctuation, reflexive pronouns, word agreement. Some things slip through the cracks, like the famous "Winston Tastes Good *Like* a Cigarette Should." No doubt it's better than ". . . As a Cigarette Should," which sounds stilted.

I once wrote "Real College. Real Careers. Real Close to Home" for Dallas Community Colleges. Naturally, the client changed the last part to "Really Close to Home," saying a college couldn't afford to advertise with errors in grammar. Despite that, I fought for the symmetry of the three "reals," but really couldn't argue with their conclusion.

This is a true conflict for the grammar-conscious copywriter — protecting the language versus the most interesting communication for the client, protecting the ad industry from criticism versus selling. The best way to resolve the conflict is to find a better, more interesting way to say it, while staying within the ground rules of grammar, much as you find a better word for expressing anger than a cuss word.

**The Look of Copy**   Your writing should be pretty to look at, whether for broadcast or print, with a format that makes your typing or printout a pleasure to read. Especially in these days of word processors, there is no excuse to turn in anything that is not absolutely perfect — no whiteout or crossouts. If your copy looks sloppy, the client will suspect that your thinking is sloppy too. Copy should also be pretty to look at from the point of view of logic. Split the headlines and the copy for sense in print; and in radio or TV, type the copy for presentation by a voice talent or actor who may be a stranger to you.

**Brevity**   Be concise. Every second of TV and radio, every inch of an ad or brochure, costs money. Even more, if you don't keep the consumer interested by moving along, you cost your client money by losing the sale.

**"You"**   Say "you" a lot. And if you must refer to the client, say "we," not "they." Consumers know who's running the ad; don't pretend you're standing apart from the client. You are a part of the client — his/her ghostwriter, his/her agent.

**Length**   Somebody in every copywriting class (accustomed to term papers) always asks, "How long should the copy be?" Lincoln, when asked how long a man's legs should be, said, "Long enough to reach the ground." Copy should be long enough to tell the story. Gum and potato chips don't need much copy. A Mercedes or an expensive house needs a lot of copy. And yet, advertising is a business with no rules for the most part, so maybe you would find a reason for long gum copy and short Mercedes copy. Unless you're told specifically to keep the copy a certain length, as in catalog copy, write until you've told the story. Then stop.

**Write Every Word in the Copy**   Write everything out. Don't say "client name and address here." You're the writer. If you don't spell out every last word in the print and broadcast, you — in effect — leave it to others to write some of your copy. This has two dangers: you look lazy and you lead others to think that it's okay to write on your copy, and they might start writing on other parts.

**"Ing" Words**   Avoid "ing" verb forms because they're weak. "Being an ice cream lover . . ." is not nearly as forceful as "I love ice cream. So I . . ."

**"But," "And"**   Some English teachers don't like you to start sentences with "but" or "and." Used judiciously, in advertising, however, they help pull the reader or listener along and make the copy more conversational.

**Exclamations**   Exclamation points, like basketball time-outs, should be used sparingly. Some writers use so many they sound as if they're yelling at you in the copy. Resist exclamation points!

**Emphasis**   If you want to emphasize certain words, avoid underlines and try to use italics or boldface. This is easier, of course, if you're using a computer. In print, art directors hate underlines, and they may be correct in saying that underlining makes the copy look junky. If you use underlining as an editing direction that means to italicize or boldface the word, explain that to the art director. It's not as big a deal in broadcast, because announcers tend to under-line words to indicate when to emphasize a word or phrase they read. You might as well underline words that you feel need an extra punch in broadcast copy.

**Phone Numbers**   If you must use a phone number on radio, repeat it twice — at the end of the spot. It would be better to refer listeners to the Yellow or White Pages. One student at SMU handled phone numbers well on a radio spot for Sweet Roll Delivery. At the end of the spot, she said, "Look in the White Pages under 'Sweet.'" People driving a car seldom have paper and pen ready for the phone number. The reference to White Pages will stick with the listener.

On TV, putting the number on the screen is better than saying it, if it doesn't junk up your final panel. Doing both is best if you can do so gracefully. In print, the phone number can be prominently displayed away from your sell copy. Be sure you don't put it inside your copy, unless there is some real reason to refer to it there.

**Paragraphs**   In ad copy, keep your paragraphs short.
Like this.
Easier to read.
More inviting to the eye.
(Of course, too much of this style reads like Dick and Jane. And it's not always appropriate. You're apt to use it more in newspaper and magazine ads than in annual reports.)

**Taste**   Good taste is a must — not only with regard to race, national origin, religion and sex, but also with regard to bumbling husbands, obsessive house-keepers, older people and other seemingly harmless targets. With the power that advertising exercises in communications, the copywriter has a responsi-bility to be sensitive to every group. A beer company recently found itself in trouble because it ran a TV commercial that put down polka music. An ethnic group often connected to that music reacted with vehemence and forced the spot off the air.

**Writing for Today**   In the early days of television — maybe in the early days of every medium — whatever was on was new and interesting, even a man holding a pack of cigarettes next to his head for a minute and talking about smoking satisfaction. But the media-conscious consumers for whom the copy-writers write and produce out there today won't accept such a commercial. Only colorization, for instance, makes it possible to talk movie-crazy children into watching a 1930s or 1940s film classic. And if you do talk them into watching the old film, and if you watch it with them (as they want you to do), you will be struck by how heavy-handed the action and other film aspects were in the "olden" days.

In terms of production, today's consumers accept cuts from one scene to another, jumps in time and space that were impossible 30 years ago. In a film

30 years ago, a man going to the drug store had to be followed walking to his car, parking and walking up to the druggist. Today, the character says, "I'm going to the drug store," and in the next scene he's in his bathroom putting drops in his eyes; and you know he went to the store, what he bought, and why. Writing for today means understanding not only the slang and styles of the times, but also how much modern readers and viewers can understand visually. Experience as a copywriter will teach you these things, but equally important will be what you learn from reading, watching TV and otherwise learning about today's pop culture.

## The Advertising Part

Although it's difficult to separate style and content ("How you say it is what you say" is a favorite adage of English teachers), my suggestions up to now have centered on how you write rather than on what you say. Let's look at some important aspects of what you say when you write advertising.

**Benefits**    Talk in terms of benefits to the consumer, not to the client. What can you do for the listener, viewer or reader who has chosen to spend some time hearing your pitch?

**Focus**    Stay conscious of what the creative strategy is, the one point you're trying to make. It's easy to get caught up in the drama and storytelling, in an idea that really appeals to you, and drift away from the creative strategy you're trying to bring to life. As the old saying goes, "When you're surrounded by alligators, it's hard to remember that your goal was to drain the swamp." The creative strategy is to drain the swamp. Focus on that. Figure 4.1 exemplifies an ad with total focus on the creative strategy.

**Sell**    Never forget that your mission is to sell. Copywriting is a science, the science of business. Copywriting is also an art — the art of making consumers happy you are selling to them. Because selling is a combination of art and science, then, don't get so caught up in science that you forget the art, and vice versa. Some marketing professionals come to believe the creative parts of advertising can be formularized. On the other hand, some **creatives** think art and writing in themselves are more important than what the art and writing are about. Both are wrong. Advertising is all about selling by a team that deals with some art, some science. Figure 4.2 shows an ad that doesn't forget its purpose.

**Mandatories**    Though we mentioned them in Chapter 2, mandatories are stressed here again because many beginning writers misunderstand the term. A mandatory appears at the bottom of copy for some clients who want you to put in their copyright, their parent company's name, other legalisms or matters that have nothing strictly to do with the main sales message. Maps, location copy, coupons, phone numbers, credit cards accepted and other things having to do with the present sell are not mandatories, but should be

© AT&T 1989
An Equal Opportunity Employer

At AT&T, how far you go—and how fast— is a matter of your ability. Whatever your specialty, we offer opportunity to move your career full speed ahead.

# No limit.

You might find yourself on the road to a career in international trade. Or setting the pace in marketing leading-edge consumer products. With choices like Finance/Business, Applications and Systems Programming, Marketing/Sales, Research and Development or Manufacturing/Operations Engineering, there's a wide choice of vehicles that can get your career in gear.

If you're a high-achieving college student with high career expectations, you should be talking to AT&T. We've got the right opportunities in the right businesses at the right time. And that makes AT&T a place where you can expect to go far. Send your resume to:

AT&T
College Recruiting
100 Southgate Parkway
Room 3A01
Morristown, NJ 07960

AT&T
The right choice.

**4.1**

*Total focus on a creative strategy promising unlimited horizons to an employee of AT&T.*

shoehorned neatly into the ad without disturbing the basic copy story. The art director is good at fitting these in, even though some may resent the effect such material has on a handsome design; you can help give the art director flexibility in design by listing these things after the main elements of an ad (see Chapter 5). If you can leave a piece of copy out of the ad or spot and still say all you wanted to say to sell the product or service, it is a mandatory.

*Good example of an ad that is interesting but never loses sight of its selling mission.*

**Visuals**   Be sure your visuals in print and TV are interesting and have a twist. A cat eating cat food is boring; a cat eating cat food while ignoring a bird in front of him is a creative idea. Whether it's a TV storyboard, an outdoor board, a brochure or a magazine ad, the visuals are half the sell. Even though an art director may ignore your visual ideas, as a copywriter you have a duty to think just as hard about the visuals as you do the words. Very often — most of the time in TV — your visuals will be used as you created them or will be modified somewhat. The actual symbiosis between copywriter and art director, and who does exactly what in creating visuals, will be discussed in more

# The secret of linking the world lies at the bottom of the sea.

As underwater lightwave transmission changes the face of global communications, *AT&T's SL SUBMARINE CABLE SYSTEMS* lead the way internationally. As a full-service provider in the design, production, installation and maintenance of these high-performance, high-capacity systems, AT&T supports the full range of network applications: voice, data, fax, dedicated and switched services.

AT&T's experience in system installation is unmatched. A pioneer in underwater transmission, AT&T has constructed more than 136,000 kilometers of submarine cable systems throughout the world's oceans and seas since 1950. Today's fiber-optic cables bring the extraordinary speed, clarity and quality of digital communications to all parts of the world.

AT&T. Experience, quality and reliability from a worldwide leader in telecommunications.

For more information, contact *AT&T SL SUBMARINE CABLE SYSTEMS,* 412 Mt. Kemble Ave., Room N400, Morristown, N.J. 07960, USA, or call **1 201 644-7852.**

**AT&T**

**4.3**

*The visual "twist" in this ad depends on the headline. Good example of copywriter/art director teamwork.*

detail in the following chapters. If you look at Figure 4.3, for instance, you'll see that it doesn't matter whether the copywriter or the art director thought up the visual; what matters is the teamwork that produced the ad.

**Ask for Business**   Ask for the business. That's why the client bought your efforts and the space or time to advertise in. Let the consumer know what you expect: "Call us today." "Consider a new kind of eating experience." "Switch to the tennis shoe that won't let you down."

It seems strange to mention this part of copywriting, when the whole point is to sell something. But a predictable number of beginning and experienced writers create fine copy and yet fail to actually ask the consumer to purchase the product or try the service. There are all kinds of ways to ask for the business, both outright and subtle. Whichever you choose, be sure the urge to action is clear. It may mean giving phone numbers or addresses or listing people to write.

**Flat Statements**   Avoid flat statements of superiority, like "We're the best restaurant in town." Who said that, except your client, through you? Who's going to believe the client? The point of the ad is to *prove* you are the best in town, not just to assert it. The fun of reading or watching advertising for the consumer, again, is to see just how you prove the claim you're making.

The proof may be a product fact, a unique selling proposition like "Exxon has HTA, an ingredient that cures hesitation." The proof may be brand image, such as "All my men wear English Leather or they wear nothing at all." The proof may be something that sets the client apart from the competition, thus creating a unique selling proposition: "Federal Express guarantees delivery by 10 A.M. or your money back." Keep in mind that you're asking consumers to switch from another brand or to try something new, or even to use an old product in a new way (such as smearing peanut butter on a banana). Consumers need reasons to buy your pitch, maybe subtle, maybe philosophical reasons — though a good hard exclusive product or service attribute is hard to beat. It's not always possible, though, to find such an attribute in this age of product and service duplication.

On the other hand, flat assertions you can prove (or that cannot be disproved) are great in copy. It makes you believable for the next **copy point.** Statements such as "The world is not flat!" won't be denied by most people. When you follow up with a pitch about your client's tires never getting flat either, the reader may be more receptive to your logic.

**Persuasion**   Indulge in humor (Figure 4.4) or in nostalgia or sadness or other sentiments in copy to set a mood, but never forget you're using them as means of persuasion. The difference between selling and persuading is subtle, but there *is* a difference. The whole ad or spot is selling something, but basing that sell on an appeal to reason or a good feeling toward your client is persuasion. If you write a letter to your folks for money, for instance, you may talk of other things along the way to the big hit at the end, where you ask for the donation. Chances are you make little remarks like "I would have gone to the concert but I was out of money, so I had jelly beans and read *Time* on Saturday night."

There is persuasion in such a side trip. Remember the yellow brick road. The scarecrow and the lion were important to Dorothy and the story. They were persuasive side trips that made it all the more important to get to Oz.

**4.4**

*Humor has been a big part of the Isuzu sell for years. Joe Isuzu's outrageous lies and claims, corrected immediately, have kept customers interested in learning the true story of the product.*

**"To demonstrate how the Lotus suspension improved the Impulse's handling, I took it for a spin on my test track."**

He's a little off track.

You don't have to go to an amusement park to try the Impulse's new handling. Just take it around your block. But hold on tight because Lotus, the renowned leader in sports car handling, spent five months giving the Impulse what *Motor Trend* calls, "a dose of handling magic."*

handling by LOTUS Ⓖ They experimented with 250 different shocks. Tested over 300 tires. Travelled over 30,000 miles. Until they found the perfect combination of shocks, stabilizer bars and wide Bridgestone Potenza tires. So you can fly around corners without flying out of your seat.

And if it's more speed you're after, try the fuel-injected, intercooled Impulse Turbo. You'd have to wait in line for a faster ride.

But the biggest thrill of all is getting the Impulse for as little as $14,109.** Now that's something to scream about.

For free Isuzu brochures call: (800) 245-4549. In California: (714) 770-3490.

**ISUZU** Ⓜ

*Motor Trend*, February 1988 **M.S.R.P. P.O.E. excluding tax, license and transportation fee. Prices subject to change.

*Proud sponsor of the 1988 Summer Olympics on NBC.*

**Shills**   Avoid **shills.** Shills are people who play a carnival game first and are allowed to win in order to encourage others to play. Afterward, the shill, an associate of the carnival person, will go around to the back of the booth and give back the prize. Certain characters in print and broadcast advertising are shills, because they are obviously shilling for the client:

MARGE:   I just can't get a clean wash.
SALLY:   Try Oxydol with green crystals.

Who talks like that? Nobody. Use voice-overs in TV and let radio announcers make the copy points if they must be made so directly. People expect announc-

# BBDO

Batten, Barton, Durstine & Osborn, Inc.

Client: PEPSI-COLA COMPANY 1988          Time: 60 SECONDS

Product: BRAND PEPSI         Title: "HOT FEET"         Comml. No.: PEPX 2056 (Stereo)
PEPX 1906 (Mono)

SFX: (LOCUST CHIRPING)

Ah! Ooh! Ah! Ooh, Ooh, Ooh!      Ooh, Ooh! (SITS DOWN) Hot!      SFX: SLAM!

Eeh — Ow — Ooh . . . Hot, Hot!      Ah, Ow, Ooh . . .      Aah, Oooh, Ow, Eeh, Ah, Hot! (etc.)

Eeh — ooh — ow — e      Aah . . . Aah      Aaah!

**4.5**

*The characters in this famous and effective Pepsi spot do all the selling for the client, not with their mouths, but with their "hot feet," which they are willing to sacrifice for a Pepsi. This shows that your characters don't have to talk like announcers to be effective salespersons.*

ers to shill for the client. Keep your characters in character; let them be whatever you have set them up to be (Figure 4.5). Just don't set them up to be announcers dressed in character clothing.

**Hard Sell and Soft Sell**    One oft-stated reason for a client's turning down copy is that "it's not hard sell enough" — as though the public were sitting out there trembling, waiting for the facts on the client's product or service, and eager for some person to yell them out. The terms *hard sell* and *soft sell* are confusing and perhaps shouldn't be used at all, because sell is all we're concerned about. What we think of as soft sell could actually be hard sell.

Take the hackneyed image of a cave man, for instance. He hits a woman on the head with a club, drags her by the hair to his cave, and has his way with her. But imagine that he hands her some dandelions, gently ties a necklace of sabre-toothed tiger claws around her neck, whispers in her ear — and *she* drags him off to the cave. Which is the hard sell and which is the soft sell? Which has a more lasting effect?

## IN CONCLUSION

If you've first completed analysis, research and the CWP and then done mental preparation for the ad or spot (thinking about your target market, finding the drama in the product and imagining a story to go with it), then you're ready to write. The guidelines for writing advertising all assume you're using means of persuasion to sell a product or service. Chapter 5 deals with using these guidelines to write print ads for magazines and newspapers.

### EXERCISES

1.  Pick a retail account and think of a story line based on the inherent drama of the product. Describe the story in several paragraphs, with a beginning, a middle and an ending. Be sure the product is the hero of the story.
2.  Do the same thing for a durable goods product.
3.  Do the same thing for a service.
4.  Do the same thing for a packaged goods account.

# CHAPTER 5

# WRITING PRINT ADVERTISING

In Chapter 4, you started on creative execution and learned some of the overall guidelines for writing advertising. Now you're finally ready to put words down for a magazine or newspaper ad. Above all, you're ready to "create," a word that connotes something magical to writers and non-writers alike. There is magic in copywriting, no doubt about it. Most copywriters would agree that, at some point in the creation of their best ads, there was a time when they had no idea which way to go; but suddenly there was an idea, and the work proceeded. No chapter in a book can teach you how to arrive at that magic moment when "suddenly there is an idea." But we can give you everything on all sides of it. If you've gone through the steps suggested in the first four chapters, particularly if you have a strong creative strategy, you're ready to create the ad.

## GETTING DOWN TO WRITING

The cursor blinks. The typewriter paper is blank. You've cleaned your office, balanced your checkbook and completed the other mental pencil-sharpening tasks that have delayed writing, a ritual for many writers as important as stretching-out exercises for a runner. The lighting, the coziness of the environment, the snacks and beverage, the music or TV or radio in the background are essential to many writers. It's not absolutely necessary for the writer to be all cozied up for the task at hand, but it doesn't hurt.

## ELEMENTS AND FORMAT OF A PRINT AD

When you write a magazine or newspaper ad, you know there will be certain basic elements in that ad. Advertising for printed collateral materials contains additional or different elements from those we cover in this chapter (see Chapter 8). The basic elements in most ads include:

Identification of client and ad

Headline

Picture (photos or drawings or both)

Subhead

Body copy (includes transition line, the first line of copy)

Snapper (ending of the body copy)

Slogan

Signature (client's name)

Logo (additional graphic to go with client's name or a graphic representation of client's name)

Address and phone number (mostly in retail ads)

Maps, credit cards, coupons

Mandatory copy (legal or other "non-sell" copy)

Rarely will all of these be in every ad you write. An ad can be as simple as the picture and logo on the Nike catalog page (Figure 1.1). But let's take a look at a sample ad format that does include all of these items, so you can see where everything would be positioned. The format of an ad is the actual way you put the elements above down on paper, and when you hand it in it's called the *copy*. The basic format follows; abbreviations and unfamiliar terms will be explained later in the chapter.

Dog-ear this page in the book (that's okay, dog-earing a book is a sign of love), so you have it for ready reference when you write an ad for an assignment. Note, by the way, that all the copy is written on the right-hand side of the page. We'll discuss the reason for this later.

CLIENT NAME
TYPE OF AD (MAG OR NSP), SPECIFICATIONS
"TITLE"
YOUR NAME
DATE

HEAD:               HEADLINE GOES HERE IN UPPER CASE (CAPS) OR UPPER AND LOWER CASE (U&LC).

PIC:                 (DESCRIPTION OF DRAWING OR PHOTO GOES HERE, IN CAPS AND IN PARENTHESES).

SUBHEAD:         If there is a subhead, underline it, or in some other way make it look different from headline and body copy.

COPY:              Indent paragraphs in body copy. Note that all the other elements are not indented.

Create frequent paragraphs regardless of grammatical implications, because this is advertising copy, not an essay.

You can even have one-line paragraphs.

Or one word.

Wow!

The last line of the copy is called the *snapper*. More on that later.

SLOGAN:          MANY ADS HAVE A SLOGAN. IT CAN GO ABOVE OR BELOW THE "SIG," AND MAY BE CAPS OR U&LC. IT WON'T BE THIS LONG.

SIG:                NAME OF PRODUCT OR SERVICE.

LOGO:             (LOGO, IF THERE IS ONE).

ADDRESS:         Not in every ad. A phone number may be included as well.

MAP:               (MAP) No map in most ads, though one often is shown in a real estate ad or an ad for a new business. Indicate it as shown (MAP); do not draw it.

CREDIT CARD PIX:   (PIC OF MASTERCARD AND VISA). Indicate as shown.

CREDIT CARD COPY:   You might have to write copy about accepting the cards. Best not to indent.

COUPON:          Not in every ad, but a good place to describe it if there is one. Write all the information that the coupon will contain, including blanks for names, etc.

MANDATORY:      © Copyright 1990 by Acme Corp., or other mandatories go here.

*Good example of the
headline also being used
as a graphic element.*

## THE FORMAT ELEMENTS

We'll discuss most of the elements listed in the order you see them. But as we go, keep in mind that you can write certain elements before or after others. Always write the identification of the ad in the upper left-hand corner first of course, but after that it's up for grabs. Some writers write the body copy first and see if they can pull a headline out of that. Others write the slogan for the campaign first, then write the headline, then the body copy.

Though they have something in mind for all the body copy, some copywriters will write the first line of copy (transition line) and the **snapper** (last line of copy) before writing the rest of the body copy. And sometimes the idea for all the elements hits the writer all at once so that it's possible to start at the top and go right down to the bottom, in the order this chapter follows.

As we discuss each element, refer to the ad by Toshiba shown in Figure 5.1. Though you can read the ad as published, it's written out here so you can see how the copy would have looked if turned in by the copywriter in the format suggested. Note that in the ad the copy has been set as one paragraph by the art director, but we have broken the lines of copy to a certain rhythm to make a point later on. We have also created a title, though we don't know what the original title was.

The original copy might have looked like this:

```
TOSHIBA RT-SX2
MAG, 1/3 PG, B/W
"COMES APART"
(NAME OF COPYWRITER)
(DATE)
```

| | |
|---|---|
| HEAD: | BOOM |
| PIC: | (TOSHIBA RT-SX2 ASSEMBLED) |
| HEAD: | B OO M |
| PIC: | (SAME MACHINE IN THREE PARTS, HEADLINE ELEMENTS RELATING TO PARTS) |
| COPY: | What really sets Toshiba's RT-SX2 apart is how it comes apart. |
| | The speakers detach for true stereo separation. |
| | And the system includes an AM/FM stereo radio and an auto-reverse cassette deck with soft touch controls. |
| | In short, it's perhaps the best boom box anyone's ever put together. |
| SLOGAN: | In Touch with Tomorrow |
| SIG: | TOSHIBA |
| ADDRESS: | Toshiba America, Inc. 82 Totowa Road Wayne, NJ 07470 |

The copywriter's thumbnail drawing of the ad layout is shown in Figure 5.2. This would be drawn right on the same page as the print copy or would be on a separate attached page.

## Identification of the Ad

```
TOSHIBA RT-SX2
MAG, 1/3 PG, B/W
"COMES APART"
(NAME OF COPYWRITER)
(DATE)
```

The information for the identification often appears in the upper left-hand corner of your page of copy, but many companies and advertising agencies put this information on the upper right or in upper center of the copy.

5.2

*Thumbnail sketch for*
*Toshiba ad.*

The basic information is the same in print as for broadcast, with one exception: the second line in a print ad may be a bit more complicated than saying :30 TV or :60 radio (a 30-second TV spot or 60-second radio spot).

The first line is the name of the client. See item 1 in the CWP in Chapter 2 to see how client names can vary. Here we have the name of the manufacturer and the specific name of one of its many products.

The second line tells what kind of publication (MAG for magazine; NSP for newspaper), the size (1/3 PG means one-third page) and the colors used (B/W for black and white). For a four-color, full-page magazine ad that will bleed (go to the outer edge of the page), the indication in the second line would be: MAG, 4/C, BLEED, FULL PG. There is no magic in the order of these indications or in the abbreviations used, although it might be useful to note the kind of publication first, MAG or NSP. The important thing to know is that every ad needs to be identified, regardless of whether it's on the second line, as here, or some other place. Often, a code number will also be assigned to the ad by a company or agency, but let's keep things simple for now.

NSP, 1/4 PG, B/W is a way to say the copy is for a newspaper ad which will be a quarter-page in space (with exact dimensions to come later, after the layout is done) and that the ad will be black and white, as most newspaper ads are. As a writer, you don't have to worry about exactly how much space, or what dimension, the quarter-page ad will take, because the art director and print production people will take care of that. You do want to know, however, approximately how much space you are writing for, so that you don't write too much copy for the art director to lay out in an interesting way.

On the third line is the title of the ad. The title should not duplicate the headline or slogan or any obvious parts of the ad. It might be a catchy phrase from the actual body copy, or might be a title you make up that you think catches the spirit of the ad, as in our example — "COMES APART." It's important to make the title catchy, just as titles on paperback books are catchy to grab your attention when you're shopping. You're trying to catch the client's eye when selling this ad in a presentation; and if you announce an interesting title as you introduce your work, you just might provoke an ice-breaking laugh or comment from the client. The title is also important in the records of a company or agency, along with the code number if there is one, as a way to retrieve the ad after it has been filed away for some time.

The fourth line is your name. Many companies and agencies make it a practice not to put the writer's name on the ad. But if you, as I have, patiently explain the pride you have in writing the ad and your willingness to be identified if the ad is not approved, most places will relent and allow you to put your name there. Why should you care? Well, as a copywriter, you are a ghostwriter for a product or service. Your name will not appear on the ad, though I agree with those who say that better advertising would be done if writers had to sign their ads. You should at least get credit for your work inside the company or agency you work for.

On the fifth line, many writers also include the date the ad was written. Some even write "First Draft" before the date, but it's better not to do that. The client and others might think there should be a second draft. And how embarrassing it would be to have a piece of copy floating around with your name on it and right below your name to have "Sixth Draft" written.

## Headlines

A headline is a word or words, in larger type than body copy in most cases, meant to (1) carry the entire message of the ad and/or (2) attract attention to the body copy. The headline in the Toshiba ad might be said to imply the entire message of the ad, but mostly it makes you want to read the body copy.

HEAD:     BOOM

PIC:      (TOSHIBA RT-SX2 ASSEMBLED)

HEAD:     B OO M

PIC:      (SAME MACHINE IN THREE PARTS, HEADLINE ELEMENTS RELATING TO PARTS)

This is an unusual headline, coming in two separate places, so we've included the PIC designation here as well.

**The Toshiba Headline**   Note that the headline words are a known pair of words, "BOOM BOOM." Using those words with a boom box shown first connected, then unconnected, is not only entertaining but also informative. The reader knows, by first looking at the head and PIC, then at the SIG, that Toshiba is attempting to sell a boom box with speakers that disconnect. This clever copywriter used words as graphic illustration as well as information and was concerned with every aspect of the ad, the visuals as well as the words.

For some readers, the HEAD, PIC and SIG may be enough information. The readers already may be convinced of Toshiba quality and now know Toshiba has a product of this type available. And off they will go to a store that carries this brand. It can happen. But perhaps other brands also have the disconnecting speaker feature. The reader may be entertained and informed by the HEAD/PIC, but need more information to make a purchasing decision. Estimates vary about how many people read body copy, but one thing is certain: if they read the body copy, they are interested, though the interest may be only the urge to be entertained some more. We'll have more to say on body copy later. Now let's investigate headlines in more detail.

**Headlines in General**    If possible, try to include a benefit to the consumer in your headline. Here, for example, are five clients and the benefits to be communicated to the consumer in the ads:

1. Better price, more features (for GE)
2. Ease of computer use (for Macintosh)
3. Unusual animals on view (San Diego Zoo)
4. Interesting science displays (Boston Museum of Science)
5. Value of keeping fit (YMCA)

Here are the actual headlines that were used to bring the reader to the body copy to learn about these benefits:

1. SPEAKER OF THE HOUSE
   (for a GE answering machine)
2. UNREQUIRED READING
   (for a Macintosh user manual)
3. THE WORLD'S GREATEST LONG JUMPERS
   ARE NOT IN THE OLYMPICS
   (picture of kangaroo, for San Diego Zoo)
4. COME TO MY BIRTHDAY PARTY
   OR I'LL EAT YOUR GERBIL
   (PIC of mean-looking owl, for Boston Museum of Science)
5. SIMPLE INSTRUCTIONS FOR
   CHANGING YOUR SPARE TIRE
   (PIC of man's fat midriff, for YMCA)

The GE headline doesn't talk about price and features, though the cleverness of the headline might be considered a benefit in its depiction of GE as a company with a sense of humor. Speaking of a sense of humor, the Boston Museum headline doesn't have any recognizable benefit—"COME TO MY BIRTHDAY PARTY OR I'LL EAT YOUR GERBIL"—but does anyone believe the copy will not be read? Is it possible to ignore a headline like this? Aren't you curious to at least read the first line of copy (the transition line) to see what on earth the museum is talking about? Headlines that are interesting or don't spell out a consumer benefit in client terms aren't necessarily bad. The other headlines (YMCA, San Diego Zoo and Macintosh) certainly, in combination with a picture, carry the entire message.

**Guidelines to Writing a Headline**    How do you write clever headlines like these? It's impossible for any textbook, any person, to tell you. I might as well try to tell you how to have courage, how to be a good person, how to face death. But there are some guidelines that might help you.

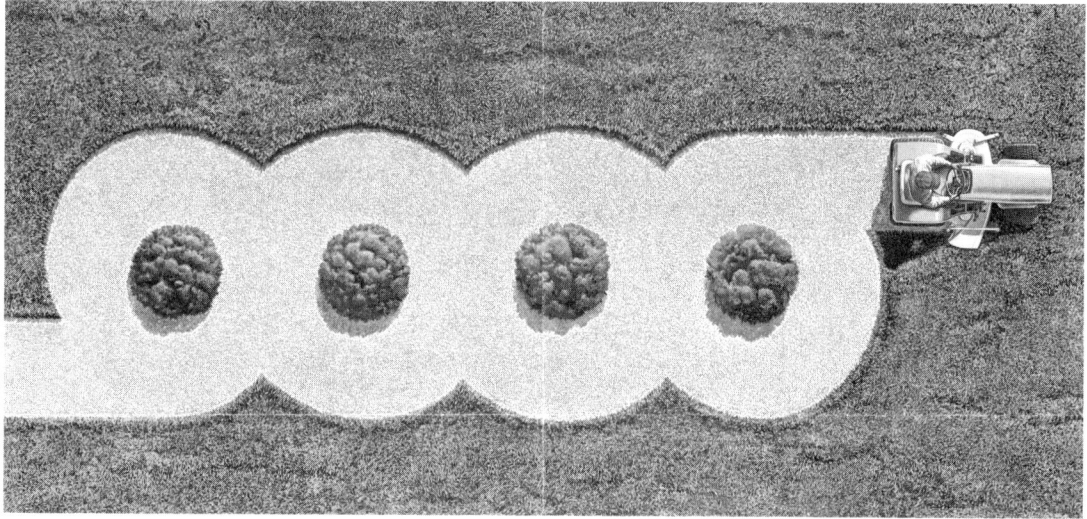

Our 430 Diesel runs circles around the competition.

Cut a few acres of grass and you'll appreciate anyone's diesel tractor. For the fuel economy as well as the diesel power.

But you only have to cut a few feet of grass to appreciate the John Deere 430 Diesel. Especially if those first few feet take you around a bush, or under a branch, or anywhere you need a highly maneuverable tractor. Because our diesel not only saves you fuel, it saves you time.

The fact is, ours may be the only diesel to combine a 26-inch turning radius with power steering and hydrostatic drive. All features that turn the 430 into a tractor that turns tight corners easily, over and over again. Virtually eliminating the need for trimming.

But while our 430 Diesel is maneuverable enough for the delicate jobs, it's also strong enough to put in a full eight hours on the toughest assignments. Thanks to a liquid-cooled 20-hp 3-cylinder engine.

You'll get the fuel economy you need day after day. And the durability you want year after year. In fact, we're so confident of the durability of our 430 Diesel that we've given it a new 2-year limited warranty.

For the name of the dealer nearest you, or a free folder on the John Deere 430 Diesel, call 800-447-9126 toll free (800-322-6796 in Illinois). Or you can write John Deere, Dept. 50, Moline, Illinois 61265.

The maneuverable John Deere 430 Diesel. Because we know that the shortest distance between two points isn't always a straight line.

Nothing Runs Like a Deere®

**5.3** *This headline relates to the picture in this one ad; the slogan can go on any ad.*

- Try hard to include a benefit (see discussion earlier in chapter)

- Write the headline for the specific ad under consideration. The headline is concerned with the one ad it is used in; the slogan relates to the overall campaign. Look at the magazine ad for John Deere in Figure 5.3. The headline ("OUR 430 DIESEL RUNS CIRCLES AROUND THE COMPETITION"), works with the visual to make a point about one particular product among the hundreds of products that John Deere makes, ending on the snapper (last line of copy) that says "Because we know that the shortest distance between two points isn't always a straight line." Deere's fine old slogan ("Nothing Runs Like a Deere") will work on all ads run by John Deere, regardless of the individual product being sold.

- Make it short. Short headlines make for more flexibility in the design of the ad and a better chance to snag the reader with a short attention span. Both the art director who designs the ad and the reader will be grateful. Examples include:

THE SOUND AND THE FURRY (for a radio in a stuffed dog)

EAT NO EVIL (monkey eating low-calorie ice cream)

Note these two headlines, though short and clever, also carry a benefit. It can be done!

- Be concise (which is not necessarily the same as short). Condense the most pertinent part of the ad to an intriguing statement. Examples:

  ARMORED CAR (for Armor All car cleaner)

  HE REALLY ONLY WALKED 2 MILES TO SCHOOL (an ad for a Dad)

  IS YOUR PILOT FLYING HIGH BEFORE HE TAKES OFF? (drug abuse ad)

- Know when to be clever. Headlines don't have to be funny, provocative or clever when there's a ready-made audience for the message. You may be selling a product or service that is new or offering something free — providing basic information, which is the basic rationale for advertising. Examples:

  OPEN SUNDAYS (for a bank)

  GOING OUT OF BUSINESS SALE (any retailer)

- Write business-to-business headlines the same way you write consumer headlines. Examples:

  AFTER 133 YEARS, WE'RE PROUD TO ANNOUNCE
  WE'VE FINALLY COME UP WITH A LEMON.

  With PIC of a lemon, this copy points out to grocery stores that Dole has a lemon it's proud to sell.

  DOLE WOULD LIKE TO SHOW OFF ITS NAVEL.

  The copy points out that Dole stocks navel oranges now. Many copywriters used to view the readers of business-to-business publications (also called trade books) as not regular people. In other words, they imagined that a reader of a banking publication would appreciate rather unimaginative copy. A reader of an engineering publication would enjoy facts and figures, and so on. The truth is, the same people watch sitcoms and read *People* magazine and play with their children. Just because they read trade books, they don't want to be bored any more than do the readers of popular culture magazines or newspapers.

- Pay off the headline. If your headline says "HOW TO KISS A COW," chances are the copy will be read. That's an intriguing headline. But if you don't tell the readers somewhere in the copy how to kiss a cow, you will have disappointed them. The readers will feel cheated, because you teased them with that headline and didn't pay it off.

- Don't use the headline as the snapper. The snapper is the concluding thought in the copy, often a twist or play on words; it may be humorous or powerful or moving or in some other way a definite and satisfying conclusion. If your headline said "GIRLS DON'T MAKE PASSES AT BOYS WHO WEAR GLASSES," perhaps in an ad for contact lenses, you have a twist on an old quote to tease someone into reading the copy. After you make your pitch in the body copy, don't repeat the headline as the last line of the body copy. If you do, you'll disappoint readers, because they've already read that interesting comment and are ready for something fresh.

- Keep the headline in the same tone as the copy, and vice versa. The "GIRLS DON'T MAKE PASSES" headline has a certain tongue-in-cheek aspect to it, a certain offhanded feeling. If you've written straight copy based on medical reasons for buying these contact lenses, this headline is inappropriate to the tone of the copy. Or, if you write this headline first, the body copy should follow through in the same tone.

As we consider other elements in a print ad, continue to study headlines you see. Learn to see their relationship to the copy, the snapper and the slogan.

## Visuals and Thumbnails

HEAD:       BOOM

PIC:        (TOSHIBA RT-SX2 ASSEMBLED)

HEAD:       B OO M

PIC:        (SAME MACHINE IN THREE PARTS, HEADLINE ELEMENTS RELATING TO PARTS)

**Toshiba Ad Visuals**   The word PIC is used because it's neutral. Some use ILLUST. You can type it on the left even before you know whether your visual will be a photo or a drawing, and it can refer to either. Note that in the Toshiba ad, there is no reference to whether the PIC is a photo or a drawing; the copywriter normally leaves that decision up to the art director.

Even so, it's a good idea for a copywriter to draw a little thumbnail sketch of a suggested layout on the print copy, just to show the art director what the general idea of the PIC is. That's what that funny little drawing was at the bottom of the Toshiba copy (Figure 5.2). In that figure, I drew a little sketch to show you what such a thumbnail would look like. I tried to reproduce the bad drawing ability of the average copywriter and meant no insult to the actual copywriter on this ad.

Whether the art director likes the copywriter's thumbnail or not, he or she will probably do a little thumbnail too, so that the copywriter and art director can come to an agreement before a more sophisticated layout is completed for agency management and the client. The computer is coming on strong, if slowly, in agency creative departments; and some thumbnails and layouts are being done on the computer. Many modern art directors, however, still sketch the thumbnail and ensuing layouts on paper, usually with marker pens and other materials used by advertising artists. Figure 5.4 shows how the art director's thumbnail might look if drawn on a computer. In this course, it is a good idea for you to draw a thumbnail of the ad layout on every piece of print copy you write (or a storyboard in the case of a TV script).

If you look through magazines, you'll see that there will often be more than one PIC, but seldom is the headline split up as it is in this ad. Most art

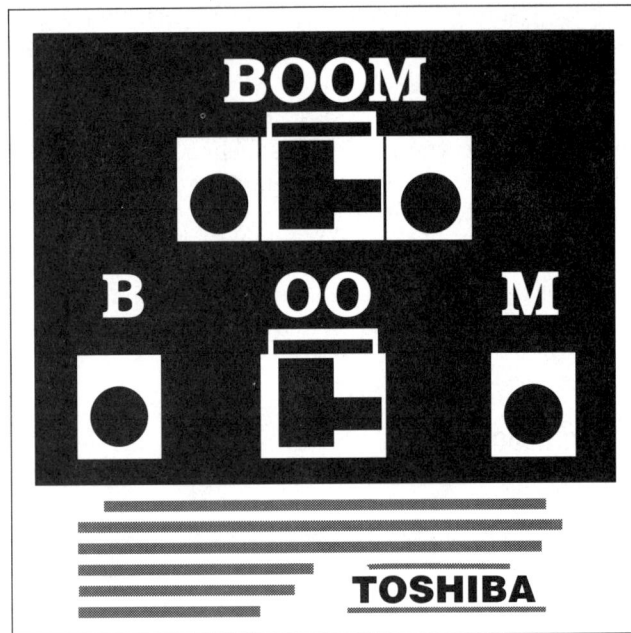

*Thumbnail for the Toshiba ad as done on a computer.*

directors don't like split heads because they take away from unity in the design, but in this case the logic of the headline demanded the split head.

**Visuals in General**    In the early days of print advertising, copywriters would create visuals for their ads and draw thumbnails or actual layouts to size. Then artists would be called upon to slavishly follow the copywriters' visual ideas. Many of these artists didn't even work for the agency, but were called in only as needed. Some of the artists so employed had better ideas than the copywriters, even if the artists weren't technically of an advertising mind. In fact, some of the artists enjoyed the advertising work they were called upon to do, and many soon did develop an advertising mind. In time, artists became art directors who not only improved upon the copywriters' suggested visuals, but also took upon themselves a variety of jobs from the first design (which is "art") through selecting type, choosing models, picking paper stock, supervising the engraving process and a score of other ad production elements (which is "direction").

Until the 1960s, art directors were still not considered equals, in many cases, with the copywriters. As late as 1967, when I first went to Tracy-Locke Advertising in Dallas, the copywriters were housed on the carpeted management floor, and the art directors were downstairs in more sterile surroundings. But during the so-called creative revolution in advertising in the 1960s, regardless of where each was housed, it became the norm for copywriter/art director teams to work together on creative strategies and executions and share equally in the creation of TV commercials and headlines. After strategies and concepts were agreed upon, they would separate and concentrate on the separate crafts of writing and art direction.

Today, some copywriters write their ads without indicating a visual idea (not a good idea); most write not only visual instructions, but also create thumbnails, even though the art director in many cases can be counted on to change the copywriter's visual in some way. Though the copywriter should not get caught up in describing every aspect of a visual or in executing a piece of finished art instead of a rough thumbnail, the copywriter should concentrate just as heavily on the visual as on the writing. Good art directors appreciate a visual suggestion from the copywriter because at the least it gives them a starting point, whether or not the copywriter's visual thinking is represented in the final product.

You saw in the Toshiba ad how simple were the copywriter's visual suggestions. Here's another example of simplicity. If the copywriter's idea for a visual is a dog scratching, the instruction should be written:

PIC:        (DOG SCRATCHING)

Note that the copywriter has not said this is a brown and white collie of about 50 pounds, sitting a certain way, with a doghouse in the background. If the visual works with any dog scratching, don't worry about the details and let the art director do his or her thing. If, however, you are selling doghouses or collies, then you would indicate a picture of a doghouse in the background or foreground or specify the breed of dog. Again, unless it really makes a difference to the ad (if you're selling Kodak film, for instance), don't say anything but "PIC" and let the art director decide whether the picture should be a drawing or a photograph. Even in the case of a Kodak ad, some creative people could rationalize the use of a drawing.

## Subheads

The main purpose of a subhead is to pull the reader from one block of copy into another one. Because most newspaper and magazine ads don't have long copy, subheads aren't used as much in those media as in brochures, direct mail, annual reports and other collateral advertising pieces. Of course, long real estate and car ads aren't rare, so you will have the opportunity to write subheads from time to time for magazine and newspaper ads. When writing a subhead for an ad, be aware of what the reader has just read and anticipate the reader's need for a little nudge into the next section of your wonderful copy. Sometimes the subheads come to you as you're writing the body copy, and sometimes you don't realize you need a subhead until you go back to review the body copy you've written.

The main danger in subheads is writing a subhead to explain the headline. If you have to explain your headline with a subhead, you haven't written a very good headline:

HEAD:           NEW GIRL IN TOWN!

SUBHEAD:        Sally Beauty Supply Opens
                First Store in Birmingham

Although you see such subheads used all the time, they give an ad a "busy" look and lend an ad a tone of voice that might be inconsistent with what you had in mind. On the other hand, a retail ad pushing a sale or multiple products and prices may employ several subheads to differentiate products from each other. But that's the point. The head and subhead for Sally Beauty may make an ad look like a sale-heavy retail ad when the intent of the ad is to establish a corporate look. Perhaps the way to combine the head and subhead effectively would be:

HEAD:     SALLY IS NEW
            GIRL IN TOWN

Then let the first line of copy communicate the information about a new store.

Subheads probably came into popularity in the early days of newspapers to create a sense of excitement and break up huge areas of gray copy. Read your local newspaper and study the use of subheads in feature stories. Apply the lessons learned to long advertising copy you might have to write, because journalism and advertising have much in common.

## Transition Lines

COPY:     What really sets Toshiba's RT-SX2 apart is how it comes apart.

A **transition line,** the first line of copy, is often a transition from the headline to the more intense sell of body copy. But some copy is only one sentence in all, so a transition line is not always in evidence.

The Toshiba ad provides a perfect example of a transition line. You have the headline coming apart, you have PICs of the product assembled and apart. The opening copy talks about what you've seen, something "apart," and uses clever phrasing (sets Toshiba's RT-SX2 apart) to drive home the theme of this product coming apart.

The first line of the copy is a bridge to the sell copy from what you always hope is an intriguing headline. The transition line acknowledges what the PIC and headline have done for the reader and shows understanding for why the reader has not turned the page. It sets the stage for the persuasion of the body copy. People in advertising estimate that only 10 percent of people read the copy; that might be true, but perhaps more than that read the first line of copy. Hook 'em while you got 'em.

Examples of heads and first lines of copy include:

IS YOUR HAIR GROWING OLD BEFORE THE REST OF YOU?
What you do to your hair you wouldn't do to any other part of your body.
(Pantene)

ARE YOU FIT TO LIVE?
These days, survival of the fittest isn't just theory, it's fact.
(St. Helena Hospital and Health Center of Napa Valley)

Notice that these first lines of copy don't come on with a heavy-handed sell, but rather are extensions of the thought in the head, to soften the blow for the pitch that is to come. Readers know the pitch is coming, but they want you to be gentle.

More examples of transition lines:

CITIZENS AGAINST HANDGUNS

PIC:       (ROBERT KENNEDY)

HEAD:      SOME OF OUR BEST IDEAS HAVE BEEN SHOT DOWN

COPY:          On June 5, 1968 one of the truly brilliant minds of our time
           was abruptly lost to us forever...

MAX LONG DISTANCE

PIC:       (MAN IN DEEP SEA DIVER'S SUIT WITH PHONE)

HEAD:      A PHONE CALL TO ATLANTA SHOULDN'T SOUND LIKE A PHONE
           CALL TO ATLANTIS

COPY:          Does your bargain long distance make you sound like you're
           calling from a tin can 10,000 leagues under the sea?

THE AMERICAN MUSEUM OF NATURAL HISTORY

HEAD:      AN OFFER FOR ANYONE WHO THINKS HERPETOLOGY IS
           SOMETHING YOU COULD CATCH

COPY:          Nobody has all the answers. But you will find the answers to
           some very intriguing questions right here at the museum...

Note in all these introductory lines of copy the setup for the pitch to come: to write for handgun information, to send in a coupon for MAX, to visit the museum. You have to set up the pitch, because people aren't sitting there waiting for a sales job. They're waiting for a great piece of writing; they're waiting to be persuaded. The opening lines of copy, the transition lines, are the first steps to persuasion.

## Body Copy

COPY:          What really sets Toshiba's RT-SX2 apart is how it comes apart.
           The speakers detach for true stereo separation.
               And the system includes an AM/FM stereo radio and an auto-
           reverse cassette deck with soft touch controls.
               In short, it's perhaps the best boom box anyone's ever put
           together.

**The Toshiba Body Copy**    Line by line, let's take a look at the Toshiba body copy. The first line, the transition line, plays off the separate elements in the second PIC. The line cleverly introduces the model number of the product, RT-SX2, by linking the number with an engaging play on words: What sets it apart is how it comes apart. That's quite a claim, by the way, because other machines come apart, too. But Toshiba claims that this feature sets its machine apart. In the broadest interpretation, you could defend yourself to the legal staff by saying you're only claiming that machines like this one are set apart from machines that don't come apart.

The second line gets right into the point of the ad, that the speakers separate. There's nothing clever about this line, though it is in fact a payoff to the first line, an answer to the tease in the first line. Notice the connection. English teachers say that the first line of a new paragraph should pick up the thread of the thought in the last line of the previous paragraph. In body copy, where space and time to sell are at a premium, each sentence should pick up from the last, to maintain a tight line of continuity and logic.

The third line contains three copy points that either the client or the copywriter or both thought important to communicate about this machine. And it may very well be that these points set the machine apart from other machines that also come apart. These copy points sound impressive, are simply communicated, and lend respectability to a pitch that started off with humor and may not have been so convincing to the consumer without a sense of humor.

The last line is a true snapper, a classic snapper, playing off the PIC and the first line of copy. It's a restatement, in an entertaining way, of the main point that the machine comes apart. Part of the entertainment stems from the double meaning of "anyone ever put together," meaning the best machine the client ever built or that the customer ever used.

In the early days of print advertising, when quack medicines were advertised as the cure for everything you could name, advertising deservedly earned a bad name for exaggeration. The key to good body copy is to avoid any hint of exaggeration, to weave a logical case as strong as any lawyer's, to entertain with lively writing while doing so, and to reflect respectability. In this Toshiba ad, the body copy comes off as reasonable, not exaggerated. Its tone, set by well-written words, took skillful crafting.

**Body Copy in General**   Many experienced copywriters develop a consistent way of thinking and writing, regardless of medium. I don't mean that the writer can't go from humor to Americana to emotion to a heavy-handed sell at the drop of a paycheck. Versatility is one of the copywriter's tools. But consistent word choices, sentence lengths, logical approaches and other factors that make it possible to recognize a certain writer's style in every medium. Given that, and understanding that, each medium still forces certain restrictions on the writer: short copy on outdoor, for instance, or unusual contractions in a jingle that may look illiterate in print, such as "gonna," "wanna," "doncha" and the like.

The point of this discussion is to steer you away from thinking you must change your style for each medium. It's not your style you change; it's your format. You're conscious of the effects of spoken words in broadcast and the effects of printed words as you write. You write one type of copy for the ears and the other for the eyes. Your approach to logic and writing doesn't have to vary for you to write for each medium. In the long run, you may find your style of writing for broadcast may actually be just fine for print, perhaps because of the effect of writing all your copy on the right-hand side of the page.

**Writing on the Right-Hand Side of the Page**   As we saw in the basic ad format on page 67, the elements should appear on the left-hand side of the page and the copy on the right. I adapt this standard format by dividing the page in half vertically and moving the copy column further to the right. Not all examples of ad copy printed in this book appear in this half-page format, and copywriters often use variations of the same basic format. However, the half-page format has many advantages. Writing copy in this half-page width will encourage you to be concise in broadcast, where time is at a premium. But space in print is at a premium, too. The client is paying for that space, and a concise writing style will enable you to either get in more good sales points or leave more room for the art director's graphic presentation. One advantage, then, to half-page writing, is preventing some part of the mind from saying, "This is print. Write all you want. Plenty of room."

Half-page writing is based on the narrow columns of newspaper stories. That newspapers have evolved to this format universally says a lot about the width of copy best suited to the reader. Another advantage to half-page writing is the rhythm it gives to print advertising; half-page writing is also based on broadcast copy, which tends to have a rhythm because it's written to be read aloud. People can sense that rhythm in print.

Go back to the Toshiba copy on page 69 and sense the rhythm of the lines as they are written. Note the sense of the lines, as well as the way the sentences are broken line for line. A copywriter should be concerned with the rhythm of the copy because it makes reading easier, which helps to sell the product. Read the Toshiba copy out loud. It was written for print, but notice how easily it would flow as radio copy.

A third advantage of half-page writing is how the copy actually looks. Big gloppy paragraphs of gray type scare people away.

But note this.

Your eye is drawn here.

Faster.

Because of this style.

You seem to read faster.

And enjoy it more.

There's no reason you shouldn't employ the same terse style in print as in broadcast, and for the same reason: impact. You do it in broadcast because you want to make the voice talent say the words exactly as you heard them when you wrote them.

To emphasize words in broadcast,

you use <u>underlines</u>,

*italics*,

and careful

breaking of sentences

from line to line.

In print, there's no reason why you shouldn't cater to the reader's eye with as much care as you do to the listener's ear. Of course, there is no guarantee the art director will design the typesetting in accordance with the way you indicated the copy breaks. (Note that the Toshiba copy [Figure 5.1] was set without paragraphs. Odds are good the copywriter probably had several paragraphs.) If you are passionate about the way you broke the copy and have a good relationship with your art director, you may be able to successfully argue your case. As you contemplate print writing and formats, then, try to develop one style that doesn't change, but only adapts to the requirements of various media. A beginning step toward this is to consistently write your copy — whether print or broadcast — on the right half-page.

**Length of Body Copy**   Even if it fills a page, body copy should be short: short words, short sentences, short paragraphs. Body copy should be as long as necessary to tell the story. Outside of the obvious limitations of the space the ad is meant to fill, stop when you've had your say. Total length is not usually a problem. Good art directors will find a way to set off your words. It's the length of time it takes you to get to the point and to the persuasion that dictates the length of copy.

Even readers who are interested in what you're selling don't want to be bored. They're doing you a favor by reading your words, and it's important to get right to the point. But don't get to the point at the expense of your reader's entertainment. You should still have a creative strategy, a plot and fun with your copy, but it needs to move along at a brisk rate. In the best of all possible worlds, your entertainment "hook" will include all the copy points you need to get across, just as the first line of the Toshiba copy included the name of the model in the midst of making a cute remark.

**Including Copy Points**   What doesn't work very well is a mere recitation of copy points, a criticism you don't want to have written on your copy by your creative director or teacher. There's nothing that makes clients feel less like paying for your copy than to have you vomit back at them the copy points they gave to you in the first place. Copywriting is more than arranging the copy points into sentences and writing a head and thinking of a picture. Copywriting is first examining what copy point dominates all others, to arrive at a creative strategy. Second, it's figuring out what other copy points are necessary to weave into your copy as supporting reasons. All the copy points are woven into a single-point story.

The third line of the Toshiba ad is probably not as good an example of integrating copy points as you might find elsewhere. Following is an example that shows how copy points can be made vital to the single-point story. Though you can read the ad in Figure 5.5, I have again written it out in a standard format so you grow accustomed to the idea of writing in this format.

| PIC: | (RABBIT CONVERTIBLE IN THE SNOW) |
|------|----------------------------------|
| HEAD: | SNOW JOB |
| COPY: | 'S no joke.<br>If we proved one thing after all these years, it's this: Volkswagens are just about perfect for winter driving. Why should the Rabbit Convertible be any different? |

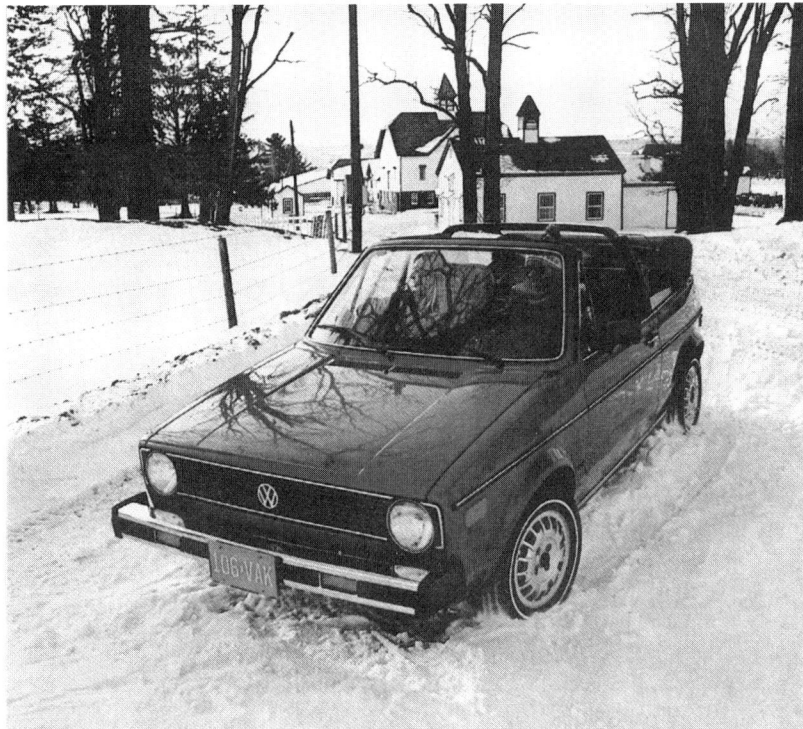

$10,595. Rabbit Convertible includes 12-month unlimited mileage, limited warranty. Mfr's sugg. retail price. Transp., tax, reg., dealer prep. add'l. Alloy wheels, whitewalls optional.   Seatbelts save lives

## Snow job.

'S no joke.

If we've proved one thing after all these years, it's this: Volkswagens are just about perfect for winter driving. Why should the Rabbit Convertible be any different?

It's a Volkswagen, isn't it? With positive-pull front-wheel drive (just like other Volkswagens). So you can go dashing through the snow when you want to. And you can turn or stop smartly when you have to. Because our convertible has an advanced suspension system and steel-belted radial tires (just like other Volkswagens).

The car certainly has its practical side. And top. Thanks to our engineers. (Their idea of having fun with a convertible is to design a top that's double insulated and fits snug. So you can keep snug. Even at 0°F.)

Some people think a car this practical can't be much fun to drive. But some people think a car this much fun to drive can't be very practical. Some people are wrong.

**Nothing else is a Volkswagen**

5.5

*This Volkswagen ad integrates five copy points into the story it tells.*

It's a Volkswagen, isn't it? With positive-pull front-wheel drive (just like other Volkswagens). So you can go dashing through the snow when you want to. And you can turn or stop smartly when you have to. Because our convertible has an advanced suspension system and steel-belted radial tires (just like other Volkswagens).

The car certainly has its practical side. And top. Thanks to our engineers. (Their idea of having fun with

a convertible is to design a top that's
double insulated and fits snug. So
you can keep snug. Even at 0°F.)

    Some people think a car this
practical can't be much fun to drive.
But some people think a
car this much fun to
drive can't be very
practical. Some people
are wrong.

| | |
|---|---|
| LOGO: | (LOGO) |
| SLOGAN: | Nothing else is a Volkswagen |
| MANDATORIES: | $10,595. Rabbit Convertible includes 12-month unlimited mileage warranty. Mfr's sugg. retail price. Transp., tax, reg., dealer prep. add'l. Alloy wheels, whitewalls: optional. Seatbelts save lives. |

**Analysis of the VW Ad**    This is nice body copy, vintage Doyle Dane Bern-bach advertising agency, 1983. Study this copy. There are at least five heavy copy points: (1) positive-pull front-wheel drive, (2) advanced suspension system, (3) steel-belted radial tires, (4) double-insulated top and (5) snug top. See also how many times the word *Volkswagen* is used in a totally natural way.

    By rising above the copy points to a story of how all VWs are good in winter, the copy points support the copy that says this model is no exception, that this model is "just like other Volkswagens." The copy points are necessary to the story, not just a gratuitous recitation of facts.

    Notice how the mandatory copy is set in small type and run under the picture, out of the way of the main story. It's a good example of copy that is required by the client, but that does little for the main story. Even so, those who would argue that price and warranty information are part of a car ad make a good point. The author's point of view is that if the ad is persuasive and works without the additional information, then that additional information should be labeled MANDATORY.

**Other Examples**    The Jeep ad in Figure 5.6 is an example of the best copy sometimes being no copy, if the art direction tells the story. It's no coincidence, probably, that the copywriter received mention as one of the two art directors on this ad.

    The headline on the Honda ad in Figure 5.7 ("MY, HOW WE'VE GROWN") is a good example of two meanings: a phrase used with kids, and one is pictured here; and a copy point about a larger car, also pictured. Note how the snapper, "That's why this car is for families who want one to grow on," relates to the first meaning of the headline. The second meaning of the head is explored in the rest of the body copy, so there is a nice payoff to the concept that intrigued the reader in the first place.

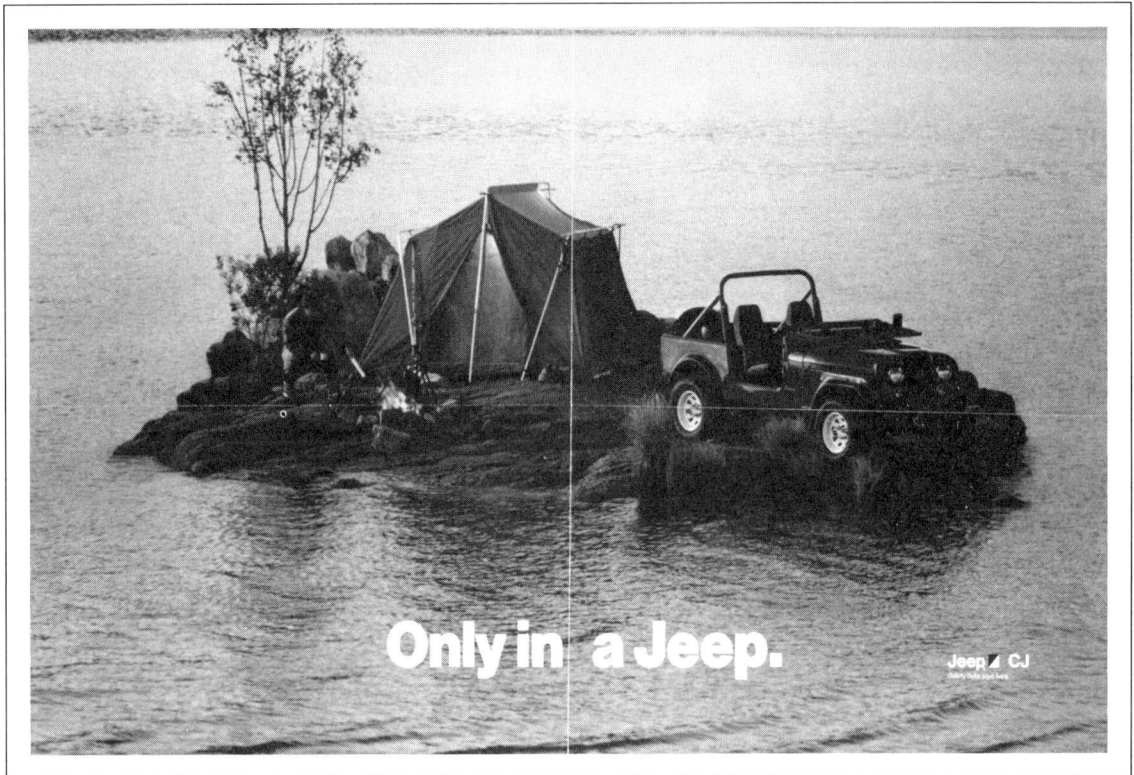

**Only in a Jeep.**

Jeep CJ

**5.6**      *Sometimes having no copy at all is highly effective.*

These examples of body copy are included to help you focus on body copy as opposed to headlines. We could fill the book with these examples, but there is no need to do so. The world around you is filled with advertising. Look at the ads you see in newspapers and magazines with new eyes, searching for the relationship between headlines and transition lines, transition lines and body copy, body copy and snappers. Remember, the main thing about body copy is to get out when everything necessary to the sell has been said.

## Snappers

The snapper is the little twist you put at the end of your copy, to cap your effort. The snapper is something moving, humorous, shocking or provocative — something that in some way surprises and/or satisfies the reader. The snapper is also a bridge that ties back to the body copy and points to the signature and slogan, if there is one. Let's look at the Toshiba snapper.

In short, it's perhaps the best boom box anyone's ever put together.

SLOGAN:      In Touch with Tomorrow

# My, how we've grown.

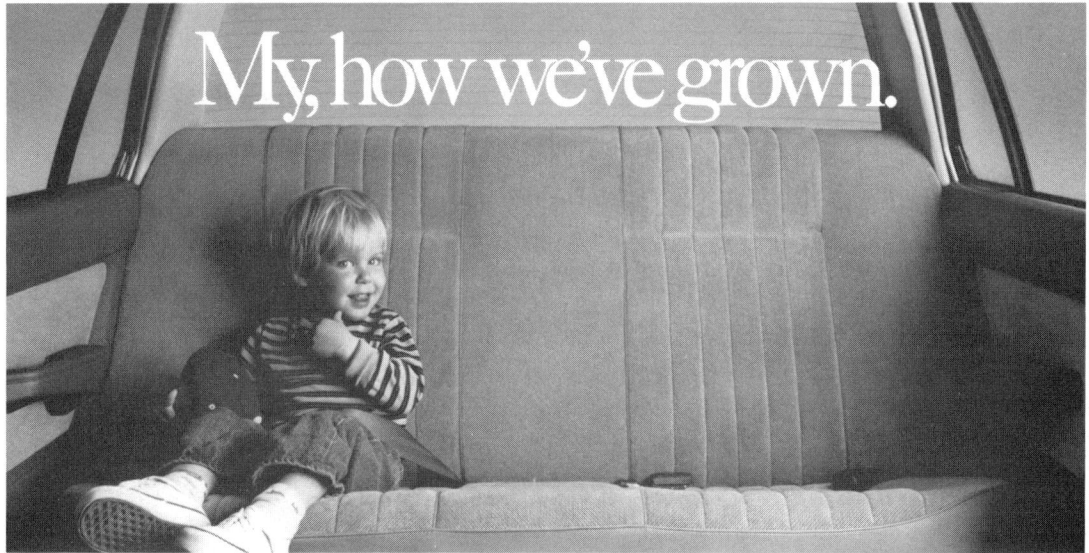

In the back seat of our Civic 4-Door Sedan, we've grown headroom, shoulder room, legroom, hiproom, and kid room.

In the trunk, we've increased our carrying capacity by an amazing 13%. Our glass area has grown, too, for better visibility.

We've included driver comforts like an adjustable steering column, child-proof rear door locks, and optional automatic transmission, as well.

But while we were doing all this growing, we didn't forget to keep the sticker price small. That's why this car is for families who want one to grow on.

The Civic 4-Door Sedan

**5.7** *Headline, visual, body copy, and snapper all work together perfectly in this ad.*

**The Toshiba Snapper**  We included the slogan here to show how a snapper can set the stage for the campaign theme as well as end the body copy on a satisfactory note. The headline and copy were all about the boom box coming apart, and the snapper wraps up that thought. But the company's slogan covers a variety of products with the more encompassing idea that Toshiba is a company with modern innovations, as expressed by "In Touch with Tomorrow." The "anyone's ever put together" thought in the snapper points mildly toward the slogan.

**Snappers in General**  If there's no slogan, then the snapper precedes the signature (name) of the advertiser. The problem with snappers is usually not writing them. Most people, copywriters or not, seem to have the gift of coming up with a snapper. The hard part is to make sure the snapper is not a repeat of the headline or the slogan, that it finishes off the copy with flair and with relevancy to the signature and slogan, if there is one (see Figure 5.8).

Although we're formalizing aspects of an ad here and picking parts out, it's important to remind you that snappers are not always the last words of copy. It could be the headline, as in an Audi ad: "ACTIONS SPEAK LOUDER THAN WORDS." (The head is followed by a list of racing events won by Audi.) The snapper could be a copy line in outdoor advertising, as in

## One ride and you'll understand why most rocket scientists are German.

There is nothing else like it. Nothing. As the intercooled, turbocharged engine spins past 3000 rpm, the raspy, throaty 282 hp flat six makes mechanical music unlike anything you've heard.

The surge of power that follows is simply astonishing. You are literally pressed back and held fast by the deep leather sports seats. Like Al Holbert, Hans Stuck and Derek Bell before you, you feel the breathtaking thrust of legendary performance.

This, after all, is the engine that conquered Le Mans and Sebring more times than any other engine in automotive history.

This is the car that *Car and Driver* tested from 0 to 60 in 4.6 seconds, and in 13.1 seconds for the quarter mile—records still unbroken by any other production car in the world in the past 20 years.

This is the car that David E. Davis, Jr., Editor/Publisher of *Automobile Magazine*, called the most likely car to become a classic in the future.

And this is the car that stands as the epitome of 40 years of uncompromised, racing-bred Porsche engineering heritage.

If you think it's a remarkable car to look at, wait until you get behind the wheel.

It may be true that German engineers have produced vehicles capable of more prodigious performance. But you won't find them on this planet.

PORSCHE

**5.8** *The last lines (snapper) of this Porsche ad refer to German engineers, saying they may have produced "vehicles capable of more prodigious performance. But you won't find them on this planet." Note the tie-in with the head without duplicating the exact words: "One ride and you'll understand why most rocket scientists are German."*

a MADD poster showing pallbearers carrying a coffin: "YOU SHOULD HAVE CALLED FOR A LIFT EARLIER." Or in a Minnesota Zoo ad showing a ferocious cobra, the snapper is "MORE SNAKES IN THE GRASS THAN KNOTS LANDING." Sometimes the snapper is the name of the client, as in the outdoor boards showing beautiful sports action in art, signed only with a small NIKE.

As usual, it's the idea — the creative strategy — behind the advertising that dictates whether your words or the client name or the slogan register the surprising impact a snapper should have. Such impact is exemplified by a billboard that has obviously been destroyed by fire, leaving enough space to say: "DON'T JUST *HOPE* YOU HAVE GOOD INSURANCE" and then lists the name of the client, an insurance company.

**Writing the Snapper Before the Body Copy**   If you come up with the snapper early in your writing of an ad, you have something to write to, something that ends and emphasizes the story you will write. Ads are written in various order by various writers, but it does make sense to consider writing the last line of the body copy first, to give you a direction, to enable you to write shorter copy because you know where you are going. How many novelists or playwrights start writing without knowing the ending?

## Slogans

Many copywriters write the slogan first if it does not already exist. Though you are reading a linear description of the writing of advertising, realize that often many of these seemingly separate parts of writing happen all at once. In the case of the Toshiba ad, the slogan probably existed before the copywriter was asked to write the specific ad we've been exploring.

SLOGAN:      In Touch with Tomorrow

It often happens with a multi-product company that you are asked to write to the corporate umbrella slogan on a specific product, such as the one in the Toshiba ad. If so, again, try to write a snapper that captures what came before and hints at the slogan to come.

**Slogans in General**    A slogan is a clever and/or memorable distillation of the creative strategy. It is not at all unusual for a copywriter to hammer out a creative strategy and have the slogan that explains that strategy pop into mind at the same time. It is also not unusual for a slogan to come to mind before there is a creative strategy and for that slogan to lead the copywriter backward to the strategy.

The slogan should be a punchy condensation of your creative strategy. It needs to be a phrase that can be sung as well as read and above all should embody the point of your creative strategy in an interesting way. It goes on every ad in a campaign. Every ad is written to it. Along with your logo and the graphic design of your print and broadcast, the slogan carries the continuity of the campaign.

**Specific Slogans**    Also called taglines or themelines, slogans often become the part of your campaign that people remember most. Here are a few:

You Deserve a Break Today (McDonald's)

The Quality Goes In Before the Name Goes On (Zenith)

Everything You Always Wanted in a Beer. And Less (Miller Lite)

We Try Harder (Avis, original)

We Try Harder to Make Things Easier (latest Avis variation)

Things Go Better with Coke

We Make People Happy (Astroworld)

Good to the Last Drop (Maxwell House)

Stick with the One You Know (Scotch Brand tape)

You can see that the name of the client may or may not be in the slogan, though it seems better if it is. If the name of the client is in the slogan, you do art directors a favor, because they don't have to add the SIG in limited spaces — outdoor boards, for instance. The name is already there.

How do you come up with a slogan? Think short. Think pithy. Think double meaning. For example:

Doing What We Do Best (American Airlines. First meaning: the thing we do best is to fly people from here to there. Second meaning: we fly people from here to there better than other airlines.)

All My Men Wear English Leather, or They Wear Nothing at All (The double meaning is obvious.)

All slogans don't have to be screamingly funny or have double meaning to be effective. These three have a simple point to make and make it with economy of language and dignity:

The Art of Engineering (Audi)

Engineered Like No Other Car in the World (Mercedes)

If You Don't Look Good, We Don't Look Good (Vidal Sassoon)

To write a slogan is to write a footline for a campaign, as opposed to a headline for one ad. Read ads. Watch TV. Look for the slogans. They pop up at the end, usually, and appear over or under the product or service name.

**Slogan Guidelines**    Like all copy, slogans are written as a result of both hard work *and* inspiration. Some guidelines to help you begin follow:

* Keep them short. They're easier to sing and easier to integrate with a signature if short.

* Cull out extraneous words. "Taste As Good As They Crunch" is better than "They Taste As Good As They Crunch."

* Make it a distillation of the creative strategy, not a repeat of the creative strategy. If the strategy has been worded as a perfect slogan, rewrite the strategy in terms that don't sound like the creative execution, which the slogan is part of.

* Make the slogan rise above specific copy points. On rare occasions a specific copy point may make for a short-term slogan — "The Only Car with Rear Wheels That Turn" — but a slogan should normally be written to last for years, in hopes that it will become part of American pop culture.

* Regardless of the point of an individual ad, write to the slogan. For people who don't read copy, the head and slogan may carry the whole message. Don't let the slogan get tacked on as an afterthought. It should be, if only remotely, a relevant last word.

* The best way to learn to write slogans is to read them — in ads, TV spots and on outdoor boards — and to listen for them on radio.

## SIGs, Maps, Etc.

Be sure you sign every ad with the name of the client, product, or client and product together — whatever is the recognizable name for this product or service when a consumer buys it. Always have a SIG, even though you also have a logo. Let the art director worry about integrating the SIG with the logo.

As for maps, addresses, phone numbers, coupons — the main thing is that you take these things as seriously as you do the rest of the copy. These are copy. Your reputation as a thorough copywriter can be enhanced by the way you take the little things seriously. Years ago a writer was forced at the last minute by a restaurant client to include the information that the restaurant would take MasterCard, Visa and American Express. As the client said: "Just tell them 'MasterCard, Visa and American Express cards accepted.'" The copywriter had to put his own mark on even that simplistic copy and wrote "MasterCard, Visa, American Express and cash cheerfully accepted." The restaurant ran that little piece of copy for years in all its advertising, long after the original agency had been supplanted by others.

## Instructions That Aren't Copy

To make it easier for the art directors and others who read your copy to know the difference between the actual words in the selling message, and technical instructions, it is traditional to put instructions in parentheses and write them in capital letters:

PIC:          (WINDING ROAD IN THE DESERT)

LOGO:        (CLIENT'S LOGO)

## PRINT WRITING HINTS

• Know the elements that go into an ad.

• Learn and use the proper format of ad copy.

• Identify your ad copy properly.

• Make the headline relevant to the ad being written, not to the entire campaign.

• Be just as creative with visuals as you are with words. Create a rough thumbnail drawing to go with every print ad.

• Be sure the transition line (first line of copy) refers back to the headline and points the way to the body copy.

• When you have said all you have to say, stop writing body copy.

• End your body copy with a provocative snapper.

• Your slogan should be an umbrella statement (distilled from the creative strategy) that rises above copy points.

• Be sure you write the little things like coupons and credit card notations with as much fervor as you write headlines and body copy.

## IN CONCLUSION

Many copywriters prefer to write radio and TV advertising over print advertising for magazines and newspapers. They enjoy a higher level of ego gratification and sense a higher level of public awareness of their mini-films for TV or their jingles on radio. But newspapers and magazines are the classic media for advertising, the media that first made advertising and advertising agencies a real business.

There are two major differences between writing broadcast advertising and writing print advertising. First, reading is a very personal one-on-one experience. There is an advantage in this when selling, because a person who is reading has fewer diversions competing with the copywriter's sales pitch. A person reading is doing it on purpose, is volunteering valuable time to read your words. Second, and most important, print writing requires a grasp of grammar and spelling — and all the other elements of literacy required of any writer. Broadcast advertising, for instance, does not require spelling skills; even more, the conversational mode of the broadcast media means writing incomplete sentences that might not communicate at all in print.

It is important that the new copywriter know that in agencies and corporate marketing setups, it is often the norm to relegate the new writer to print writing, while many of the more experienced hands are writing the more glamorous broadcast assignments. If you have the proper respect for classic print writing, you know that should not be the case. In these situations, then, new copywriters who might excel at broadcast could fail at print and so never get a chance to show what they can do. Many universities are concerned about developing a stronger program to produce graduates who are better at writing in general, the feeling being that broadcast news and entertainment has lessened the interest in reading and writing that college graduates should have. Those who will pay you for copywriting have no less an interest in your print writing ability.

## EXERCISES

1. Choose a local retail account, write a Creative Work Plan for it, then write a quarter-page newspaper ad, making sure you have a slogan, a snapper, a headline, a transition line and body copy.

2. Do the same for a full-page magazine ad, in full color, for a durable goods, packaged goods or service account.

# WRITING FOR TV

Writing copy for television commercials, also known as TV spots, doesn't mean writing in a new style, as we've already said. It does mean writing for the ear (as well as the eye) and working more closely on the actual production of the spot.

If you're writing a campaign, you may have started the creative execution with the print part of the campaign, so that by the time you get to the TV spot you already have a slogan to write to and end your spots with. If you start creative execution with TV, you would go through the preliminary thinking described in Chapter 4 and the creation of a slogan would proceed as described in Chapter 5. We shall assume in this chapter that you do have a slogan to write to.

Technically, if you have absorbed the lessons of Chapters 1–5, you're already a terrific copywriter and now you're only expanding your horizons about specific media. Let's start with the elements and format of a TV spot.

# ELEMENTS AND FORMAT OF A TV SPOT

Because of TV's exclusive combination of sight, sound and motion, beginning copywriters tend to be overwhelmed by the variety of terms and the never-ending aspects of this medium. Relax. It's all quite simple if you take it a little bit at a time.

Following are the main elements found in a script. The list does not include some specific camera shots and other terms we shall learn later, because shots and terms are subordinate to the overall structure of a script.

Identification (in upper left corner)

SIGHT heading

SOUND heading

Description of actions you can see, under **SIGHT** heading

Descriptions of things you hear, under **SOUND** heading

Final scene, to include client or product name, and slogan, telephone number or other important information. But not all at once, because the final scene doesn't have much room.

Let's take a look at an actual TV spot that was turned down by the client. This will give us an opportunity to flesh out the elements noted above and give you a sense of the format of a TV script. Study this script carefully. You're familiar with the identification in the upper left-hand corner, and you know it varies by company or agency in how it is displayed. The rest of the script more or less reflects the advertising industry standard for how a script should be constructed.

FRITO-LAY, JALAPENO BEAN DIP
:30 TV
"CHARACTER"
Jim Albright
19 September 1991

| **SIGHT:** | **SOUND:** | |
| --- | --- | --- |
| 1. OPEN ON: CU OF CAN OF JALAPENO BEAN DIP. | SFX: | (DISSONANT CELLO) |
| 2. PULL OUT TO SEE TOP OF CAN OPEN AND HAND OF AN ANIMATED CHARACTER STICK OUT. | CHAR: | (AGONIZED VOICE, CRACKING) Water . . . |
| 3. CHARACTER CLIMBS OUT AND SLITHERS DOWN SIDE OF CAN. | | Water . . . |
| 4. SEE CAN ALONE IN MIDDLE OF SCREEN. | VO: | One thing about Jalapeno Bean Dip. It's a little hot . . . |

SFX: *(DISSONANT CELLO)*

CHAR: *(AGONIZED VOICE, CRACKING) Water*

*Water . . .*

VO: *One thing about Jalapeño Bean Dip. It's a litte hot . . .*

SFX: *(LID SLAMS SHUT)*
VO: *. . . but they always come back for more.*

SONG: *JALAPEÑO BEAN DIP THEY ALWAYS COME BACK FOR MORE!*

**6.1** *Copywriter's thumbnail storyboard for Jalapeno Bean Dip commercial.*

| | | |
|---|---|---|
| 5. CHARACTER RETURNS AND JUMPS INTO CAN AND PULLS TOP DOWN. | SFX: | (LID SLAMS SHUT) |
| | VO: | . . . but they always come back for more. |
| 6. ZOOM TO: NAME ON LABEL. SUPER: They Always Come Back | SONG: | JALAPENO BEAN DIP, THEY ALWAYS COME BACK FOR MORE! |

Figure 6.1 is the copywriter's **storyboard** for the Jalapeno Bean Dip commercial. If you draw the storyboard on paper, the copy under the panels can be handwritten, because it is a waste of time and premature to type the copy on a thumbnail storyboard at this point. Some people believe both visual and sound indications should go beneath the storyboard panels, but I believe the board itself should represent the visuals, and only sound indications are necessary, as shown.

## Upper Left-Hand Corner

The only difference in the identification between print and broadcast is the second line. The second line tells whether it is radio or TV, and the length of the commercial. Some people indicate whether the commercial is to be shot on film or tape with :30 TV, FILM, or :30 TV, VTR (video tape recording). If the script is for a slide show or 10-minute film, the second line should reflect that.

## The Sound Side

The two columns on the right describe the kind of sound and the sounds or words themselves.

**Some Terms** **Dialogue** is speech by a character or characters in some sort of plot, indicated by MAN, BOY, WOMAN, DOG or even by names if the names are important to the plot. To describe a character's mood or voice sound, go by this example:

| SIGHT: | SOUND: | |
|---|---|---|
| OPEN ON: CU TEENAGER'S FACE | TEEN: | (WHINING) Oh Dad! |
| CUT TO: CU DAD'S FACE | DAD: | (SADLY) You lost my hammer. |

**Voice-over (VO)** is a disembodied voice that speaks over the action on the screen. In radio it's called **ANNC** for *announcer*, but in TV the term VO is usually employed. Example:

| SIGHT: | SOUND: | |
|---|---|---|
| SEE CAT PLAYING WITH TOY | VO: | Get your cat a toy that works. |

Although VO usually refers to an unidentified voice without a body speaking as a salesperson for the client, there is another kind of VO: when a character talks on camera (OC) and the same character's voice is over (VO) a scene in which the character does not appear. Example:

| SIGHT: | SOUND: | |
|---|---|---|
| MAN TALKS TO CAM | MAN: (OC) | Hi! |
| CUT TO DOG | MAN: (VO) | How's my dog? |

By reserving VO, VO1, VO2, etc., as a bodiless voice or voices and using parentheses, (VO) and (OC), for characters, not only you but also the people who read your script will avoid much confusion. A character will never be followed by either (VO) or (OC) without *both* being used in the script. When MAN or WOMAN, whatever the character, is used without (VO) and (OC) in a script, it is assumed that character is always on screen when speaking.

**SFX** means sound effects, and can be anything from a dog coughing to a description of the character's tone of voice to instrumental music. Examples:

| | | |
|---|---|---|
| OPEN ON: COUGHING DOG | SFX: | (DOG COUGHING) |
| CUT TO: MAN'S FACE | MAN: | (IN HUSKY VOICE) <br> I just gotta quit smoking. |
| CUT TO: DOG NODDING AGREEMENT | SFX: | (INST. OF COUNTRY MUSIC, UP & UNDER VO) |
| CUT TO: MAN PATTING DOG | VO: | Yes folks, smoking is harmful, and ... |

Do not repeat SFX in front of a series of sound effects that are not interrupted by something else, such as a character talking or a VO or a song. Example:

| | | |
|---|---|---|
| WRONG WAY: | SFX: | (BIRDS SINGING) |
| | SFX: | (OWLS SCREAMING) |
| | SFX: | (PEOPLE SNORING) |
| RIGHT WAY: | SFX: | (BIRDS SINGING) |
| | | (OWLS SCREAMING) |
| | | (PEOPLE SNORING) |

Only if a series of sound effects is interrupted would you insert a new SFX designation, as in this example:

| | | |
|---|---|---|
| OPEN ON MAN SLEEPING | SFX: | (OWLS HOOTING) |
| HE OPENS ONE EYE | | (HEAVENLY SINGING) |
| HE SITS UP | MAN: | I want Niblets. |
| CORNER OF ROOM GLOWS | | Who ... who are you? |
| GLOW TURNS INTO ANGEL | SFX: | (HARP STRUM) |
| ANGEL WALKS TO BED | ANGEL: | I am the angel of licorice ... the Niblets department. |

The same rule of repetition applies to a character or VO with multiple lines of copy. You don't need to repeat MAN or WOMAN or VO in front of every line of copy until the copy is interrupted by SFX or SONG or another character. In the example there are two sound effects but only one designation SFX. Note there is also only one MAN, though he has two lines of copy.

A favorite device in many movies and some commercials is what is known by some people as a **flash forward sound cut,** which means that the sound from the next scene comes on before the present scene is over. For example, a mom and son may be sitting in a living room, talking about going to a carnival; and before that scene is over, carnival music starts up. No special designation is necessary for a flash forward sound cut, because you can indicate SFX anytime you want to, at any place. Example:

| | | |
|---|---|---|
| OPEN ON: MOM AND SON IN LIVING ROOM | SON: | So Mom, where are we going? |
| | MOM: | It's carnival time guy. |
| | SFX: | (STRAINS OF A MERRY-GO-ROUND, UP & UNDER MOM AND SON) |
| CUT TO: MOM AND SON AT CARNIVAL | MOM: | Well, here we are! |

SONG is an indication of the lyrics for a jingle. If using only instrumental music without lyrics, many writers write SFX: (INST. MUSIC or just **INST.**). Lyrics are always written in CAPS. Example:

| | | |
|---|---|---|
| OPEN ON: HIGHWAY FROM HIGH UP | SONG: | CARS AND BUSES DOWN BELOW, MAN THEY SURE ARE MOVIN' SLOW, |
| CUT TO: WOMAN IN PLANE SEAT EATING A MEAL, LOOKING OUT WINDOW | | LOOK AT ME AWAY UP HERE, FLYIN' STANDBY ON FRONTIER. |
| CUT TO: EXTERIOR, PLANE FLYING THROUGH CLOUDS | SFX: | (INST. UNDER VO) |
| | VO: | Yes folks, blah blah blah . . . |

In this example, it is assumed the INST. is the same style as the music just sung. But when indicating instrumental music (INST.) with no other reference point, it's better to identify the music by general style — country, rock, classical, etc. — rather than to name a specific piece of music. The music may be impossible to buy from the copyright owners when the time comes. You can get into specifics after selling the script, unless the music is truly keyed to the point of the spot, as in the California raisin spots that featured the song "I Heard It Through the Grapevine." In that case, you would have to find out the availability and cost of the music before pitching the idea to the client.

**The Right-Hand Side**  Write your dialogue, voice-over copy, sound effects and song instructions in a column on the right-hand side of the page. As with print copy, this forces you to be concise. The short right-hand copy is also easier for voice and acting talent to read, because you can write the four or five words per line you want to have emphasized, and the talent — without coaching or direction — can fall into your rhythm. This is important to you, because sometimes other people will produce your script without you in attendance, and you want to be sure the reading is close to your concept.

**Spacing, Caps and Parentheses**  Single-spacing or double-spacing in a script is a matter of personal choice; just be sure to have more than normal spacing between scenes of the SIGHT side for easier storyboarding later on. Dialogue and VO copy should be upper and lower case (CAPS and small

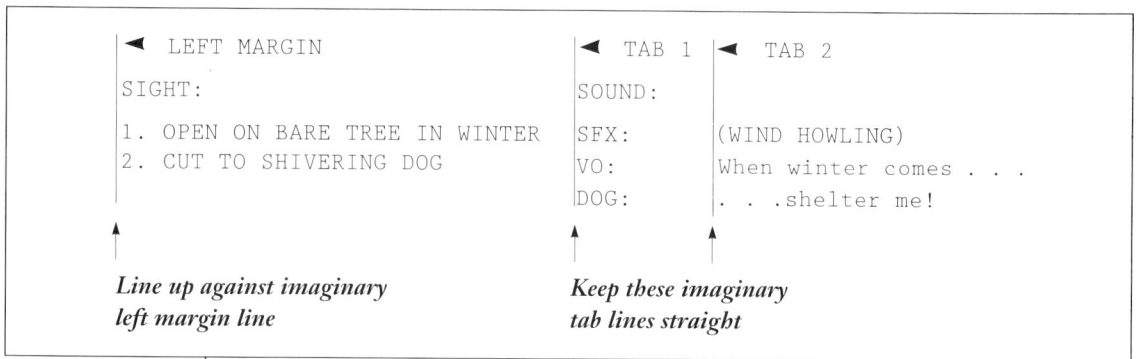

```
   ◄ LEFT MARGIN           ◄ TAB 1  ◄ TAB 2

SIGHT:                      SOUND:

1. OPEN ON BARE TREE IN WINTER   SFX:    (WIND HOWLING)
2. CUT TO SHIVERING DOG          VO:     When winter comes . . .
                                 DOG:    . . .shelter me!
 ▲                               ▲       ▲

  Line up against imaginary     Keep these imaginary
  left margin line              tab lines straight
```

**6.2**          *Setting tabs for TV scripts.*

letters); all instructions are upper case, in parentheses, and indications like SFX or MAN or SONG are always in upper case. The sound recording person is accustomed to looking at a script, knowing that upper and lower case copy indicate talent to be recorded and that the upper case copy in parentheses will be directions to the sound person.

**Names of Characters**   Note that the animated character in the bean dip spot is called simply "Character," rather than "Thirsty Sam" or whatever. (One reason for the turndown of the script is that the client did not like the idea of a character crawling around in its food. The other reason, even more legitimate, is that we were claiming the product was spicier than it really was.) In most cases, you don't need to name characters in a script unless it's really integral to the point of the script, such as an airheaded character's getting someone's name wrong; in this case, the names are integral to the script.

There is too much broadcast advertising where the writer has come up with names like Harry and Bess and Stanley and so on. Are these names funny to you? They're not if you're named Harry or Bess or Stanley or if your relatives are so named. They're usually funny only to the writers because of their particular personal history and association with such names. Such names add nothing to the plot, take up valuable time, and stand in the way of crisp communication.

**Lining Up the Tabs**   Note in the bean dip spot how the SFX and other indications are lined up directly under SOUND, which is the first tab you set. If you tab about ten spaces to the right of that first tab, you will have room to use character names and sound indications, although you may have to abbreviate them, as CHARACTER is shortened to CHAR and SOUND EFFECTS to SFX. Figure 6.2 shows how to set tabs. Note how the designations under SOUND line up against an imaginary line descending from TAB 1, and the actual copy and instructions line up against the imaginary line descending from TAB 2. Keep those lines straight by starting the first letter of the words on that line under the tabs. You might think we're paying undue attention to a minuscule point, but such attention to this detail will ensure a more readily understandable script and a more professional look. These tab settings will also work for print, radio and collateral copy, saving you energy over many years and ensuring a consistent look to all your copy.

**Placement of Sounds vis à vis Scenes**   In Figure 6.2, there are single lines across from each other, but in the bean dip spot, you see the word "Water . . ." across from the first line of scene 3. Even when the scenes run longer (deeper) than the sound descriptions, be sure to place the first line of the sound descriptions directly opposite the first line of sight description in each scene. If this results in a lot of white space under the sound descriptions, don't worry about it. It's also possible for sound descriptions to be longer than the sight scenes, and there could be white space on the left. It's important that it be perfectly clear what each different scene on the left is (hence the numbering of scenes) and what the corresponding sound for that scene is. By keeping the sound directly to the right of the scene, on the same line, a person reading the script knows exactly what sounds or words occur when that scene comes on screen. If there is no sound or dialogue as that scene comes on screen, simply say (SILENCE) across from the first line of the scene. And when some sound does occur in that scene, put the sound on a line directly across from where the action takes place.

## The Sight Side

The words SIGHT and SOUND are the author's invention. You will also see VIDEO and AUDIO used by some copywriters; SIGHT and SOUND are somewhat broader terms that cover both film and tape production. Some people think of VIDEO and AUDIO as strictly TV terms.

**Caps and Underlines**   On the left-hand side of the page, write the visual instructions — what happens on the screen — in upper case letters (CAPS) under SIGHT. If there are words to appear on the screen, such as the words following SUPER (a superimposition of words or pictures over what is already on the screen) in the bean dip spot, be sure to underline them. That way, an art director creating the storyboard can tell at a glance what words to draw on the panels of the storyboard.

**Indicating Camera Moves**   You may also want to indicate certain camera moves (more details on those later) that are necessary to your vision of the script, but in general let the film director worry about what camera shots are needed in order to accomplish your vision. Notice that the bean dip spot says OPEN ON CAN OF JALAPEÑO BEAN DIP, but does not indicate close-ups, angles, etc., though the copywriter's storyboard does express such an idea.

  In the bean dip spot, instead of the direction to PULL OUT TO SEE TOP OF CAN, the script could just as easily have called for a CUT TO: TOP OF CAN. There are many ways to tell a reader what is happening; the main thing is to keep it simple and not to fall in love with terms like CUT, DIS-SOLVE (DISS), PAN, TRUCK and the others to be explored later. Just tell a simple story, with minimum use of these terms. Your thumbnail storyboard will show what you have in mind generally; the specifics of how you get to these pictures shouldn't matter to you.

**Separate Scenes for Separate Actions**   The scenes under SIGHT are not only obviously separated from each other, but also have only one action apiece, which makes it easier to create a storyboard later. One action doesn't refer to length, but rather to camera setups. You might have only one scene description for the whole spot, such as MEDIUM SHOT, MAN FISHING AND TALKING TO CAMERA (CAM). That's one action. The camera is set up once, that man talks, and there's your commercial. It's easy to draw one panel on a storyboard of that one action.

If the camera zooms into the man's face for a close-up, then zooms back out to a long shot, it still may be only one camera setup, but now you have three actions: (1) a medium shot of the man sitting in the boat, (2) a close-up of his face on the zoom in, and (3) a long shot of the man in the boat. These are three separate scenes on your script and on your storyboard.

If you write OPEN ON MAN FISHING, CATCHES FISH, DRAGS IT INTO BOAT, it will look like one scene on your script. But as you can tell, there are three scenes in that description that should be separated. If the man is saying one sentence of copy during those three scenes, you just divide that sentence into three parts opposite the three scenes.

**The Last Scene**   The last scene in the script is very important and can be compared to the signature on a print ad; it often combines the client name, a product shot, a slogan and other relevant information. In print advertising, there is more room to design all these elements around the signature. But on TV, space is limited, and too much information in the last panel might look like a record offer, with a screen filled with phone numbers and credit cards and more. Good design is good persuasion. Too much junk in a panel that appears on the screen for only 3–5 seconds—the normal time you should provide for a final panel—will confuse the viewer.

At a minimum, the last panel should contain the client or product name. If the name is clearly readable and in the client's normal logo style on a package, so much the better. Then you have two elements in the last panel in the design space of one element, as in the bean dip spot. Often, when you have a slogan, you will want it to be included in the last panel, as a final reminder of your pitch and as a major element of continuity in a campaign. In the bean dip spot, the slogan is on the screen at the end, as well as in the viewers' ears, being sung. This can be effective—a double hit—but it may not always be necessary.

Another school of thought says you can get separate but complementary use of the time available by saying (or singing) one thing while showing something else. The answer to whether you show and say the slogan will depend on the product and the given situation—whether it's a new product, a well-known slogan, a spot asking for immediate response, and so forth. Be sure you underline the slogan and any other words that go on screen when you write the script.

The client or product name, a picture of the product and the slogan in the last scene are going to provide the art director with enough design challenge, but there are times when a telephone number is also essential to the sell. Sometimes you can avoid showing the phone number in the final scene and be more effective by building it into the visuals that come earlier. Or, because there's no sense putting anything into a script that isn't showcased in some way, you can sometimes create two final scenes, one with the phone number and one with the name and slogan.

## Additional TV Terminology

There is no glory in knowing the technical terms you are about to read; there is only glory in coming up with a dynamite idea. Technical terms are for technicians; ideas are for creative people. Even so, the terms we discuss constitute the minimum technical language you need to know to appear well-informed when dealing with the production people who will shoot your commercial — the director, sound person, camera persons and so on. Also, you should have some idea how to indicate certain shots when they are truly necessary to an understanding of the script. This terminology should be appropriate in writing (or shooting) either a videotape or film commercial, though there are on the whole big differences between shooting a tape or film spot, as we shall see later in this chapter.

**Camera Shots**    The following terms are used to describe the camera shots, what the viewer will see on the screen:

**ECU:** Extreme close-up of a person's face.

**CU:** Close-up. A normal close-up would be understood by most TV or film crew members as a person's head from the neck up.

**MCU:** Medium close-up, perhaps from the chest up.

**MS:** Medium shot, from the waist up.

**LS:** Long shot. A full person or, if scenery, to infinity. If showing a full person at the base of a mountain, you can use a term like ELS (extreme long shot).

**UP-SHOT** or **DOWN-SHOT:** Refers to the angle, shooting from the ground up or from overhead down.

**SNORKLE LENS:** Basically a little lens on the end of a long snaky flexible cable. With a snorkle lens, you can get down among knives and forks and make the tine of a fork look as big as a house.

**Camera Moves**    The following terms refer to the way the camera moves while shooting the scene:

ECU: *Extreme close-up of a person's face*

CU: *Close-up. A normal close-up would be understood by most TV or film crew members as a person's head from the neck up.*

MCU: *Medium close-up, perhaps from the chest up.*

MS: *Medium shot, from the waist up.*

LS: *Long shot. A full person or, if scenery, to infinity. If showing a base of a mountain, you can use a term like ELS (extreme long shot.)*

**PAN:** Swinging the camera lens from left to right or right to left, as across a row of bottles. The camera itself stays in one place, and only the lens moves.

**TRUCK:** Moving the camera itself from left to right or right to left across the same row of bottles, while the lens stays fixed in one position.

Figure 6.3 shows how pans and trucks work. The following sample copy shows how you'd use these terms:

| | | |
|---|---|---|
| 1. OPEN ON FIRST BOTTLE OF A ROW OF BOTTLES | VO: | Here are all the brands of soda. |
| 2. PAN ACROSS BOTTLES, L TO R | | As you can see . . . |
| | OR | |
| 2. TRUCK RIGHT ACROSS BOTTLES | | As you can see . . . |

The difference between a pan and a truck is a subtle one that must be seen to be understood. To many copywriters, the truck is a prettier move.

**ZOOM:** To go from a wide (long) shot to a close-up, using the movable camera lens (a zoom-in), or vice versa (a zoom-out).

**DOLLY:** To move the entire camera into or away from the subject, not changing the lens (as in a zoom).

Continuing with our copy, here's how you'd use these terms, which are illustrated in Figure 6.4.

| | |
|---|---|
| 1. OPEN ON ROW OF BOTTLES | VO:  Here are all the brands of soda. |
| 2. DOLLY IN TO CENTER BOTTLE | Here's one you'll like . . . |

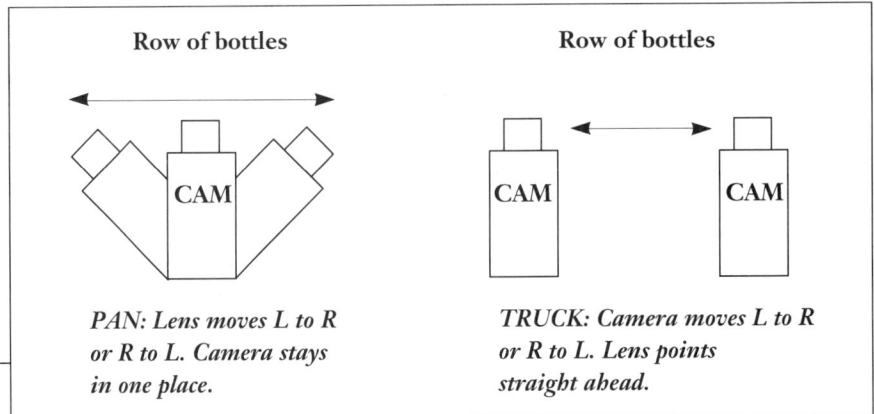

PAN: Lens moves L to R or R to L. Camera stays in one place.

TRUCK: Camera moves L to R or R to L. Lens points straight ahead.

**6.3**

*Pan and truck shots.*

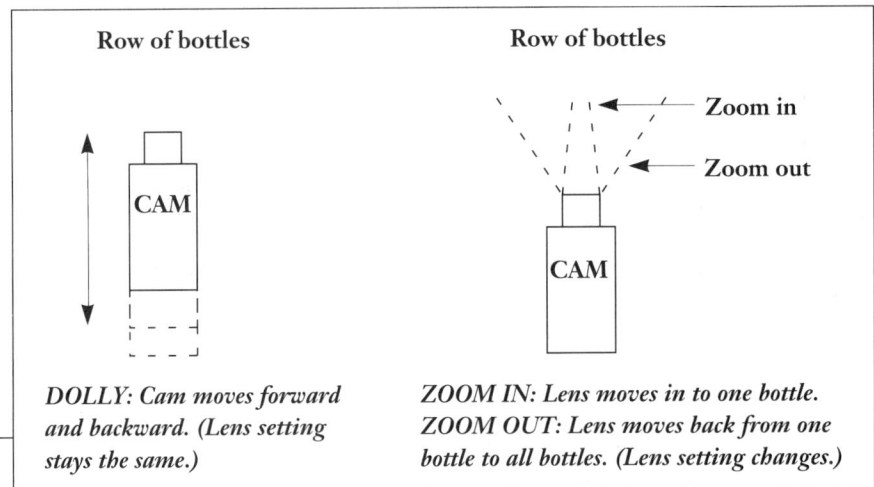

DOLLY: Cam moves forward and backward. (Lens setting stays the same.)

ZOOM IN: Lens moves in to one bottle. ZOOM OUT: Lens moves back from one bottle to all bottles. (Lens setting changes.)

**6.4**

*Zoom and dolly shots.*

|   |   |   |
|---|---|---|
|   | *OR* |   |
| 1. OPEN ON CENTER BOTTLE IN A ROW OF BOTTLES | VO: | Here's a bottle of soda. |
| 2. ZOOM OUT TO SEE WHOLE ROW |   | Here's a bunch of them . . . |
|   | *OR* |   |
| 1. OPEN ON ROW OF BOTTLES | VO: | Here's a bunch of soda bottles. |
| 2. ZOOM TO CENTER BOTTLE |   | But this is the best one . . . |

As with the truck, the dolly is considered by many producers to be a classier move. Pans and zooms seem lazy, whereas the peripheral movement on the edges of the screen on truck and dolly shots is particularly satisfying. However, if you want to feature a person across a wide canyon, then move in close to that person's face, there is no way, without exorbitant expense, to dolly across the canyon; a zoom is really your only choice.

**SNAP ZOOM:** A zoom in or out that is so fast you don't see the in-between things, but only have the sensation of a violent change.

**SUPER:** Not actually a camera move, although it comes out as such on the screen. A super is created in a lab on film and in the control room when shooting on tape. The effect is that of one scene on screen being added to by another scene or words, as when a product is shown and the name of the product is "supered" under the product, or when a person is thinking of another person and the other person appears on the screen. Figure 6.5 shows an example.

| | | |
|---|---|---|
| 8. SEE GLASS OF TEA | SFX: | (INST. UP) |
| 9. SUPER: REFRESHING TASTE | | (INST. OUT) |

| *TV scene before super* | *TV scene after super* | **6.5** |
|---|---|---|
| *(Other scenes or pictures, as well as words, can be "supered" over a scene)* | | *Example of a super.* |

**6.6**

*Example of a cut.*          *Scene before a cut*          *Scene after a cut*

**Sight Transitions**   Transitions in television are just as important in television as they are in print.

>**CUT:** The most widely used transition from one scene to another, where the former scene disappears and is instantly replaced by the next scene (see Figure 6.6).

5.  CUT TO TROPICAL ISLAND          SFX:          (INST.)

6.  CUT TO PERFUME BOTTLE                    (DOG BARKS)

>**DISS:** Written as DISS, but pronounced "Dissolve." Never say "Diss." This transition from scene to scene denotes the passage of time or a leisurely or moody feeling.

A dissolve is a ghostly effect, whereby the scene slowly appears through the old scene, which dissolves as the new scene comes on (Figure 6.7). The new scene "dissolves" onto the screen, and the old scene "dissolves" off the screen at the same time. It can be a fast or medium or slow dissolve. If it is too fast, it will look like a cut.

1.  OPEN ON TROPICAL ISLAND          SFX:          (INST.)

2.  DISS TO PERFUME BOTTLE                    (CONTINUE INST.)

>**QUICK CUTS** are a series of cuts, usually timed to music or fast word patter, such as a rap. Each scene is hard to see this way, but the totality gives an interesting impression. An example is a series of different kinds of baseball hats while a VO talks or music plays. *Time* magazine circulation commercials often employ quick cuts ad nauseam.

PULL BACK TO SEE or MOVE IN TO SEE: These may not be conventional transition terms, but technicians will understand them. Sometimes you have a scene where you want a dramatic change, but you don't want to cut or dissolve to a new scene. Perhaps it's a baby close-up, with mountains in the far background, and you want the baby to get small as the mountains come into view. You would say PULL BACK TO SEE MOUNTAINS. Or, if you have the mountains dominating the scene and

| Scene 1 before dissolve | Scenes 1 & 2 during dissolve | Scene 2 after dissolve |

**6.7**      *Example of a dissolve. Scene 2 replaces scene 1 by coming through scene 1.*

a teeny weeny baby in the foreground, and you want to see the baby close-up, you would say MOVE IN TO SEE BABY'S FACE.

## STORYBOARDS

A storyboard is a series of (usually) hand-drawn TV **panels** that show the key scenes in a TV spot, usually with all sound indications (including copy) written beneath the panels. The panels are, of course, in the dimension of a TV screen, roughly a 4 x 3 proportion. The panels could be 8 inches wide by 6 inches high, double that, half that or any other size, depending on the requirements for the presentation of the storyboard (across a desk to one person or to a room containing ten people).

In most cases, the storyboard for presentation will be 6–12 colored panels on a stiff black board that the copywriter or art director can point to while explaining the script. Sometimes the presenter will read the copy and explain the sound effects or music; other times these elements will have been roughly recorded and will be played as the presenter points to the appropriate panels. After writing a TV script, you will do yourself a great favor if you create a rough "thumbnail" storyboard. This act will reassure you about the clarity of the script, and help you explain to an art director (who will create a much more sophisticated storyboard) what you have in mind.

### The Jalapeno Bean Dip Thumbnail Storyboard

Look back at the copywriter's thumbnail storyboard for the bean dip spot (Figure 6.1). I created the storyboard on a computer. Though I'm no great shakes on a computer, I'm even worse with hand-drawn thumbnail sketches, and comfort myself in the (perhaps false) belief that most other copywriters are pretty bad at drawing too, or they would have become art directors. Though a quick hand-drawn copywriter thumbnail historically came with many copywriter scripts to explain to the art director how the spot really should look, as you can see the computer almost makes the copywriter (in this case at least) look like an artist. Consider using the computer for your thumbnail storyboard when you have the opportunity to use one.

Note the relationship between the scenes as written in the script and the panels of the storyboard. The way the scenes on the script are numbered and separated by white space makes it a lot easier for the copywriter to figure out a thumbnail storyboard and for the art director to create a more polished storyboard later.

A key thing to remember when creating the visuals on your script (and subsequently for your storyboard) is that the action on a TV set happens in the middle of the screen. Make your visuals interesting, of course, but render them big and bold on the screen. There are a lot of little TV sets in America; think about them when you're creating a storyboard. This is not to say you can't create a striking visual of a broad western landscape, sun going down, and a silhouette of a rider far in the distance. Just make sure the rider is in the middle of the scene or at least is the focal point. TV spots go by very fast; normally only one piece of business can be absorbed by the casual viewer, and many viewers are casual.

In the bean dip spot, notice that the name of the product and the product can are on screen all the time. It would be boring to have 30 seconds of a can on the screen by itself; but the story of the little character wanting water because the product is so spicy makes the product natural to the action, and it actually needs to be there. The product is the hero of the story. Your goal when writing any advertising, certainly including TV, is to think of a story that will make your product indispensable to the action.

## Why Use Storyboards?

The need for a storyboard often comes into question when the cost of making the storyboard comes under review. Individual panels can cost far in excess of $100 each for an artist to draw, and the time spent by art directors and others assembling the boards is usually billable. Many creative people (writers, art directors and broadcast producers) say the boards are not for them because they can read the script and imagine the scenes as indicated on the script.

But the cost of a commercial can be so much — hundreds of thousands of dollars; in some cases, even a million dollars — that the relatively small cost of a storyboard can easily be rationalized to avoid misunderstanding by the client, who is paying for the production. Storyboards can reflect clothing styles, ages, hairstyles, production techniques, locations and many other aspects of the "shoot" the client may or may not understand from reading a script.

The clients' advertising or marketing directors, who themselves are a little nervous about approving such large production costs on behalf of their corporations, or sole owners committing their own money want to protect their investment as much as possible. They will compare the storyboard they approved to the footage shot for the commercial to be sure what was approved was actually shot. "Shoot the board!" has become a hated phrase to many creative people who would like to experiment a little bit during a shoot when something better may occur to them. (But they experiment only a little bit, because production is too expensive to try to "wing it.")

The storyboard also gives a production house, which films or tapes a commercial, a good basis upon which to bid the project. Once awarded the bid, the production house will often create its own "shooting board," broken down much more finely than the 6–12 panels on the average agency storyboard, into maybe 30 or 40 or more panels, some representing only a fraction of a second of shooting time.

## Storyboards Are Not All Boards

In the broad scheme of things, a storyboard can be as simple as black and white marker-drawn panels on layout paper. In its most sophisticated form, the storyboard could be a videotaped presentation of elegant drawings, with music, sound effects and complete voice track. Or the storyboard might be put on slides and projected on a huge screen, while a sound track roars out of giant speakers as a dissolve unit gives motion to the changing slides. The success of a presentation depends on the client's perfect understanding of the commercial before approving the TV spots; hence the dog and pony shows.

The "dog and pony show" phrase used to describe advertising creative presentations may have come about because of the elaborate presentation of storyboards (and, before TV, presentation of print, radio and collateral materials). That most TV sets still do not have the large screens used for slides or fine sound systems (though stereo TV is coming on strong) does not occur to the client, who is bowled over by such a presentation, though many clients are too smart to equate a huge screen and stereo sound with a small black and white TV set with a tinny sound.

When you're seeking your first job as a copywriter, a storyboard like that in Figure 6.1 will do nicely in your sample book.

## Storyboard Examples

Figures 6.8, 6.9, 6.10 and 6.11 are storyboards, all of which are a step up from the copywriter thumbnail storyboards, ranging from hand-lettered art director efforts to photoboards that pick out key scenes from a finished commercial. The photoboards are often created after a commercial is completed to persuade franchisees to run the commercial created by the parent company, as in the case of the Isuzu storyboard (Figure 6.10), which was sent to car dealers.

## TV WRITING

When you're writing for TV, the main thing to keep top-of-mind is that TV is a medium of sight, sound, motion and emotion. In today's advertising, emotion seems to dominate more and more.

There are among us fellow citizens who work for us...

... and whose work is so dangerous they have to strap on a gun when they go to work, to protect themselves ...

The Dallas Police. We can't do for them what they do for us. But we can show our appreciation. Friends of the Dallas Police

with your help will sponsor an annual awards banquet to honor those who protect us.

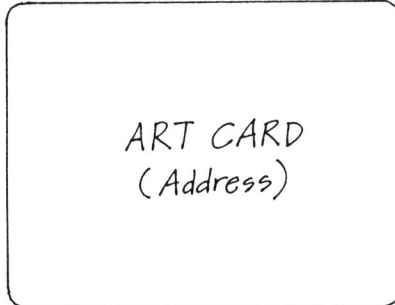

ART CARD (Address)

Please send a contribution to the address shown here.

The Dallas Police. Give one time to those who give so much... every day.

**6.8**

*This Friends of the Dallas Police commercial features former Dallas Cowboys quarterback Roger Staubach. Note how simple the storyboard is; it was adequate to explain the commercial to a client without a huge budget for art.*

SFX (Instrumental Exxon music est + under)

POPS: Well, well, well. What brings the famous Exxon Tiger to my proud station?

TIGER: Actually ... it's that sign ... wonder if you'd like to take me on?

POPS: You? Hm ... well, you know anything about selling gasoline?

TIGER: Yes sir.
Dr PS: Do you know the problems of new cars with emission controls?
TIGER: Yes sir.

POPS: Do you know we put HTA in Exxon gasolines to help reduce hesitation caused by uneven gasoline flow?
TIGER: Yes sir.

POPS: Did your homework, eh?

TIGER: Yes sir.

POPS: (HMMS AS HE THINKS ABOUT IT) OK. Give you a chance at it ...

TIGER: Hey, thanks!

POPS: ... allright. Here's a uniform.

TIGER: How do I look?

POPS: A little too much like a tiger. Better wear this mask.

Although, heh heh, there's a little Tiger in All us Exxon dealers ...

SINGERS: Dontcha know that Exxon keeps things movin'

Movin' right across the U.S.A.

6.9

*This Exxon spot was an animated commercial. But the artist's rendering is not much different in style from what you might see for a commercial that would be live action. Many storyboards have a cartoony look, even if they are to be live action.*

# "Dr. Isuzustein"

New :25/:05 second television spot designed to introduce the new Isuzu Amigo.

The "mad" Dr. Isuzustein plans to create an entirely new kind of vehicle.

He's going to combine the best of a sports car and the ruggedness of a 4 x 4 pickup.

The "doctor" throws the magic switch!

The new Amigo emerges from the smoke.

Dr. Isuzustein gloats over his marvelous creation:
**JOE:** "It's alive. . . it's alive!!!"

"Dr. Isuzustein, you've created a monster!"

Price: $8,999

**6.10** *This Isuzu photoboard contains five seconds of black at the end (noted on the board but not shown here), so a local car dealer can customize the commercial with the dealer's name, address, etc.*

## One Point

Though it's important to stick to one point in every medium, in TV it's even more important. You can reread print advertising; broadcast advertising goes flying by in a minute or less and does not sit there for casual review. Here's an example of a TV spot that sticks to the point:

(A teenage girl karate-chops some concrete, and sings) BEFORE I BUST THROUGH SOLID CONCRETIES, I GET THE EATIES FOR MY WHEATIES!

PANEL 1
AUDIO: Mom: It was Stephen's first birthday party.

PANEL 2
VIDEO:
AUDIO: Mom: It was happy

PANEL 3
VIDEO:
AUDIO: Mom: and messy

PANEL 4
AUDIO: Mom: The cake was chocolate, very chocolate.

PANEL 5
VIDEO:
AUDIO:

PANEL 6
VIDEO:
AUDIO:

PANEL 7
VIDEO:
AUDIO: I honestly believed his jumper was ruined!

PANEL 8
VIDEO: Mom:
AUDIO: I poured Liquid Tide on the really bad spots . . .

PANEL 9
VIDEO:
AUDIO: Mom: and washed.

PANEL 10
VIDEO:
AUDIO: As you can see Tide saved the outfit!

PANEL 11
VIDEO: Icon
AUDIO: Anncr: If its got to be clean, its got to be Tide.

PANEL 12
VIDEO: Sincerely,
AUDIO: Lisa K. Mathieson

**6.11** *Here's a Tide storyboard that shows some revisions, as evidenced by the different-sized type under some panels. The small frame around the baby in panel 7 indicates a zoom out to the full panel. This storyboard has a place for video under the panel; note only the sound side is represented, as in all these storyboards.*

(A guy mountain-climbing sings) BEFORE I CLIMB TWO THOUSAND FEETIES, I GET THE EATIES FOR MY WHEATIES!

Then the voice-over says, "The eaties for Wheaties. That undeniable, irresistible urge for the crispy, crunchy, whole wheat taste of the Breakfast of Champions."

(Tony Franklin, ace barefoot placekicker, enters and kicks a football, singing) BEFORE I KICK WITH MY BARE FEETIES, I GET THE EATIES FOR MY WHEATIES!

(Then they show a package of Wheaties and the super EATIES FOR WHEATIES with a bite taken out of the word *Eaties*. The voice-over says, "Part of your good breakfast."

Note two things about this spot, which is part of a campaign of similar spots. First, the point is simple and never strayed from: some active people don't do their active things until they eat their Wheaties. Second, the spot recalls, for the older market, the historic tie-in Wheaties has always had with athletes and active people, back to the days of radio when Wheaties sponsored Jack Armstrong, The All-American Boy.

## Length

Keep copy to a minimum. Let visuals and drama and music do the work. (These hints assume a reasonable budget. For a no-budget effort with, say, a slide and a voice-over, you must rely on mighty fine copy to get the job done.) If you must write wall-to-wall copy, that still means only 20 seconds of copy on a 30-second TV spot, or 50 seconds in a 60-second TV spot, because you need time for dramatic pauses, pictorial presentation and other time-consuming aspects of film or tape presentation you may not have considered when writing the spot.

Consider this 30-second TV spot with less than 10 seconds of copy. More copy probably couldn't add anything to the persuasiveness of the spot: The scene is a long shot of a farm house on a stormy night, with sounds of thunder and lightning and a child crying. A light comes on in the house and the voice of a mother says, "Shh. It's okay. It's just thunder. You're ok. Shh." Then the announcer's voice over the scene says, "It's nice to know you can take us for granted. Texas Power & Light Company."

## Timing

Time your scripts. Time them over and over. It's amateurish to run long or short in production in the studio or on location. And it wastes the client's money because of the time it takes to rewrite while expensive production crews stand and wait. One of the things you promise as a copywriter includes professionalism, that you know this spot will run as long as you say it will. People twiddle their thumbs and mumble about you while you rewrite. Even worse, if you're not attending the production, somebody else will do the rewriting, and you'll be losing control of your vision and script.

## Tell a Story

"Telling the story" is the telling phrase in writing. Nowhere is this more true than in the TV commercial, which combines the movie-like elements of storytelling. A commercial is, after all, a short movie, often utilizing the same people and equipment used for feature films. Take advantage of that. Keep the copy short, make the visuals have impact and keep the story clear.

When you write commercials, tricky camera moves may appeal to your sense of accomplishment, but in fact they only get in the way. Shakespeare lives today because, among other reasons, he set scenes that could be produced as easily in west Texas as in England. Scene I, Act II, of *A Midsummer Night's Dream* is introduced as: "A wood near Athens." How simple! In the west Texas scrubland, that "wood near Athens" might be a grove of mesquite trees for an outdoor production or might be indicated on stage by five or six potted ficus trees. In England, those trees would surely not be mesquite. What this means is that the director of a Shakespeare play has not been overly dictated to by the author, that the director can comfortably set the scene knowing that the intent of the writing has been carried out.

Here's an example for setting a scene the way Shakespeare would do it, if he were writing a spot for Chevrolet:

| SIGHT: | | SOUND: |
|--------|---|--------|
| 1. OPEN ON DESOLATE RURAL ROAD. | SFX: | (OUTDOOR SOUNDS) |
| 2. CHEVY PICKUP APPEARS. | | (ENGINE SOUND) |
| 3. CUT TO DOG SITTING UP, HITCHHIKING. | | (SOUND OF CAR SLOWING DOWN) |

Note that the road could be anywhere between Oregon and Florida or even in Alaska or Hawaii for that matter. There is no indication of which direction the pickup is coming from. No breed is assigned to the dog. OUT-DOOR SOUNDS is a matter of choice for the area, and so on. The copywriter has written a scene description that will work 400 years from now (if there are still pickups and dogs then), just as Shakespeare wrote (400 years ago) scenes that work in west Texas today.

It's hard to walk the fine line between setting a scene to take full advantage of the director's creative talent and writing a description that's too general. But it's a line that eventually must be walked by instinct in the craft of copywriting.

## Coming Up with the Idea

One more time, no textbook can get you through the magic part of creation. Watch TV, have a strong strategy, try to do something that's never been done before, make the product or service the most important part of the commercial. Write and rewrite. As Edison said, it's 99 percent perspiration and 1 percent inspiration.

Following are two of the best advertising ideas from the last few years. The first is a script for Bugle Boy jeans. The script identification is reproduced as it came to me to show you the similarity to and the difference from the model you have been shown. I've slightly changed the format of the Bugle Boy script to make it consistent with the model in this chapter, but not a critical word under SIGHT or SOUND has been changed. Note how the

**6.12**   *This is a scene from the 1988 Bugle Boy spot scripted in the text. This spot was a distinct departure from the Levi's 501 jeans campaign and other jeans campaigns of the time. Bugle Boy came up with a completely different tone in its advertising, rather tongue-in-cheek and, some say, liberated.*

writer (not identified, by the way) has created the SIGHT side without using a single bit of technical terminology. Figure 6.12 shows a scene from the filmed spot.

CLIENT: Bugle Boy
PRODUCT: "Thank You."
MEDIA: :30 TV
W.O. NO: BBIGENB82514/QIBU 8075 :30
DATE: June 30, 1988

| **SIGHT:** | **SOUND:** | |
| --- | --- | --- |
| 1. OPEN ON LONELY ROAD IN DESERT. A PERSON IS STANDING BESIDE ROAD. | SFX: | (MUSIC) |

| 2. CAR APPROACHES AND PASSES PERSON. | | (NATURAL SOUNDS) |
|---|---|---|
| 3. CAR STOPS AND BACKS UP. | | |
| 4. CAR WINDOW ROLLS DOWN. | | |
| 5. CUT TO GIRL DRIVER INSIDE OF CAR. SHE ASKS PERSON OUTSIDE A QUESTION. | GIRL: | Excuse me. Are those Bugle Boy jeans that you're wearing? |
| 6. PERSON OUTSIDE RESPONDS. | GUY: | Why, yes . . . they are Bugle Boy jeans. |
| 7. CAR DRIVES AWAY LEAVING PERSON STANDING BY ROAD. | GIRL: | Thank you. |
| SUPER: <u>BUGLE BOY JEANS</u> | SFX: | (MUSIC) |

db

mac

1

As of this writing, the Levi's 501 Blues campaign for Levi's 501 jeans (Figure 6.13) ran for five years, with over 100 executions, all with original music tracks. Research shows over 90 percent of the target market is aware of and likes this campaign. Sales doubled.

# PRODUCING THE TV COMMERCIAL

In many agencies and corporations there is a person known as the broadcast producer. Often that person is one who studied radio-TV-film production in college, worked in TV, worked for production houses on film and tape projects, or in some other way learned enough about **broadcast production** to be of service to an agency or corporation broadcast department. The broadcast producer may or may not have had experience with the concepts of advertising creation as related in this book and may have picked up those concepts after going to work for an agency or corporation. Even if the broadcast producer is not as learned as you will be on the subject of advertising by the end of your training, the producer should have at least a minimum knowledge of the purposes of advertising and how those purposes are forwarded through radio and TV commercials — at least enough advertising skill to add to or cut scripts during production.

## The Producer

When you see "producer — so and so" listed on a credit for a commercial, you know that the person named has at least the background just described. Up through the middle of the 1960s, most agency producers had such a background. A few people started out as producers and then dove head-on into

# Levi's
## 501® JEANS

CLIENT: LEVI STRAUSS & CO.
AGENCY: FOOTE, CONE & BELDING
COMML NO: LZMB5323
COMML LENGTH: 30 SECOND

"SUBWAY VISION"

(MUSIC UP)

SINGER:
*I've been crazy
for you girl since we
were terrible two's.*

*In our button fly,
shrink-to-fit 501 blues.*

*Now, our bodies grew up
different, and I love
your ways and means.*

*Because Levi's
always understood...*

*it's all in the jeans.*

(MUSIC UNDER)

*It's all in the jeans.*

*The 501 jeans.*

(MUSIC UNDER AND OUT.)

**6.13**

*There have been over
100 executions of this
campaign, with the
key message, "Levi's
501 jeans give you a
uniquely personal fit."
The campaign has been
described as "showing
people just being
themselves."*

copywriting. It was not unusual for these copywriters to assume the job of producer, even when there were traditional producers on staff because, after all, these copywriters knew their way around a studio and it made sense for them to do that job also.

But copywriters who had never been producers started going along on shoots (and, in fact, copywriters for years had gone along in case a rewrite on the set was necessary) more and more, until they began to learn the production process, at least in general terms. There is a lot of nitty-gritty to broadcast production that copywriters do not distinguish themselves at. These things include assembling (and sticking to) a budget, requesting and certifying that certain kinds of equipment are used, that certain kinds of film or tape are available, that certain labs are used and that certain personnel are available.

## Roles of Copywriters and Art Directors

In the more visible aspects of production, copywriters (and art directors) excelled in:

Casting

Choosing a production house or individual directors and crew members

Location and prop search

Knowing the good makeup people and home economists and choreographers and when they were necessary to a shoot

Sound effects and music production

It came to be that for certain radio and TV spots, usually low-budget jobs, copywriters (and more and more art directors) became quite adept at directing, even though they were called agency producers and even though they were supposed to be "just" copywriters or art directors. For a while, in the creative revolution of the 1960s and early 1970s, there would be no traditional producers even on giant shoots, or the producers who were there would be relegated to the status of coffee-carriers and budget and detail persons. But so many art directors and copywriters displayed an arrogance with the client's money that there was a mini-revolt by many clients, who insisted on bringing back the (by now) traditional producers.

Today, you see a blend, depending on the agency, in the producing function. You see art directors and copywriters going to shoots as "advisors," but in truth still handling the producing functions they're best at. But the traditional producer has his or her title back and performs valuable functions that the copywriter and art director disdain anyway.

## What Should a Copywriter Expect?

You can be expected to produce or not to produce, whatever your wont. The reason copywriters wanted to produce in the first place was to protect their work, to see it through from concept to final execution. Furthermore, many copywriters felt the producers did not understand the advertising concepts as well as they understood technical production and were consequently missing nuances of commercials that the art director and copywriter had sweated over. In truth, some producers may have been overlooking important details; but in fairness, there were many producers who knew exactly what they were doing and did it well.

Suppose you're at an agency, on your first job, and one day the boss asks you if you want to produce this little radio spot.

"It's only a :30, and we don't have the budget for a production house. We're going to produce it down at the radio station. Want to produce it?"

**"YES!"** you should scream.

It's your chance to get some experience in a low-profile place. And you couldn't do any worse than the radio station's on-staff producer, who in many cases is not normally concerned with advertising. If you want to be a producer, you should go ahead and take the job, even if you're ignorant of the subject. After all, you wrote the commercial; you know what it should sound like. Now all you have to do is work with the engineer and coax the right reading out of the talent.

If you wish to stay clear of production altogether, you can probably still have a career as a copywriter — but not as good a career, because the more you know about production, the more you know what can be done when you write a script and the less chance you have of making a fool of yourself.

## Guidelines for the Agency Producer

Here, then, are guidelines for the agency producer, avoiding as much as possible the technical aspects of production. These guidelines are intended to make you sound as intelligent as possible so you don't break protocol in producing situations, so you don't waste the client's money and so you can do the best possible job of bringing your vision to life.

**The Agency TV Producer/Writer**   TV writing was covered earlier, but here are a couple points that need repetition. They are intended to make it easier for you to produce your TV spots. Try to write short slogans. You should do that anyway, but if you want to have a clean-looking final panel on your spot, where there may be a beauty shot of the product and the client's name, a short slogan makes it easier for the art director to design that final panel. Along the same lines, try to keep copy to a minimum, leaving time for dramatic pauses and action on the screen.

**Pre-production**   The **pre-production** stage is where copywriters and art directors often fell down as producers in days gone by. Because they didn't have enough discussion with production houses and directors on how the shoot would be accomplished, the copywriters and art directors had more hassles on the set during the actual production, when the money clock was running.

Everything needs to be considered, from who will prepare the cue cards or program the automatic prompter to location to props to everything, everything, everything. Does this seem too emphatic? Consider this: whether it's a $5,000 videotape production at a local TV station or production house, or a $500,000 Hollywood film production, every detail you don't consider beforehand and have to face on the set is costing your client money. In many cases the client will be there on the set and can see you losing time doing things you should have done before the production. This is not good for your career.

**Dealing with Talent**  Though you will have help from film directors and casting people on a film commercial, you and the art director in almost every case will have the final word on casting; in videotape production, the director will have little to do with casting and you and the AD will have even more responsibility for the talent. Be sure you get your talent to memorize the script. Only a fool (this may be a little strong) makes a talent read from a cue card or a prompter. You can always see the talent's eyes looking off-camera on cue cards or shifting back and forth on a prompter. Any talent worth his or her salt should be able to memorize.

Talents are fascinating creatures, but it's unprofessional to hang around talking to them, on the set or otherwise. All the talent often really wants is to sell you on hiring him or her on the next job. Don't get this wrong: Talent can save your TV spot and make you a hero; a good talent is worth his or her weight in gold. But the set is no place to socialize. You will look amateurish if you do so.

**Dealing with the Director**  There is a rigorous caste system in tape and film production. Everybody there works for the director. She or he gives orders. If you ask grips (stagehands) to move something around or sound persons to do certain things, you're making a serious mistake that could threaten your whole production. You are, of course, not barred from responding to questions from crew members who are in the course of performing their jobs.

Production is a tedious process, particularly in high-cost film commercials, and also in videotape. It takes forever to get things just so, to rehearse camera angles and moves, to get the timing down. When the director is trying to set up a camera move is not the time to ask him or her to have the talent's hairstyle spruced up. When the director is timing the production is not the time to ask to have the talent read lines differently.

The director will always turn to you at the appropriate time each step of the way and ask what you think. After all, you (through your company or agency) are paying for this gig. The director isn't going to shove it down your throat.

**The Writer/Producer as Director**  In tape production, the directors usually leave it up to you to direct the talent. Don't rely on the director at all in tape production. It's your job. If you can't handle it, don't be producer. In film, you hire a director who is good at directing talent. He or she will resent your talking directly to the talent. But you can whisper to the director if you don't like the way the reading is coming out. If you dislike it too much, however, it's all your fault for hiring that particular director.

The reasons for this difference are historical, for the most part, and may disappear in time if all commercials are made on tape. Historically, the director in TV was more technically minded, with three or more cameras to coordinate at once. Advertising agency people, who for years created radio and TV programs, became accustomed to directing the talent in those programs and in commercials. In movies, whose traditions and facilities have been adapted by film commercial makers, the director has been the one to direct the talent.

**Never Accept a Glitch**   That little imperfection in your commercial will haunt you the rest of your life every time you show your sample reel—if, indeed, you do show that commercial.

**The Actual Order of TV Production**   You write the script with the approval of your art director (AD), then sell it to your creative director and agency management. If they approve, you sell it to the client. If the client approves, you're ready to start production.

You are appointed the producer or advisor to the producer. You, often in concert with your AD, take the storyboards to production houses, ask them to bid on the job, then pick a production house to actually shoot your commercials. If there is a jingle, you go through the same process with a music production house.

You cast the spot, meet the actors, give them scripts to memorize. (You may or may not use a casting service or the agency casting facilities—there are many ways to do this. You may cast talent you already know or have seen. You may ask for videotapes of talent reading your script. You may have the talent read for you and the AD in person.)

You have pre-production meetings with the production house producer (a different kind of producer from you), the director and others to determine every aspect of the shoot—props, locations and so forth. You write reports to agency management as you go along, to be sure you are not committing the client to something that was not agreed upon.

On the day or week of the shoot you sit around a lot, watching everything, always available. You may have gone on location searches or prop searches or costume searches or all of the above. You may have looked at "beauty bags," special packages without prices for use in the commercial, or other cleaned-up products which will be featured in the shoot. Most of this is relevant to film shooting. In tape you may have similar matters to attend to on a smaller scale, and in addition you direct the talent.

In film, you look at "rushes" the day after a shoot and select the best takes. In tape you can see whether the shoot is okay at the time. In film or in tape you are available for editing the various scenes and putting them in order. Sometimes you do this at a post-production studio. (Note: Even if shooting on film, it is quite common now to transfer the film negative to tape and finish editing on tape, to get the best out of both technologies.)

At some point, you show what you have to the client. Some clients want to see the footage in the early stages. Others trust you and wait until your final finished cut, but still want to see it before release prints or tape dubs are made. After approval by the client you go home and brag about it to your spouse and kids and then wait for the kudos to pour in.

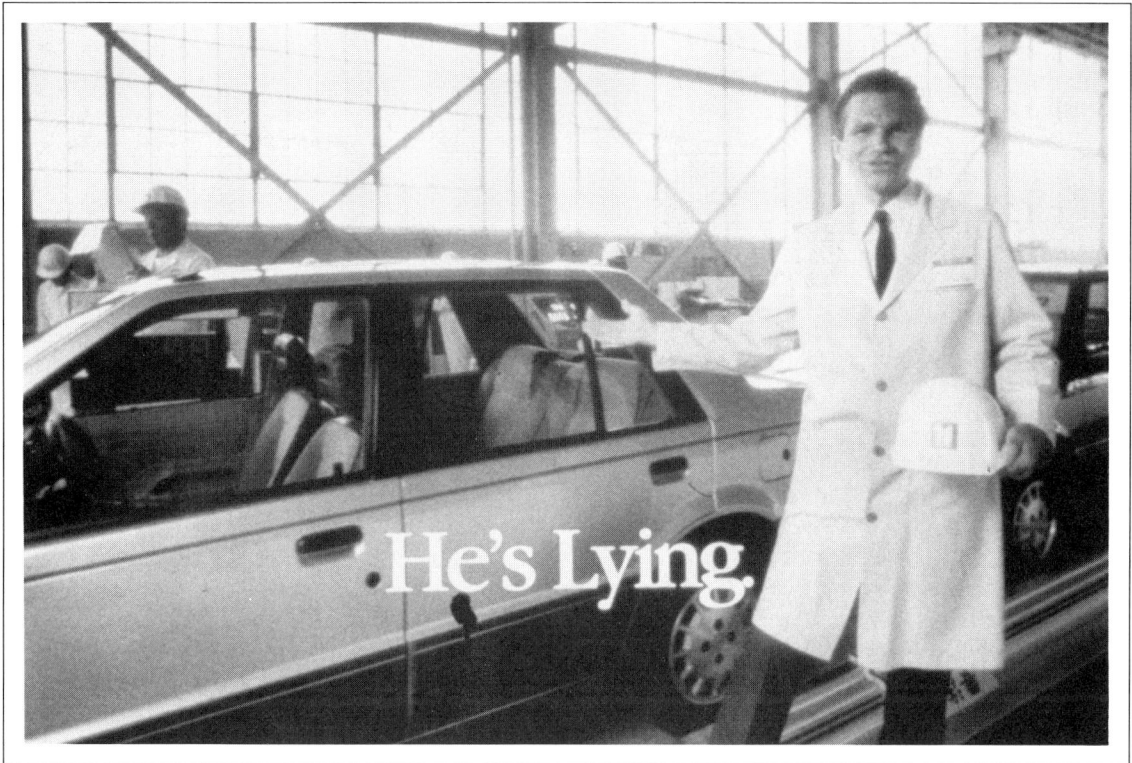

He's Lying.

*David Leisure as Joe Isuzu not only made the agency of Della Femina, McNamee WCRS, Inc., even more famous for their production skills in the late 1980s, but also gave himself a big career boost, showing up later on a TV sitcom.*

## Agency and Corporate Producer — A Rare Breed

It is tempting here to list a bunch of technical terms and effects you may want to call upon in the writing and production of your TV spot — things like split screens, match dissolves, wipes, skip framing, rack focus and so on. But that would be the effects tail wagging the dog.

If you write a TV spot with a clear vision of the visuals, and if that spot calls for an effect that requires the use of some of the technical effects available, the production company will know how to employ these effects to achieve the result you seek. This concern for what comes out on the TV screen rather than how it comes out is what separates the agency or corporate producer from the production house, TV station or network producer.

There's no doubt that you should know some basic capabilities of the medium, print or broadcast, so that you don't write or attempt to produce something that cannot be accomplished. But it's your skill as a writer and your taste as a producer that make you a successful writer/producer. If you go

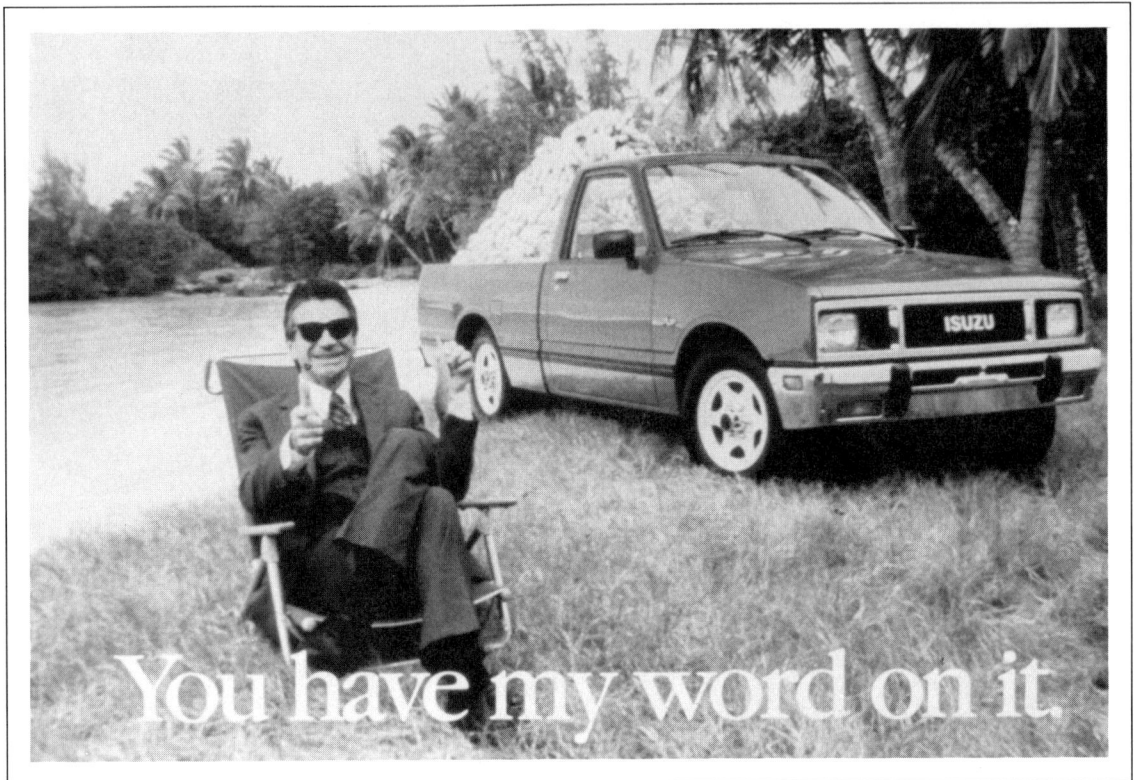

6.15 *Another spot from the Isuzu campaign.*

through the drill of consulting with your art director, your creative director, agency management and the client about a TV spot, it's rare that someone in that chain won't spot a questionable production suggestion.

Good as it might make you feel to know as much technical data as those you pay to know that data, never forget that you as the agency or corporate producer are the one to say, "Okay, that's the way we want it." Theoretically, if you've done pre-production correctly, there's nothing to do but sit back and watch in a film shoot, and coach talent and watch in a tape shoot. If you find yourself getting wrapped up in the technology rather than watching the acting and production as a whole, you may miss what you're there for — the faithful execution of your script onto film or tape. Figures 6.14, 6.15, 6.16 and 6.17 illustrate TV spots with excellent writing and production techniques.

## TIPS ON WRITING AND PRODUCING THE TV COMMERCIAL

• Know the script format so well you don't have to refer to an example of it.

# BBDO
### Batten, Barton, Durstine & Osborn, Inc.

| Client: PEPSI-COLA COMPANY | | Time: 60 SECONDS |
| --- | --- | --- |
| Product: BRAND PEPSI | Title: "GLASNOST" | Comml. No.: PEPX 2226 (Stereo)<br>PEPX 2236 (Mono) |

(MUSIC THROUGHOUT)

FATHER: Noise! Noise! You call that music?

FRIEND: Hey, Dude! Totally awesome day!

ANNCR: Not very long ago, America introduced Pepsi to the Soviet Union.

LADY: Look! What's this craziness?

FATHER: Look at you! Do you have to dress like that?

ANNCR: And while it may be just a coincidence . . .

ANNCR: a lot of refreshing changes have taken place ever since.

FRIEND: Yo! Mickey!

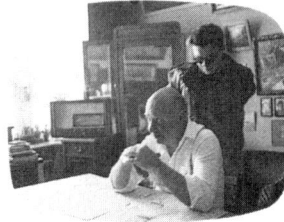

FATHER: Don't you have any normal friends? Kids!

ANNCR: Pepsi. A Generation Ahead

WIFE: Yuri . . . come on, lighten up.

**6.16** *This Pepsi spot is not only a good example of the ongoing strength of Pepsi writing and production, but also an example of the value of keeping up with the news and its relationship to advertising messages.*

# "CARRIER" :60

(DRAMATIC MUSIC & SFX UNDER)

OFFICER: Have we gotten our orders yet?
MAN 1: As far as I know, Sir,

they've been sent.

Now we just have to wait.

MAN 2: I have something, Sir.

An aircraft on the 250 radar...

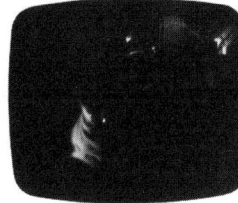

OFFICER: Gentlemen, our orders. A Whopper, no pickle, large fries.

Chicken Tenders and onion rings. Double Cheeseburger with...

Alright which one of you guys ordered a salad with Russian dressing?

**6.17** *Burger King's "Sometimes You've Gotta Break the Rules" campaign relies on humor and surprisingly few food shots, a breaking of rules in itself for fast food commercials.*

- Know the terminology you need to know so well you don't have to look up definitions.
- Pay attention to writing on the right-hand side, to what should be capitalized or not, to what should be in parentheses, and to what should be underlined.
- Don't name characters unless absolutely necessary.
- Write only one action per scene, and keep scenes separated for easy storyboarding.
- Be sure to include at least the client or product name in the last scene and the slogan when appropriate; time the last scene at 3–5 seconds.
- Create a thumbnail storyboard for every script.
- When writing visuals, make them as interesting as the copy.
- Keep copy short; focus on one point; time your scripts and tell a story.
- Rely on a strong strategy to lead you to a good idea for your execution.
- Volunteer to produce, even if you don't know how.
- Be obsessed with thorough pre-production to prevent problems on the set.
- Love talent for what they can do, but don't hang out with talent on the set.
- Pass all suggestions about the shoot on to the director, not to his or her crew members.
- Direct talent in tape production; direct talent through the director in film.
- Keep clients and agency bosses informed all through the production process.
- Remember it is your taste, not technical knowledge, that will make you a good agency or corporate producer.

## IN CONCLUSION

Writing for and producing TV advertising seems very complicated compared to, say, radio. But it is only complex because of the hundreds of details involved; writing and producing effective radio may in fact be harder, because of the single focus on the ear. As has been noted by TV salespersons, television offers sight, sound, motion and emotion. It takes a large team of people to bring off TV production; one person, theoretically, could write, star in and engineer a good radio commercial. Not so in TV.

Don't be daunted by the hundreds of details. Individually TV is as hard or as easy as any other kind of advertising. And, in the minds of copywriters, it's more fun because of the show business aspects of the business.

1. Write a Creative Work Plan for a local retail store, bank or car dealer and a :30 spot that executes your creative strategy.

2. Do the same for a durable goods, packaged goods and service account.

# CHAPTER 7

# RADIO WRITING

**M**any beginning copywriters think of radio as TV without pictures. There is a certain similarity in broadcast scripting, but generally radio is a completely different ball game. It's harder for people to absorb information by ear alone, so radio calls upon you to create vivid mind pictures to drive the advertising message home.

Let's start with the few elements in a radio script.

## ELEMENTS AND FORMATS OF RADIO SCRIPTS

The basic elements of a radio script are

ANNC (announcer)
SFX
SONGS
INST. MUSIC
Characters (men, women, children, talking animals and inanimate objects)

That's it. It's pretty simple compared to all the elements in a TV script. But as in all things, there is a trade-off for this simplicity, because such simplicity makes the need for heightened creativity a must in radio.

Take as your model for the format of a radio script the following three basic radio executions. Note that the format is consistent in all three examples, but that each spot features a somewhat different approach based on announcer and sound effects, dialogue and sound effects, and announcer and song.

## Format 1, Announcer and Sound Effects

BAT-A-MOUSE
:30 RADIO
"MROWER"
Jim Albright
27 August 1991

| SFX: | (LOW, THREATENING GROWL OF A CAT STALKING SOMETHING, UP & UNDER ANNC) |
|---|---|
| ANNC: | S l o w l y  the cat stalks<br>the toy mouse.<br>He gathers himself to spring.<br>He springs,<br>bats the mouse with a mighty paw,<br>and . . . |
| SFX: | (SURPRISED "MROWER" OF CAT) |
| ANNC: | The mouse jumps back at the cat. |
| SFX: | (CAT BEGINS TO GROWL AGAIN, UP & UNDER) |
| ANNC: | Again he stalks.<br>And again and again,<br>when you buy your cat<br>a Bat-A-Mouse.<br>The amazing cat toy<br>that jumps back every time<br>it is batted by a cat.<br>Bat-A-Mouse, at fine toy stores everywhere.<br>You supply the cat . . . |
| SFX: | ("MROWER") |
| ANNC: | . . . and we'll supply the mouse.<br>Bat-A-Mouse. |

Note that the SFX of the cat growling is actually something you can hear and understand. Not like one writer's SFX written as (SOUND OF AN OIL SLICK). Though the growl could be any animal, the announcer's first words explain what you are hearing. Although designated ANNC, don't confuse this voice talent with a radio disc jockey or the like. A proper reading of the copy calls for an actor, not a person who gives the weather—for someone who can interpret your copy as you heard it in your mind when you wrote it. To get the reading the way you heard it, emphasize certain phrases, by underlining words or by spacing ("s l o w l y"), which helps explain how you hear the word being read. All good copy is left open to interpretation, and a professional actor will not resent your underlines or other explanations of emphasis. Indeed, a good talent appreciates the direction.

On the other hand, hard on your ego as it might be, some voice talents on a first reading will interpret your words differently . . . and better! Be smart enough to know when the reading is better the talent's way than your way. You'll still get the credit in the end.

In the SFX directions, the notation of UP & UNDER tells the recording engineer that the growling sound is up on a volume level with the announcer copy for a moment, then continues under the voice of the announcer copy. If you don't say UNDER, the recording engineer will assume that the sound effect only happens in that one spot and does not continue or, worse, may assume it continues at full volume, drowning out the announcer.

Writing for announcer and sound effects is a rewarding experience. In essence, you have someone saying your words; and when a mental image is to be reinforced, you just plug in the sound effects as you feel the need. There are only the two elements to think about. Many radio commercials employ this format.

But, remember, this approach — like most — isn't planned. A writer doesn't necessarily sit down and say, "I think I'll write something for announcer and sound effects." The writer writes, and then one of several approaches results. Of course, sometimes a budget restraint announced to the copywriter at the beginning of the job lets the writer know that there will be only one voice talent, no music, etc., which tends to push the copywriter toward this rather simple, yet potentially effective, format.

As to the identification in the upper left-hand corner, note only the second line is different from what you've learned before — ":30 Radio" or ":60 Radio" says it all for a prerecorded radio spot. You might want to add the word *Live* if your commercial is to be read live, something rare on a national or regional level, but still done for some local advertisers.

## Format 2, Dialogue and Sound Effects

BILL'S CAR REPAIR
:30 RADIO
"CALENDAR"
Jim Albright
19 September 1990

| | |
|---|---|
| SFX: | (CAR BACKFIRES AND STOPS RUNNING) |
| BILL: | Mister, you ain't drivin' that car outta here today. |
| MAN: | Aw shucks. |
| | Gee. |
| | I gotta get to work. |

| BILL: | My son will drive you. |
|---|---|
| MAN: | Golly. Lucky I pulled in here. |
| BILL: | It's more than luck . . . it's fate. |
| MAN: | This is like . . . like . . . the old days. I mean, you're right downtown. |
| BILL: | That's the whole idea Mac. We even got a calendar in the back there. |
| MAN: | Can I see it? |
| BILL: | You better get to work. |
| ANNC: | Bill's Garage at Main & Locust. Service like the old days at a fair price. |
| BILL: | And this year's calendar. |

The hard part about dialogue is keeping the characters from sounding like shills for the client (see Chapter 4). If you want copy points to come tumbling out of a character's mouth without shame, why not just use an announcer? That's what Format 2 does when it's time to ask for the business. Here's an example of shills at work:

| WOMAN: | Well, big boy, where are you taking me to lunch today? |
|---|---|
| MAN: | To the Budget Bar. |
| WOMAN: | Oh good, you mean the place at 1234 Main Street. |
| MAN: | That's the one. And they've got a huge selection of fish, beef, chicken and other specials. |
| WOMAN: | I love their salads, starting at 95 cents . . . |

Yuck. You think that's an exaggeration? You can hear it everywhere in America, every day. It's the kind of advertising that gives us all a bad name. Why couldn't they just pick a great voice talent and let him or her read some good copy? There would be no artifice about that. As it is, this script insults the audience with a typical announcer pitch disguised as a dialogue. Why did someone think a dialogue was important in the first place?

It's true the characters in the Bill's Garage spot do make the copy points desired — old-fashioned place, good service, nice people — but we hope those points are made while entertaining the listener. The copy points are designed to be subordinate to and support a loftier message. As pointed out in Chapter 6, the product must be the hero and must naturally be a part of the commercial. In this case, we have constructed a script that makes it natural for the man to be interested in what the garage has to offer.

Note the use of the snapper coming back after the pitch by the announcer. This is a fairly common technique and holds an element of surprise and interest for the listener, who usually hears a little playlet and then an announcer at the end, and that's it. In that way of ending a spot, the listener may tend to drift off when the announcer comes on, listening mostly for the byplay between the parties that comes first. That one last little bit of comment or humor can make the listener who has heard the spot before listen more attentively to the announcer's pitch, knowing a snapper is coming.

## Format 3, Lyrics and Donut

SWEET ROLL DELIVERY
:60 RADIO
"IN THE BOOK"
Jim Albright
28 May 1991

| SONG:<br>(30 seconds) | WHEN YOU'RE SLEEPIN'<br>IN ON WEEKENDS,<br>AND YOU JUST DON'T WANTA COOK,<br>BUT YOUR HUNGER<br>IS A-GROWIN'<br>YOU CAN FIND US IN THE BOOK<br><br>WE'LL BE WALKIN'<br>TO YOUR DOORSTEP<br>WITH A TRAY OF BREAKFAST TREATS<br>WE ARE SWEET ROLL DELIVERY<br>IN WHITE PAGES UNDER "SWEET"<br><br>SWEET ROLL DELIVERY<br>THE WEEKEND BREAKFAST TREAT<br>SWEET ROLL DELIVERY<br>MAKIN' WEEKENDS SWEET |
|---|---|
| ANNC:<br>(15 seconds) | Sweeten up your weekend mornings with hot rolls, juice, butter and beverages. Sweet Roll Delivery brings it to your door half an hour after you rise and call us. Credit cards and cash cheerfully accepted. Sweet Roll Delivery. Look in the white pages, under sweet. |
| SONG:<br>(15 seconds) | YES, WE'LL BE WALKIN'<br>TO YOUR DOORSTEP<br>WITH A TRAY OF BREAKFAST TREATS<br>JUST CALL SWEET ROLL DELIVERY<br>IN WHITE PAGES UNDER "SWEET"<br><br>SWEET ROLL DELIVERY<br>THE WEEKEND BREAKFAST TREAT<br>SWEET ROLL DELIVERY<br>MAKIN' WEEKENDS SWEET |

When you have a song to sing and interrupt with announcer copy, the announcer's part of the script is called a *donut*. When the music is recorded, an "instrumental bed" of music bridges a gap of so many seconds between song lyrics for later inclusion of an announcer in that donut. As one student has pointed out, that gap in the lyrics should really be called a "donut hole," but such is life; it's called the "donut."

It's not usually necessary to point out that after the end of the first song lyrics, the announcer will have instrumental music playing underneath. But some writers do point that out, so as to leave no question about what is happening.

## Variations in Format

The three formats shown are basically those found in radio advertising, but there may be many variations. You could have a full lyric version in 30 or 60 seconds. You could have an announcer talk for 30 or 60 seconds with no music or sound effects or characters; this is called a "straight announce" script. You could have the characters carry the entire message without an announcer at all. But basically, what you write will fall into the three formats shown.

# RADIO WRITING

## Be Intrusive

Radio is an intrusive medium. Just think about what it's like when people have the radio on. A very large proportion of the radio audience is driving in a car, though there is a substantial home and office audience as well. The automobile listener can be distracted by conversation with other passengers as well as traffic. Even at home or at the office, there are plenty of distractions. The copywriter must recognize these environmental impediments to listening and prepare scripts intrusive enough to halt conversation with a passenger, block out whatever is happening at home or at the office, and draw attention to the advertising message. No wonder, then, that radio commercials often consist of terrific music and lyrics, humor, bizarre situations or frightening messages — something with impact.

## Be Unique

When you're planning creative strategy, you're trying to find something unique to say about your client's product or service. Now you're striving to make your *execution* unique. You should, of course, be unique in every execution for every medium. But to overcome the extra distractions radio carries, you must be extra unique — or intrusive — in that execution.

Some clients and copywriters insist on thinking people are just sitting out there in Radioland waiting for their advertising message. That might be true if the message were:

ANNC:     Free one-carat diamonds today at Jones Jewelers.

Any radio spot that sets the scene like that will hold the listener's attention to the end, no matter how boring the copy or terrible the talent reading the message. But when you are one of 20 real estate companies on the air or 10 drug stores or 5 colas — your intrusion into the listener's consciousness needs to be unique. Many tools are available to help you get the listener's attention in a unique execution.

**Music**   Both music and lyrics make for an execution that can make any spot unique; you can even create a type of music that will match a station's format — classical, country-western, heavy metal, and so on. We'll say more on this later; but remember, if the client can afford a jingle, it's an excellent way to be intrusive — maybe the best way.

**Writing**   In the long run, in radio, as in all media, there is no substitute for great writing. If your words and ideas are clever, a straight announcer of average talent, with no music or sound effects to back him or her up, can sell the product. A great talent can sell even more. Great writing entails simplicity. Again, it's *hard* to get through to a person's ears alone. Most of us just haven't learned to absorb a complicated message without some sort of accompanying visual.

But to tell you a tool of radio is great writing — to tell you to write great scripts — is like telling you to relax. Use all the tools we discuss and pay special attention to each and every word in a radio script, no matter how small, and you'll be on your way to producing great writing.

As an example of radio writing at its best, radio writing that successfully intrudes on the listener, it's hard to beat the Motel 6 commercials starring Tom Bodett, which won Clio awards in 1988 and 1989 and *ADWEEK* magazine's selection as the best radio advertising of the decade.

MOTEL SIX
:60 RADIO

| | |
|---|---|
| SFX: | (FUNKY INST. UP AND UNDER) |
| TOM BODETT: | Hi. Tom Bodett for Motel 6 with a new vacation road game. |
| | The object is to guess the names of people in cars that pass you. |
| | Along comes a '68 wagon for example. |
| | You know, the kind with the fake wood sides. |
| | There's a lovely couple in it. |
| | She's knitting one and purling two, |
| | working like crazy on some little booties, |
| | and he's got both hands on the wheel. |
| | My guess is that their names are Ruth and Charlie. |
| | OK, here comes the fun part. |
| | Follow them until they stop for gas, |
| | then pull up to the pump and introduce yourself. |

If they reply with
"Hi, we're the Creekmores.
I'm Charlie and this is my wife Ruth,"
well you win.
If not, nothing lost.
It's a good way to meet people
and pass the time until you get
to Motel 6.
Where you can relax in a clean,
comfortable room for around 24 bucks,
the lowest prices of any national chain.
I'm Tom Bodett for Motel 6,
give my best to Ruth and Charlie
and we'll leave the light on for you.

**Sound Effects**   While they can be very effective tools of uniqueness, remember that sound effects should be like the scoring of music in a drama, something to set the scene and flesh it out without being obtrusive. It's natural at first to fall in love with all those thousands of sound effects in the library of most recording studios, and the new copywriter is tempted to feature the sound effects themselves, as if birds tweeting or firecrackers exploding were inherently interesting. They're not. They're useful only in the context of your plot to set a scene or complement the action. (A bird tweeting on Mars would be of enormous interest, of course, and have great dramatic impact.)

On the whole, if you concentrate on writing, the sound effects will suggest themselves to you as necessary. But if you start out letting a sound effect mandate the script you write before you've even figured out the plot, you may end up with a shallow effort.

**Production Values**   If you choose a first-rate studio and first-rate talent, including the recording engineer, you can make your commercial unique just through professionalism. Much of the recording we hear every day is not up to professional standards.

## Set the Scene

You can create visuals in the imagination of the listener. You set the scene—the visuals of imagination—at the beginning of the radio spot. When your character says, "Well, here we are on Mars," the listener's own concept of what Mars is like takes over. You can then go ahead and write the advertising message without worrying about describing Mars; each listener supplies the visual for you.

For a radio spot about a man and a woman in a bar, you can easily set the scene with some tinkling glasses and a murmur of conversation in the background, as a character says something clever like "What's a nice person like you doing here?" You wouldn't actually say something that corny, but the dialogue helps to set the scene. In TV, of course, you set the scene with pictures and sound. In both TV and radio, the action of setting the scene is very much like writing a headline for print.

In radio, sound effects don't necessarily communicate the scene by themselves, as noted earlier in the reference to the oil slick. Many beginning copywriters will write a radio spot that sets the scene by starting like this:

SFX:       (DOGS BARKING IN KENNEL)

BOY:       Here Rover!

How does the listener know the dogs are in a kennel? They might be a pack of mad dogs in the countryside or on a city street.

A better opening for Rover, if this is a spot (no pun intended) for a dog boarding service, would be:

SFX:       (DOGS BARKING)

ANNC:      The Doggy Hotel ...

BOY:       There's Rover!

There are more sophisticated and natural ways to set a scene; but this works, and in the listener's mind there is now a scene of dogs in a specific place, albeit a place designed and furnished by the imagination of the listener.

Now you can spin a yarn in context:

DAD:       No son. That looks like him, though.

Now you know the relationship between the man and the boy by the simple use of the word "son." In only 6 seconds we know that a man and his son are in a place called the Doggy Hotel and that the boy doesn't even know what his own dog looks like. The plot thickens. That leaves you 24 seconds in a 30-second spot to complete the story.

In the days before television, when radio was the entertainment medium in the home, people sat and "watched" their radios every night. Then, as now, simple suggestions made the plot work:

COWBOY 1:      What the? ... a gun!

SFX:           (CLICK OF HAMMER)

COWBOY 2:      Yeah, and ...

SFX:           (GUN FIRES)

COWBOY 2:      ... that rattlesnake almost got you, podner.

The same principles apply to today's commercials: set the scene quickly and clearly, then move on. And move on fairly quickly. Some writers take too long setting the scene and wait a long time before getting to the point.

Radio copy still contains a slogan, a snapper and an opening line of copy after you set the scene, but there is no headline. As we've said, the words that set the scene take the place of a headline. Here are two examples of openings for Molson Golden beer that take the place of headlines and set the scene:

Molson Number 1

| | |
|---|---|
| HIM: | Hi. |
| HER: | Hi. |
| HIM: | Well, don't suppose you work here? |
| HER: | No, nobody works here. |
| HIM: | Very casual resort. |
| HER: | If I worked in a place that looked like this, I wouldn't work either. It's beautiful. |
| HIM: | I love this place but it's ridiculous. |
| HER: | It's hot on the beach and I'm thirsty. |
| HIM: | Very laid back. |
| HER: | I'm going to do this myself. The bartender's not coming. What can I get you? |
| HIM: | Ah, a Molson Golden . . . |

See how they crept up to the sell, yet how the situation was apropos to a beer sell, being in a bar.

Molson Number 2

| | |
|---|---|
| HIM: | Hello? |
| HER: | Hello. |
| HIM: | Hi, I'm your neighbor, next door neighbor. |
| HER: | Yeah. |
| HIM: | I missed you when you moved in, I guess. |
| HER: | Really? |
| HIM: | I wanted to explain about that shelf in your refrigerator. |
| HER: | The shelf? Oh, you mean the bottom shelf. The one with the whole case of Molson Golden. Boy, what a great surprise that was moving in. |
| HIM: | It was my Molson Golden, my Molson Golden . . . |

Longer than a headline, true, but just as arresting.

## Make One Point

The most important thing to keep in mind when writing your radio spot is to make only one point. That doesn't mean that you say the same thing over and over, which is tiresome. It means there is a thread of continuity. You develop one subject in any way you wish — with humor, music, drama, etc.

Remember that radio is very easy for the listener to ignore. Find the one thing you wish to accomplish in your spot (come to this store, remember this ingredient, learn this location, whatever) and create a setting and a plot to get that point across.

# SAMPLE RADIO SCRIPTS

## Sanyo

The following Sanyo script is an example of a well-written, unique radio commercial, a spot that employs a combination of sound effects, dialogue, music, humor and, most of all, very fine and concise writing.

| | |
|---|---|
| SFX: | (RACING CAR ENGINES) |
| INTERVIEWER: | I notice you have a radio/cassette player in your race car. |
| DRIVER: | Yes, that's right. |
| INTERVIEWER: | Isn't that a little unusual? |
| DRIVER: | No, it's a little Sanyo. |
| INTERVIEWER: | Sanyo? |
| DRIVER: | Neat, huh? |
| INTERVIEWER: | Very nice. |
| DRIVER: | Thank you. |
| INTERVIEWER: | But don't you have trouble listening to it? |
| DRIVER: | You kidding? It's practically automatic. |
| INTERVIEWER: | Automatic? |
| DRIVER: | The radio has push-button memory tuning. |
| INTERVIEWER: | Uh . . . |
| DRIVER: | The cassette player has an automatic music select system. |
| INTERVIEWER: | Yeah, well what I meant was, don't you have trouble hearing it? |
| DRIVER: | Oh no, this Sanyo puts out some big sound, man. |
| INTERVIEWER: | I'm sure it does, but — |
| DRIVER: | Lots of power, plenty of presence. |
| INTERVIEWER: | Fine, but don't you have trouble hearing it above the roar of your engine? |
| DRIVER: | The roar of my what? |
| INTERVIEWER: | After all, race cars make a lotta noise. |
| DRIVER: | Well, to tell you the truth, I've never started this thing. |
| INTERVIEWER: | You what? |
| DRIVER: | I just come out here and sit in it, listen to my Sanyo, do a little lap time. |
| INTERVIEWER: | Wait a minute, how can you do a little lap time without starting it? |
| DRIVER: | Well . . . |

| SEXY FEMALE: | Hi Bill. How are ya doin'? |
| DRIVER: | Oh, hi Veronica. Like to get in and listen to my Sanyo? |
| SEXY FEMALE: | Oh, I'd love to. Where am I gonna sit? |
| DRIVER: | Well, you can always sit on my lap. |
| SEXY FEMALE: | Lap? |
| DRIVER: | Lap. |
| SFX: | (MUSIC UP) |
| SINGER: | SANYO. MAKES YOUR CAR SOUND BETTER! |

One point—that the Sanyo system sounds great in a car—is made over and over here, regardless of all the peripheral humor. You can make one point in a commercial without being boring, as this spot shows. It *is* hard to stick to one point. There were five copy points to make, as we shall see in a moment. How, then, do you make one point? The answer is to rise above the copy points, to integrate them into the plot. The one point in this spot is that this person enjoys his Sanyo system so much that he does something bizarre: he sits in an unused race car to hear Sanyo. The copy points are only supporting proof to the main point.

Old-timers will tell you to get the client's name in the copy early, as in all media. But a recent trend has developed (and has been pronounced successful by Video Storyboards of New York) where the client name is not introduced until later in the commercial. The theory is that you get the listener hooked on your presentation, then slip the name in at an appropriate point. In this technique, the actual client name becomes a snapper itself, because it is the payoff to what has come before.

**The Humor in the Sanyo Spot**   Most radio spots these days are 30 seconds long. For a 60-second commercial, it takes great music or humor to hold the listener's attention. Sanyo holds attention by being humorous. We know this is a humorous commercial by the fifth line, when the DRIVER says, "No, it's a little Sanyo," in reply to the INTERVIEWER'S "Isn't that a little unusual?" The humor is based on a gentle twist of double meaning, a standard kind of humorous wordplay you can hear in something as old as Marx Brothers movies. This kind of humor is not new, but used in the context of the Sanyo spot, it is new to the listener and effective. More importantly, the continued insistence by DRIVER to take another meaning from the INTERVIEWER'S questions gives the writer a perfect opportunity to make copy points without turning the character into a shill.

It is possible Sanyo told the copywriter: Be sure to tell them about (1) push-button memory tuning, (2) automatic music select, (3) power, (4) presence, (5) loud sound. These copy points sound academic, and they are, but note the cleverness of the copywriter in including the copy points as humorous misunderstandings rather than as a mere listing of copy points. To come back with the client's input, as many commercials do, and only list the copy points is not copywriting. Copywriting is taking those points and making them integral to the spot—in this case, as humorous answers.

This commercial is a good example of another point to consider when dealing with humor: don't use a one-time joke. If a friend tells you a joke, do you enjoy hearing it more than once? No. You've heard the punch line. Repetition of the joke won't make you laugh again. But, if the humor is low-key and runs throughout, and if the actor who delivers the lines has an unusual delivery, the humor bears repetition. Many great comedians have made their mark by the way they tell the story, rather than with a punch line. Humorous storytelling should be your goal, rather than a one-time, one-laugh punch line at the end.

Now, that seems to contradict the theory of the snapper, but it doesn't. Although the snapper has sometimes been described as a punch line, it is really the conclusion of a series of humorous thoughts, in a humorous effort. Or, the snapper is a serious and thoughtful last point or an emotional culmination. The snapper is the punch line only because it brings the listener back to where you started, with a bit of a twist.

**The Product As Hero**   Note that the point of the spot is Sanyo's automobile sound system. Without the insistence of this strange DRIVER on sitting in his unused race car just to listen to the Sanyo sound system, there is no spot. Sanyo is the reason for being there.

**How Specific Should You Be?**   The Sanyo script gives no indication as to what sex the announcer (INTERVIEWER) is or what kind of voice is needed. Also, there's no indication of what the singer's voice is like, what sex the singer is, or what style of music to use. If there's some reason why these considerations are integral to the spot, obviously the writer must insist on specifying such things.

Some creative directors insist on a production note at the top of the page of copy, indicating such specifics, and that is a legitimate demand. But often, when the copywriter is not too specific about production directions, the account executives, research or media people or clients might make a suggestion that makes the commercial even better than what was originally written. Copywriters should stifle their egos enough to accept such a possibility, for the sake of a better piece of communication. They still get the credit for that commercial in the long run, even if others had some suggestions.

## Uniformed Firefighters Association

In the following example of radio writing, there are no sound effects, no songs, no dialogue, no humorous stuff—only a straight pitch by an announcer. It's a monologue, if you will. Don't discount the effect of one great voice talent dealing with an important subject. Yes, there is a sell here. Yes, the client has something to say, with persuasion. But the way it's written is what captures the attention of the listener.

ANNOUNCER:     Mayor Koch, the Uniformed Firefighters Association,
               which is bringing you this message, is shocked at the
               Citizen Budget Commission's recommendation to reduce the

number of firefighters on a truck from five to four during certain so-called non-peak hours of the day. The number of firefighters needed on a truck has absolutely nothing to do with when a fire breaks out. Let's see what it means to have only four men on a fire truck. One man has to stay with the truck to maintain water pressure, only three go into the burning building. Two of these are on the hose at the point of fire and both need relief every two to eleven minutes, but only one man is left to relieve them and protect them, and this man also has to make sure there are no kinks in the hose, has to lead victims to safety, warn the men at the hose of possible fire behind their backs . . . and deal with the unexpected. Mayor Koch, please don't let thoughtless budget cutters endanger the lives of our firefighters and our citizens. Brought to you by the Uniformed Firefighters Association.

If there is a snapper to this, it is the next-to-last line, addressed to the mayor. The last line may seem bland; but given the subject matter, it comes off as a powerful plea by dedicated men and women. Whatever your feelings about unions, the rationality of this spot must appeal to anyone with a sense of fair play in his or her soul.

This spot is a good reminder of the importance of considering what the client is selling. This is not a way to sell bubble gum. It is a good way to sell the concept of endangering firefighters and citizens by what the client considers to be a misguided public policy. This commercial is also a good example of why the copywriter must spend most of the time thinking about the spot before beginning to write.

# JINGLES

We discuss jingles in the radio chapter because they are for the ear, but realize that jingles are often used for TV as well. Many copywriters don't get involved in jingles that run with radio and TV spots. They let others in the agency with a reputation for jingle creation write and produce them. Or they hire specialty jingle houses to write and produce their commercial music. The truth is, you could have a career as a copywriter and never mess with jingles, but you would be missing out on what might be the most fun there is in the copywriting business.

## Don't Call Them "Jingles"

Though called jingles by many people, the true experts prefer to call these songs advertising music. A "jingle" connotes a bouncy little collection of words, much like one of the first acknowledged jingles of advertising, back in the 1930s.

PEPSI COLA HITS THE SPOT,
12 FULL OUNCES, THAT'S A LOT
TWICE AS MUCH FOR A NICKEL TOO,
PEPSI COLA IS THE DRINK FOR YOU.

It may have not been the Beatles' "Revolution" soundtrack for Nike, but it was a history-making little . . . jingle.

In today's advertising, you find not only classic songs and instrumental renditions of same, but also original music often composed by creators of pop tunes. These songwriters are not making jingles. The same composers, in addition to creating and producing the music for a song or an instrumental track (music without lyrics), may also be called upon to score a commercial. A score is music for effect, much as movies have scoring to indicate horror or lighthearted moods, transition of time, and so on.

What we call jingles, then, really break down into three categories of advertising music: songs, instrumentals and scores. But for all of that, if you promise not to tell the advertising music people, and for ease of writing and understanding, we'll call them jingles in this chapter. We'll use the term with respect, however, because some of the finest advertising songs have in fact become popular songs, earning a place on the charts. "I'd Like to Give the World Some Love" pops into mind, a song that was originally "I'd Like to Buy the World A Coke," sung by an international group of youths on a hillside in Italy. It doesn't happen that often, but some advertising music has jumped over to general usage, as did the Gillette razor blade song "To Feel Sharp," from the 1950s. College marching bands would frequently strike up that jingle during football games.

## Who Writes Jingles?

Copywriters who are interested in jingles write them. Few writers get to college without having tried their hand at poetry in high school. If you were able to conjure up well-strung-together words for your love or for your Mom and Dad on their birthdays, you probably still have the inclination for verse, and that's just a short hop from jingles.

The interest is most important. Just by making a brave attempt to write a jingle when creating an advertising campaign, you'll finally produce one and will begin to gain a reputation as the "jingle person" in the agency. (When speaking of the copywriter writing jingles, we are actually speaking of the lyrics, not the music.) Agency bosses will encourage you to write lyrics; because although it's standard to hire outsiders to compose and produce the music for a jingle, it's a harder sell to get the client to pay even more for an outsider to write the lyrics. Often (in the mind of the client), whatever is being paid for copywriting should cover the cost of writing lyrics as well.

If you do write and have a jingle produced, you have saved the client money, you have made the agency look good and you have given yourself entry into a wonderful world of musicians and studios and the dull glow of red lights and booming speakers. Most important of all, if the copywriter on the account writes good lyrics for jingles, they are often better or more easily produced, because lyricists hired from outside the agency will have to be educated about the account. For the time and trouble that will make, why not let the copywriter go ahead and write the jingle?

It's hard on the copywriter's ego, but many art directors are often as good at writing lyrics as they are at headlines, so you should enlist their aid on the project. Art directors have a capacity to state things in very short sentences, maybe because so many of them are intimidated by words and so write their copy short for less exposure.

## The Story

"They all tell a little story, Hon," a nice west Texas woman said to me a long time ago. She was discussing country-western music. And, in truth, the main thing about lyric writing is that you do tell a good story, and you do it concisely. The actual crafting of the lyrics takes time and juggling, but there is plenty of help once you have a good basic idea for the lyrics. And most of the time that idea has already been created by you for the advertising campaign the jingle is intended to be a part of.

## Some Tips on Writing Jingles

- Get the slogan into the lyrics, particularly in the last line, if possible. In fact, when you first write your slogan for any campaign, consider whether you'll someday have a song for that account, and then make sure that the slogan is singable.
- Try to have the same number of syllables in each corresponding line. For instance, in this jingle that ran for Frontier Airlines when their standby fares were actually cheaper than the bus:

> CARS AND BUSES DOWN BELOW (7)
> MAN THEY SURE ARE MOVIN' SLOW (7)
> LOOK AT ME AWAY UP HERE (7)
> FLYIN' STANDBY ON FRONTIER (7)

The "(7)"s behind each line show you how many syllables are in each line. (You won't do this on the script.) Experienced jingle writers might intimidate you by saying that such syllabication is dull and simplistic, and maybe that's true. But for the beginning jingle writer, without the built-in talent and/or experience of a veteran jingle writer, it's best to get the rhythm right the first time through, before you show the lyrics to anyone. It helps you to sell the lyrics if they feel right.

The Frontier song was a coincidence in the way all four lines were the same syllabication. The main thing is to keep it consistent on the same lines in the song, as in this example:

> LIVIN' ON TOLLWAY CHANGE, (6)
> IT'S THE BEST I CAN ARRANGE, (7)

GOT NO BUCKS, (3)
I'M OUTTA LUCK, SO (5)
I'M LIVIN' ON TOLLWAY CHANGE. (7)

Note the syllabication varies, and that's fine. What's important is that the second verse is consistent, line for line, with the first verse.

LIVIN' ON TOLLWAY CHANGE, (6)
AND MY DOG HAS GOT THE MANGE, (7)
WE'RE A PAIR (3)
THAT'S GOTTA EAT AIR, 'CAUSE (6)
I'M LIVIN' ON TOLLWAY CHANGE. (7)

- Don't sing copy points. Stay on a higher intellectual level about the most important things. Sure, Sheraton Hotels had a great campaign song with "1-800-325-2525," and that was the copy point. These exceptions are rare. Most of the time it's very difficult to sing phone numbers and addresses, just from the point of view of rhyming and rhythm alone. If these things are important, let the announcers do it right with straight talk.

- Write the full lyric version first, with an eye on the donut. The donut, or bed, is that part of the song where the instrumental music continues under an announcer, VO, characters in dialogue, sound effects or all of the above. Obviously, after you write a full lyric version, you will have to remove a verse to make room for the donut. This can be hard, because if you write important lyrics, how can you arbitrarily take them out? Or if you write lyrics that can be easily removed, how can they be good enough to leave in? The answer is that you shouldn't write too many different lyrics, but write a few good ones that can be sung over and over. So when you need to drop some lyrics for a donut, it won't hurt so much.

- Emphasize the same idea over and over. Here's an example of how the jingle will work with just a few well-chosen words and the occasional addition of a new thought in a new verse. Most of your lyrics will be a variation on the theme, to wit:

NOW YOU'RE TALKIN' HIKING,
NOW YOU'RE TALKIN' BEER,
NOW YOU'RE TALKIN' GOOD TIMES
AND STROHS IS SPOKEN HERE.

NOW YOU'RE TALKIN' STROHS,
NOW YOU'RE TALKIN' BEER,
NOW YOU'RE TALKIN' GOOD TIMES
AND STROHS IS SPOKEN HERE.

Note the small variation between the first verse, which related to the plot of the spot, and the second verse. And note most of all how the product is integral to the theme of the song, even though the theme also connotes a philosophy of friendship. With such minor variations between verses, you will have no trouble dropping a verse for a donut, still retaining the theme of the song.

On the whole, the donuts, particularly in a :30, should occupy less time than the song, though there are times when the whole spot will be talk and only the key lines will be sung: "AND STROHS IS SPOKEN HERE."

- Use chorus and verses to best effect. Sometimes writers put VERSE and CHORUS before certain lines of the song. The verse is the story that continues; the chorus is a repetition of the same words each time, usually the high point of the song in dramatic intensity, as in the following song:

VERSE:     I PUT OUT THE TRASH (5)
AND MADE SOME HASH FOR (5)
SOME MEALS ALL ALONG, (5)
I VACUUMED THE RUG (5)
NEVER GOT A HUG (5)
WHERE DID I GO WRONG? (5)

CHORUS:   WHERE DID I GO WRONG?
AIN'T THIS WHAT SHE WANTED
ALL ALONG?
I'M A LIBERATED AND
SENSITIVE MAN,
WHERE DID I GO WRONG?

VERSE:     SHE WANTED TO SHARE
THE JOBS OF HOUSE CARE
AND I WENT ALONG,
SO SHE'S WORKIN' LATE
WHILE I'M BAKIN' CAKES
WHERE DID I GO WRONG?

CHORUS:   WHERE DID I GO WRONG?
AIN'T THIS WHAT SHE WANTED
ALL ALONG?
I'M A LIBERATED AND
SENSITIVE MAN,
WHERE DID I GO WRONG?

VERSE:     SHE READS WHILE I COOK
AND SLEEPS WITH A BOOK
WHILE FOR HER I LONG,
I'M DOIN' THE WORK
BUT FEEL LIKE A JERK,
WHERE DID I GO WRONG?

CHORUS:   WHERE DID I GO WRONG, LORD?
AIN'T THIS WHAT SHE WANTED
ALL ALONG?
I'M A LIBERATED AND
SENSITIVE MAN,
WHERE DID I GO WRONG?

(REPEAT CHORUS)

It doesn't matter if you don't label verses and choruses, because both will be obvious. As to structure of the song, you might consider a format like the following for a :60:

20 seconds of song

20 seconds of donut

20 seconds of song

or for a :30, 10 seconds of each.

As to the actual writing, whether verses or choruses or what, this could serve as a guide in a :60:

(VERSE, 10 SECONDS)

I SING TO YOU A SIMPLE TUNE,
ABOUT THE OLD STATE U,
ABOUT THE J-SCHOOL THAT WE LOVE,
AND WHAT WE'RE TEACHIN' YOU.

(CHORUS, 10 SECONDS)

WRITE THAT JINGLE DOWN TONIGHT,
APPLY WHAT YOU BEEN LEARNIN',
J-SCHOOL MEANS YOU DO IT RIGHT,
AND KEEP OUR TORCH A-BURNIN'.

ANNC: (20 SECONDS OF COPY)

(VERSE, REPEAT, 10 SECONDS)

(CHORUS, REPEAT, 10 SECONDS)

In a :30, you would have maybe the verse at first and the chorus after the donut, or maybe two choruses or two verses. The preceding verse and chorus are silly little words made up for you, just to make a point about organization. Even so, count syllables and learn the organization of the lines.

Consider making the rhyme scheme ABCB, in which the second and fourth lines rhyme. It might sound hokey when every line rhymes and sound as if it's missing something when no lines rhyme; and yet successful songs have been done both ways.

• Be economical with words. Try to eliminate all but essential *a*'s, *an*'s and *the*'s. Don't force rhythm with words like *really*, if they don't add anything to the song. Look at the samples given to see how free of all nonessential words the lyrics are.

• If you're unsure about the rhythm, use a song you know to write lyrics to. But don't tell the music person (the composer) what song you wrote lyrics to. One time I told the music person I had written some Astroworld lyrics to the rhythm of "Lookin' Out My Back Door," by Credence Clearwater Revival, and the melody and orchestration sounded just like the original in the resulting jingle. I'm still waiting to get sued on that one.

The point is, a song in your head that you know well is a great guide to syllabication and lyric length. At least you know your lines are fairly rhythmical when you're done writing. What songs should you use? Few students listen to country-western, but those songs have a unique way of telling a story in a short time. (If you listen to country-western, you'll find that the syllabication is good, too.) Herewith, to give you a break while reading this at three in the morning, an amusing list of a few country-western titles and/or lines:

> She Never Met a Man She Didn't Like
>
> All I Want from You Is Away
>
> Pardon Me, But You Left Your Tears on the Jukebox, and I'm Afraid They Got All Mixed Up with Mine
>
> For Better or for Worse, But Not for Long
>
> If I Said You Had a Beautiful Body, Would You Hold It Against Me?
>
> Your Wife's Been Cheatin' on Us Again
>
> You're So Cold I'm Turnin' Blue
>
> When Your Phone Don't Ring, It'll Be Me

- When you time your lyrics, read them aloud at a medium-slow pace. You need to build in time for orchestration and holding notes.
- Put prepositions at the front of a line, if possible.
- Reason is more important than rhyme. If given a choice, don't use awkward phrases that nobody uses ("and in the house I went") to force a rhyme.

Jingles are something you have to get into and do with a lot of bravado. But like poaching an egg, it's something you can get good at after a few tries.

Following are commercials featuring jingles, some with donuts or beds for copy, some without. Study them to see the structure of real jingles that have been heard all over America. An old saying in the advertising business by adpersons who thought jingles were silly went: "If you don't have anything to say, sing it." Jingles have become legitimate since then.

```
BUGLE BOY JEANS
:55 JINGLE
Rubin Postaer and Associates

SFX:      (HELICOPTER SOUNDS)

ANNC:     Bugle Boy.

SONG:     I'LL DO EVERYTHING I CAN
          I'LL DO ALL IN MY POWER
          TO FIND THAT GIRL
          WHO LEFT MY HEART ON FIRE
          THE ONE WHO SAID TO ME
          ARE THOSE BUGLE BOY JEANS?
          SHE'S A NUCLEAR LADY
          PUT A SPELL ON ME
          THINKIN' ABOUT IT CONTINUALLY
          THE ONE WHO SAID TO ME
```

ARE THOSE BUGLE BOY JEANS?

ARE YOU WEARIN' BUGLE BOY JEANS?
(BUGLE BOY JEANS)
ARE YOU WEARIN' BUGLE BOY JEANS?
(BUGLE BOY JEANS)
ARE YOU WEARIN' BUGLE BOY JEANS?

AMERICAN AIRLINES
:60 JINGLE
by Ken Sutherland

| | |
|---|---|
| SONG: | THE AMERICAN WAY,<br>MAKIN' IT EASIER. |
| ANNC/DIALOGUE: | (INST. UNDER, FIVE SECONDS) |
| SONG: | THE AMERICAN WAY,<br>WORKIN' HARDER.<br>THE AMERICAN WAY,<br>DOIN' IT BETTER<br>EVERY SINGLE DAY. |
| ANNC/DIALOGUE: | (INST. UNDER, FOUR SECONDS) |
| SONG: | DOIN' IT BETTER<br>IS THE AMERICAN WAY. |
| ANNC/DIALOGUE: | (INST. UNDER, TEN SECONDS) |
| SONG: | WORKIN' HARDER,<br>MAKIN' IT EASIER,<br>LIGHTS ON GO EVERY DAY,<br>DOIN' IT BETTER<br>IS THE AMERICAN WAY! |

AMALIE
:30 RADIO
by Ken Sutherland

| | |
|---|---|
| INST: | (UP AND UNDER ANNC) |
| ANNC: | Here's one sweet deal from Amalie. |
| SONG: | AMALIE! |
| ANNC: | Right now, you can get Amalie's brand of quality and the best deal yet. Get a three-dollar rebate from Amalie on every case. And in every case, you'll be getting protection no ordinary motor oil can give. Three dollars a case, that's a quarter a quart. |
| SONG: | HA! |
| ANNC: | And that's |
| SONG: | OOOOO . . . |
| ANNC: | better than it has to be. Amalie. |
| SONG: | AMALIE!<br>AMALIE . . . |

BORDEN
:30 JINGLE
by Jim Albright/Ron McQuien/R. H. Brians

SONG:    IF IT'S BORDEN,
IT'S GOT TO BE GOOD.
WE GUARANTEE THAT IT'S GOT TO BE GOOD.

WE GUARANTEE THAT
WE'LL DO WHAT WE SHOULD,
'CAUSE OUR NAME IS BORDEN
IT'S GOT TO BE GOOD.

OUR NAME IS BORDEN,
AND WE'VE LED ALL THE WAY.
WE'VE BEEN HERE
FOR A HUNDRED YEARS,
SO YA KNOW WE'RE HERE TO STAY!

ANNC:    (INST. UNDER, 15 SECONDS)

SONG:    IF IT'S BORDEN,
IT'S GOT TO BE GOOD.
WE GUARANTEE THAT IT'S GOT TO BE GOOD.

WE GUARANTEE THAT
WE'LL DO WHAT WE SHOULD,
'CAUSE OUR NAME IS BORDEN
IT'S GOT TO BE GOOD.

I wrote that song with two other fellows for a Borden corporate campaign. My best memories of it are not the compliments we got when the campaign ran, but rather the cozy night by the fire when the three of us worked on the song. That's the beauty of jingles; from creation to the day the musicians waltz in to record your work, it's fun. And why work at something that isn't fun?

PEPSI COLA COMPANY
(Author Unknown)

SONG:    HELLO TOMORROW,
YOUR CHILDREN ARE HERE.
CAN YOU HEAR THE NEW DRUMMER,
THE FUTURE IS CLEAR.

WE'RE TAKING OUR PLACE NOW.
WE'RE GRABBIN' HOLD
ON A RAINBOW OF PROMISE
WE ARE YOUR GOLD.

A GENERATION OF HOPE.
A GENERATION OF LIGHT.
A GENERATION OF DREAMS,
SHINING SO BRIGHT.

A GENERATION OF COLOR.
BLACK, WHITE, YELLOW, RED.

A GENERATION OF PEPSI.
A GENERATION AHEAD.

WE SPEAK THE SAME LANGUAGE.
WE SHARE THE SAME VOICE.
WE FEEL THE SAME FEELINGS.
BUT WE MAKE OUR OWN CHOICE.

WE'RE CROSSING THE BORDERS,
NO TIME TO WAIT.
OUR DIFFERENCES ARE
WHAT WE CELEBRATE.

A GENERATION OF CHANGE.
A GENERATION OF SONG.
A GENERATION OF LAUGHTER
COMING ON STRONG.

A GENERATION OF LIFE . . .
NOW, LET IT BE SAID
A GENERATION OF PEPSI.
A GENERATION AHEAD.
(REPEAT)

These Pepsi lyrics are a good example of how to move ahead with a fine philosophy in a changing world, while still holding on to the great generational aspects of past Pepsi advertising.

If you become a copywriter, you will eventually be given the opportunity to write a jingle. Seize the moment. There aren't many people willing to take the risk of looking foolish, but jingles are a lot easier than you might think; and if you're a good copywriter, it only takes a couple of experiences to get good at writing them. It will set you apart from the other copywriters and give you a mystique; that's what all copywriters want.

# RADIO PRODUCTION

Many of the suggestions made in Chapter 6 about TV production also apply to radio, particularly the part about being thorough in pre-production, dealing with talent, and the general order of production from script to final result. But there are, of course, certain fundamental differences between radio and TV when you're the agency or corporate producer.

## The Radio Engineer

Your engineer, instead of the film or tape director, is your most important person in radio. She or he has all the sound effects at her or his fingertips, including the music you've brought with you, the sound levels, and all the equipment to bring it together. Best of all, the engineer has the *ear* to hear things you often can't. Cultivate an engineer and try to use the same one every time, if possible, in a favorite recording studio that offers both voice and music production (for your own convenience).

When you walk onto a TV set, there are people everywhere. When you walk into a radio recording studio, there are the engineer, your voice talent, you and all that recording equipment. Sometimes you'll also have the company of the account executive (AE) and the client. Sometimes it's better to record without them, but there's one good thing about having them there: instant approval. If you get through the session with their okay on everything you do, they'll go back and sell your recording for you, for they were part of it. (The same thing is true about TV production.)

But most of the time it's only you, the engineer, the talent, whatever music you may have brought along — a jingle previously recorded, perhaps — and sound effects you and the engineer have previously chosen and recorded in sequence to be plugged in when necessary.

## The Session

If your script requires music and sound effects and a voice or voices, the engineer will let you know whether he or she prefers a "live mix"; that is, mixing in all those elements while recording the voice talents. Or you may record the voices and dismiss the talent; then you and the engineer go about mixing everything together piece by piece.

Before you start recording, ask the talent to read the script. Most of the time the talent should have the script in advance, as should the engineer, though this doesn't always happen. Listen carefully. The talent may not read the script the way you heard it in your head; the reading may even be an improvement. If the talent doesn't read the script the way you heard it and the talent's reading is not as good as the way you heard it, coach the talent.

Then you run through the production for time and, if it is a live mix, to rehearse the mixing in of the music and sound effects. Though you're theoretically rehearsing to get the timing right, you're also listening carefully to the talent's interpretation of your words.

Don't look at your script during this time, because you won't hear the presentation correctly. Just listen, the way a radio listener would listen. If there are technical flaws in the talent's reading — misstatements of facts or mispronunciations — you can check the script for them after everything is running smoothly and make corrections before the final take.

## Respect the Talent

Being respectful of the talent means (in TV too) that you don't make personal observations about the reading over the intercom. Always have the engineer shut off the mike, and go where the talent is and speak in low tones about how you feel. It's embarrassing to the talent, otherwise. An embarrassed talent is not going to read at his or her best.

If you use voice talents you have been successful with in the past, you'll know how they work. The very best don't have to do many takes, and you should know when to quit. This takes taste on your part and respect for the talent's own opinion of his or her work. Good talent will say, "I can do it better," even when you're satisfied with a take. Go with them, and you'll often get something above and beyond what you were expecting.

If dealing with a new talent, albeit one whose voice you have heard, remember that in most cases the talent improves with each reading. Wait until the talent has become familiar with your coaching and the script before you start making small changes. If you start out with small changes after each reading, you don't allow the talent to achieve a pattern, a tone that overall is what you want.

## Listening to the Playback

Big speakers are great for selling a client, but most of your consumers will hear the commercial through little speakers. Listen to the playback on both sizes. There could be something vital that you hear on the big speakers but not on the little ones.

## Don't Be Cheap

Too many people hire a studio for a minimum amount of time. You need the luxury of working with your talent and taking advantage of his or her suggestions, the engineer's or client's suggestions, or the AE's suggestions on how the spot may be improved right there and then. In such cases, it's nice to have extra time.

## Taste

Note there has been no mention of the AD here. Sometimes they go to radio recording sessions; but as a rule you're on your own, and that makes it fun. It's fun, that is, until you go back to the office and play the spot for the AD, and he or she doesn't like it. As to how you develop the taste to know when to accept the commercial, it's like all the rest of advertising. You have to saturate yourself in advertising, including radio. Listen carefully to bad commercials and figure out why they're bad. Even negative learning is a positive learning experience.

## Music Production

After your lyrics are approved, and you get the go-ahead to produce a "demo" (demonstration) track of your lyrics, it's a most crucial time. The demo could consist of the **music person** playing a piano and singing your lyrics "live" in front of the client and agency people. It could be a fully orchestrated track (with every instrument you can think of) that may not have to be re-recorded if the demo is bought. Or it could be a simple track with drums, bass and guitar. It all depends on the budget.

What determines the quality of your music is your moment alone with the music person (probably with the AD along), when she or he reveals the melody created to go along with your words. It's hard to be critical in such a situation, because music persons are intimidating. Even so, you have to gut it out and tell the music person exactly how you feel. Once you buy the melody you are committed to large expenditures (assuming the agency and client also buy the melody, on your say-so and their instincts). Nobody can teach you to know what music will go over with the client and/or public. It's instinct. If you feel you lack that instinct, don't get into music production.

## The No-Change Point in Music

Once you say "yes" to the melody, "charts" (the music) are made for musicians, and little change is possible once you're in the recording studio. Your presence there ensures that the orchestration is performed as promised and that what you and the music person promised to client and agency is done. There's certainly nothing you can do about the finer points of music (unless you're a music person too), but you definitely can't let anyone (the AE or client) change the melody. If you've called for a harmonica and the music person tries to sneak another instrument past you, you can do something about that. That's your jurisdiction.

If you're working with a music person you trust, you don't actually have to be in the studio when the music is recorded, but agencies and clients want to have a representative at a recording. You're the most logical one.

## Your Music Suppliers

Develop friendship, based on respect, with two or three music persons. It's the only way to get the job done without disappointment. Music is mysterious and difficult (though fun) to produce. Only by dealing with good people can you make sure you get something that won't embarrass you.

Nothing else in advertising will give you a bigger thrill than riding down the road with your radio booming, listening to your own lyrics with good music behind them. Nothing.

Good music people get a lot of their money up front, because the creation of the melody is the whole ball game; and the actual recording with musicians later, though exciting, is secondary. Buying music is a crap shoot. It is similar to commissioning a portrait, not really knowing until it's done whether you like it. All you have to go on are other portraits the artist painted.

The same is true of music. All you have to go on are past jobs with the music person and/or the sample reel. There's a lot of trust in this part of the business, more trust than hard-eyed business people like to have to rely on when spending thousands of dollars for something.

## Involvement in Broadcast Production

For the copywriter broadcast production affords much greater involvement and responsibility than does print production. This may be because obvious art talents are involved in print production or because copywriters jumped into the broadcast technology ahead of the art directors. Without implying that a copywriter should not get involved in print production, I want to urge you to take advantage of any opportunity to be exposed to broadcast production in your internship or summer jobs. It will pay off later.

## RADIO TIPS

- Be intrusive by being unique in radio writing. Be bolder, take more chances.
- Know the radio format and the tools available before writing.
- Guide voice talent with underlines and special instructions on the reading.
- Make it very clear what SFX are, or explain them right away.
- Be open to suggestions on script and production by clients, AEs, engineers and talent.
- Avoid shills in dialogue.
- Set the scene; consider your opening as a headline.
- Stick to one point throughout; let copy points support that one point.
- For :60 radio, consider a song or humor.
- Make the product the hero, natural and necessary to the action.
- Be only as specific as necessary as to sex of announcers, music style, etc.
- If you must use a number, save it for last, and give it at least twice.
- Have the courage to write a jingle, if the opportunity arises.
- Rely on your radio engineer in recording sessions.
- Respect and be gentle with talent.
- Book more than enough time in the studio.
- Listen to playback on small speakers.
- Don't watch the script while listening to the production; check the script carefully against a good "take" before letting the talent go home.
- Remember, when you agree on a melody, there is seldom a chance to change it later.
- Develop friendships with two or three music persons you trust.

## IN CONCLUSION

Radio can give the copywriter a chance to work without the art director tagging along, though more and more art directors are good at radio creation and execution. In fact, if the radio is part of a multi-media campaign, it's very likely the creative strategy and overall creative execution would be determined in concert with the art director. But more often than not, the copywriter tends to create and produce radio alone.

Radio writing is fun. There's something neat and clean about writing for radio. There's no art or photography or layout to worry about as in print. There's no visual side of the script as in TV. It's all for the ear.

Radio is a big ego-booster because you can be totally responsible for so much of the spot, but remember that it is harder to reach out and grab the listener in radio, compared to media using sight or sight and motion.

On the other hand, to achieve the intrusiveness you desire, radio gives you the opportunity to be as bizarre as you wish, and that doesn't happen as often with the other media. Take advantage of it!

## EXERCISES

1. Write a number of openings for various products and services that clearly set the scene for what is to come.

2. Write a Creative Work Plan for a local retail account, and execute it in a :30 radio spot.

3. Do the same for a durable goods, packaged goods and service account.

4. Write a country-western song on the subject of drinking, bad men, bad women, children, jail or trains.

5. Write a :60 radio commercial featuring a jingle for a local retail or national durable goods, packaged goods or service campaign.

# CHAPTER 8

# COLLATERAL—PRINT AND BROADCAST

The term *collateral* describes non-media advertising materials prepared by a corporation, an advertising agency, an art studio or other suppliers to the advertising business. "Non-media" means that collateral materials are not seen in media such as radio, TV, outdoor, newspaper, magazines, transit advertising and other outlets for ads, commercials and posters. To most advertising people collateral means printed pieces such as brochures, annual reports, point-of-purchase displays, catalogs, direct mail, Christmas cards, calendars and much more—a full range of advertising created and produced by the client alone or through an advertising agency—materials not run in primary media. Collateral also refers to broadcast materials like films, tapes, slide shows, records and cassettes and to stage productions for auto and other trade shows, sales training materials and more.

Writing collateral material is different from writing media advertising like TV, radio, newspaper and magazine advertising because there is no editorial matter surrounding the advertisements. That means you're creating an unsolicited piece of sales material, and so you must be an extraordinary writer to get people to read what they commonly call junk mail (if the piece is direct mail) or to pay attention to any of the other collateral pieces mentioned. Even if the material is an annual report, it's a selling piece, and you're asking people to volunteer for a pitch. (Though outdoor and transit advertising have no surrounding editorial matter, they are still considered media rather than collateral.)

Many copywriters eschew writing collateral materials, because they have less public exposure and don't enjoy the status of TV, radio and four-color magazine ads. In fact, you have greater creative opportunities with collateral because the material must be unusually persuasive, and so you have more freedom to create material that would seem off-the-wall or bizarre in traditional media. And collaterals can lead to a profitable free-lance career.

When I was the writer and creative director on Korbel champagne and brandy, I wrote TV and radio and magazine ads for them — the high-powered stuff. But when the client needed a film for a sales meeting, I was asked if I could recommend someone to write a 45-minute sales film about Korbel, featuring Dick Cavett. The AEs thought it was beneath my dignity to write a sales film after all that high-powered stuff, but I jumped at the chance and wrote the film.

It was a good move. When I was called by a production house and asked if I had an interest in writing a film for Conoco, and heard the money they were paying was a month's pay, I said "yes."

"Do you have any samples of your work?" they asked.

"I have a film I did for Korbel, starring Dick Cavett," said I.

That did it. I got the Conoco film, then another one. The next person who called was able to see three films I had written, and so it went.

Some agencies have copywriters who write nothing but collateral material. But if the same copywriter who has created good broadcast and print advertising for a certain account also writes the collateral material, account executives in the agency and/or the advertising director in the corporation feel reassured. They like it when the copywriter for collateral material is already familiar with the account through writing print and broadcast advertising.

For some reason, though, the inexperienced writers are often assigned the collateral writing, probably on the theory that they aren't ready yet for the radio or TV or magazine "status" work. Despite this bad thinking, new copywriters have a great opportunity to show their ability. And again, because there is no editorial matter or programming surrounding the effort, writing collateral forces the writer to get to the heart of the sell in an interesting way — something that should be done on all advertising, but is absolutely essential in collateral advertising.

# PRINT COLLATERAL FORMAT

The number of different kinds of collateral pieces is enormous, and an entire textbook could be devoted to talking about each. But when it comes to the format in which you write print collateral, it is the same no matter what the piece is. For the purpose of exposing you to collateral format, we show a four-page direct mail piece, but please don't think this is the only kind of collateral there is. The difference in format from print advertising (Chapter 5), is not great, but it is significant. Pay careful attention.

The upper left-hand corner designation, on the second line, depends on you to use common sense. If the piece is a four-page direct mail effort, the example used here for format, the upper left-hand corner might read:

(Page One)
MR. WHISKERS CATFISH RESTAURANT
SELF-MAILER, 4-PG, 2C
"FRESHWATER SEAFOOD"
Jim Albright
19 May 1991

The main thing is to explain, as simply as possible, just what it is you are creating. If the client has been using some name for the piece like "The Fall Calendar," call it that. If no name has been used in the past, make up something descriptive.

Note also the page number above the four-line designation. This describes the actual sheet of paper your copy is on in this project, for the sake of someone who might get the pages mixed up. By placing the numbers for the actual sheet of paper at the top left, you avoid confusion with the page numbers of the piece spread throughout the piece you are writing. Sometimes, as in the following example, there are several page numbers on one page. Here's a complete example of how to write and designate parts of a direct mail piece. In this case it's a self-mailer, which means that one page of the piece is used for an address, because it doesn't come in an envelope.

(Page One)
MR. WHISKERS CATFISH RESTAURANT
SELF-MAILER, 4-PG, 2C
"FRESHWATER SEAFOOD'
Jim Albright
19 May 1991

COVER (page one):

| | |
|---|---|
| HEAD: | TEXANS THINK |
| | CATFISH IS |
| | SEAFOOD |
| SUBHEAD: | So What? |
| PIC: | (CATFISH WITH SHARK FIN) |

PAGE TWO:

HEAD: FISH BY ANY OTHER NAME . . .

PIC: (CATFISH PLATTER WITH HUSH PUPPIES, FRIES, CORN BREAD, LEMON, BUTTER AND TARTAR SAUCE)

SUBHEAD: . . . Can Taste As Sweet

COPY BLOCK "A": And that goes double for Mr. Whiskers Catfish. No river-bottom feeding for our babies. They're raised in clean fresh-water ponds no more than 50 miles away.

They're fed special feed to make them more plump and sweeter than Mother Nature ever thought of.

When a "seafood" fan breaks through the crispy fried batter to the soft white meat, he or she will say "Mr. Whiskers, where have you been?"

PAGE THREE:

PIC: (INTERIOR OF RESTAURANT)

HEAD: A "SEAFOOD" ATMOSPHERE

COPY BLOCK "B": If part of the fun for you is the seaside-style bar and fishnets and timbers overhead, this is the place to enjoy catfish.

Whether you're already a catfish lover, or a newcomer to the taste, have we got an introductory deal for you!

Just bring in this coupon anytime for lunch or dinner (open every day 10 A.M. to midnight), and two can eat our catfish dinner for the price of one.

COUPON: ...........................................................................
(COPY BLOCK "C") 2-FOR-1 CATFISH DINNER

Hand this coupon to the waitperson before you order two delicious dinners for one price. Beverages extra. Offer expires at the end of this year.

Mr. Whiskers Catfish Restaurant
...........................................................................

PAGE FOUR:

UPPER LEFT: A Great Catch at:
MR. WHISKERS CATFISH RESTAURANT (LOGO)
12 Pine Lake Road
East, Texas 75001
(214) 555-4526

ADDRESS: (MAILING LABELS FROM MAILING LIST)

UPPER RIGHT: (BULK MAIL IMPRINT)

The copywriter's thumbnail is shown in Figure 8.1.

Bulk Mail

A great catch at
MR. WHISKER'S CATFISH
RESTAURANT
12 Pine Rd.
East Texas 75001
(214) 341-4526

Mailing Label

Texans think
Catfish
is
Seafood

So What?

Fish by any other name...

...can taste as sweet

(A)

Interior of Restaurant

A "Seafood" Atmosphere

(B)

2 for 1 Catfish Dinner

(C)

MR. WHISKER'S CATFISH RESTAURANT

8.1

*Thumbnail sketches to accompany copy for Mr. Whiskers brochure.*

Here are a few things to note about the format:

- The page numbers (including "COVER") of the brochure itself are in CAPS and underlined. This is the main difference between the format of an ad and a multi-page piece. On the ad, everything appears on one page or part of a publication page. With multi-page pieces, you must add page numbers so art directors, among others, know where they are in the piece when reading the copy. Sometimes, after a discussion with the art director (or upon your own initiative), you may want to use both inside pages (pages 2 and 3 in Figure 8.1) as one large area for design. This happens often. When it does, then use "PAGES TWO AND THREE:" preceding the appropriate head, copy, PIC and so on. In our example, pages 2 and 3 were used as separate layout pages.

- Copy blocks are marked "A," "B," etc., because they will be on different pages of your copy and of the piece and might be hard to locate. When you indicate copy blocks on the thumbnail and mark them as shown in Figure 8.1, it's easier for the art director, account executive, ad manager, client, typesetter and other readers to see exactly where the copy goes in the piece.

- You will feel the need for subheads in a brochure because (1) the copy is often long and requires breaking up for design reasons, (2) new ideas or changes in copy direction occur or (3) subheads help pull the reader's eyes from copy block to copy block and lend an air of importance to what follows. Subheads can be written in caps or upper and lower case, or italicized, or underlined, as in the Mr. Whiskers piece. It's up to the writer. As you can see, I prefer upper and lower case and underline. The same is true of heads, though many writers use caps just to show that it is a head, even if the art director might later change the head to upper and lower case.

- Though not technically a format point, notice that the cover page is a teaser page without the client name. The theory is that the reader will get to the name soon enough, if the cover is intriguing enough. At other times it might make sense to have the client name and logo on the cover.

- Note once more that the PIC in each case does not dictate a photo or a drawing to the art director, nor any other instruction. If there is something special — if every catfish comes with a little top hat, for instance — perhaps the copywriter would mention that.

- You see that the copy is written the way you would write any copy for print. The big difference is that each copy block is a story unto itself, though all the blocks make reference in some way to the overall theme. (In Mr. Whiskers, the overall theme deals with catfish being for seafood lovers.)

- This piece has no slogan. If it did have one, it might be set up in the copy; at the least it would be included at the end of the copy or perhaps on the address page in the upper left-hand corner. In a piece this short, a slogan might be extra baggage and so unnecessary to create. But if there is an ongoing slogan for the client, it would be mandatory to include it and cash in on the money spent to establish the slogan elsewhere — to maintain continuity, in other words.

- The coupon is complete. Never write this:

COUPON:        (COUPON)

When you do that, it looks as if you think someone else will write the coupon. Someone else will, of course, and then will start rewriting your copy. You're the writer. Write everything. Even in the coupon, note the little copy pitch in ". . . before you order two delicious dinners for one price." That little extra effort in the most prosaic copy like a coupon marks you as a copywriter who pays attention to details in a creative way — a fine reputation to have. If the coupon requires lines for a person's name and address, include the lines. It's all part of copywriting.

- The same point can be made for the return address on page 4, where there is a little copy lead-in to the client address and logo (A Great Catch at:). That little pitch just might make the difference between the recipient's opening the piece or throwing it away. And, as you can see, the thoroughness extends to the recipient's address and the method of postage. (My personal bias is not to open anything that doesn't carry a first class postage stamp, because I think my time spent reading an ad is worth first class postage. But that can be very expensive in a large mailing. A good fallback position is to get the client to use a bulk-rate postage stamp, hoping people won't notice. At other times, the bulk-rate imprint must be used.)

- If the piece were to be put into an envelope, you would include the envelope in your copy and do a thumbnail for it as well. In such a case you would also include the client name, address, phone number, logo and so forth on the piece itself, because the envelope might be thrown away.

- Don't forget to consult with an art director, if possible, before starting the piece. Discuss the piece and agree to its general thrust; perhaps the art director will provide you with a little thumbnail before you start writing, a great help.

## THE TERM *DIRECT*

Before we discuss several kinds of collateral, we need to define three terms that often cause confusion.

- *Direct advertising.* Also called direct marketing, direct advertising is another way to describe collateral advertising. It is not a medium in the classic sense, but an umbrella term for advertising materials that do not run in broadcast or print media. Direct advertising is its own medium, whether it takes the form of a direct mail piece, a rack brochure at a travel agency, a pencil with a client name on it or an in-store video.

- *Direct response advertising.* Record offers on TV, some direct mail pieces, the cable channel that sells products, magazine or newspaper clip-and-send coupons all fall under the definition of direct response advertising, which is a way to buy, to respond, usually by phone or mail, without leaving your home. Direct response may or may not fall under the definition of direct advertising. A direct mail piece is direct advertising; magazine coupons or TV offers are not, because they use a medium. Direct response is both fish and fowl, media and non-media.

- *Direct mail.* Direct mail, a giant advertising medium, is advertising that is mailed directly to the target market. It always fits under the umbrella of direct advertising. If the direct mail piece asks for you to phone or send for something to be sent to you, the direct mail piece also fits the definition of direct response advertising. If the direct mail piece asks you to vote for a candidate, to visit a lake project, or to come to a store for a special event, it's not direct response, but it's still direct mail.

## DIRECT MAIL

Direct mail may be anything from a simple postcard announcing a clothing sale to an elaborate multi-piece lake development announcement. Because you're going to send this writing to a mail box, you'll also pay attention to the envelope carrying your work, and you'll spend creative time figuring out what will entice a person to open this obvious sales pitch.

Computers have made it possible to use the recipient's name on the envelope and throughout a letter or to print what may look like a credit card that peeks through a window. The technology that can help you create an envelope that will persuade your prospect to open the mail includes pop-ups, scents and even a "talking ad," pioneered in late 1989 by Texas Instruments.

Although it's easy to do your thumbnails for TV or print ads after the writing, it's important to create thumbnails for multi-page collateral pieces before you start writing, so you know in advance how many pages are available and where various headlines and copy blocks will go. Without this blueprint, you'll be confused as you write, and so will the art director who must design and lay out the piece from your writing. You don't have to create a highly detailed thumbnail before the writing, but you should at least take a piece of paper and fold it into the number of pages available; that will give you something to follow as you write. After the writing, you can create a more detailed thumbnail like the one in Figure 8.1.

Usually you know how many pages and what size the pages will be; sometimes it's left up to you to suggest that information. As usual, your visual ideas are subject to change by the art director or by the client who doesn't want to pay as much as your idea would require.

## ANNUAL REPORTS

Annual reports are issued by companies primarily to let stockholders and potential investors know how the company did financially in the past year. In banking and many other corporate situations, annual reports are mandatory, depending on state and federal laws. Though the main purpose of an annual report is to give a financial accounting, which may take several pages, smart companies found out years ago that the annual report is an opportunity to paint a good picture of the company, thereby reassuring current stockholders and perhaps enticing additional investors. The annual report may also fulfill a public relations function by a company that may have been under public attack because of environmental or other issues (doing business in South Africa brought many corporations under attack in the 1980s).

Some annual reports are full of four-color pictures, stories of innovations and advances, company philosophies and strong writing to support these items. The challenge to the copywriter on such a project is formidable. You are not writing the one-page ad or TV spot. Often the client will give you a rough draft for you to "clean up" or, more likely, for you to use as supporting data for your well-integrated long story with a central theme. Many times, however, you will have to spend hours and days with the client digging out all the information that goes into the annual report in addition to the financial information, which the client provides. You may even have to travel to get the entire story.

Not only does this mean the heartache and effort of heavy research, but whether provided with data or starting from scratch, the copywriter is also faced with a client who is extremely sensitive to the effect the annual report will have on the target markets. The result is that the copywriter will do more rewriting than she or he might have to do on a TV spot, where the same client might allow comparatively looser language.

Copywriters with the brains and skill to write a great annual report face a rather ironic problem. So few are the copywriters who can write annual reports well that the copywriter will be in demand for more and more similar projects. You could be typecast, as it were, as the "annual report writer" and not get as many opportunities to write the more high-profile advertising. But if you're already the writer for TV and the other media, and you volunteer for the annual report job and write it well, it will be a boost to your career. You'll end up understanding the client better and you'll be seen as a complete copywriter, regardless of assignment.

## BROCHURES

Brochures, or pamphlets, range from four-page, one-fold black and white 6-inch by 8-inch pieces to 20-page, four-color pieces, such as you find at an auto dealership. Brochures are designed for many uses. If they are mailed, of course, they become direct mail. They may also be found in a rack, as in a travel agency. They may be handed to people who have toured a real estate project.

The main design difference between a self-mailing direct mail piece and a brochure is that the brochure has no address page. If it's mailed, it will go in an envelope. A main content difference is that a brochure is normally taken voluntarily, and the reader is looking for information presented in an interesting way.

Whatever the eventual use for the brochure, it's considered a collateral piece. It can be fun to write, because you garner information or are given information, including the reason for the brochure and copy points, and you are in effect sent off to write a tiny book. It's up to you to develop a creative strategy, a single thrust for the tiny book, and then execute that strategy with

*Back (page 4)*          *Cover (page 1)*

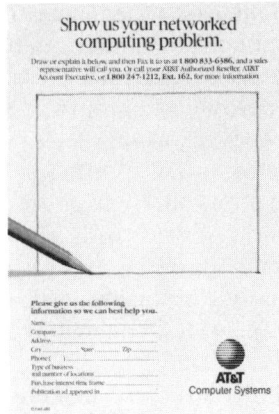
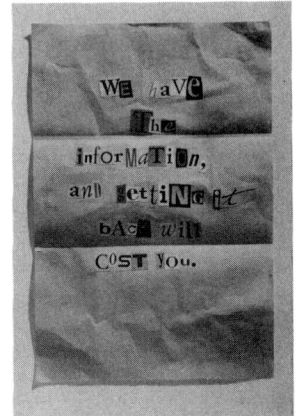

**8.2**          *AT&T brochure back and front cover.*

*Page 2*          *Page 3*

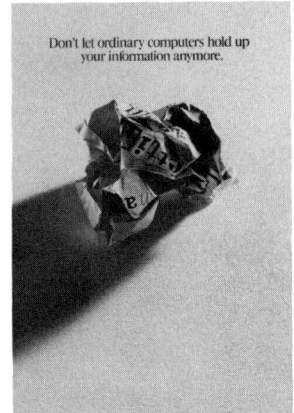

**8.3**          *AT&T brochure pages 2–3.*

eye-catching visuals and an interesting story. Again (and again) only your writing will attract customers, unless you're giving away diamonds, because there is no editorial matter surrounding your work.

Although you're burdened with the responsibility of interesting a prospect in reading a selling piece, all the principles of writing discussed previously are applicable. The writing will be longer and broken into more sections, and it will usually include more visuals. But it is still the persuasive writing which is at the heart of any copywriting job.

The AT&T Computer Systems brochure shown in Figures 8.2, 8.3 and 8.4 is a good example of how important it is for the writer to at least figure out the pages, with thumbnail drawings or not, along with the art director, before writing. We'll see a computer drawing of the page outline as well as the actual page from the AT&T brochure.

*Page 5*      *Page 6*      *Page 7*      *Page 8*

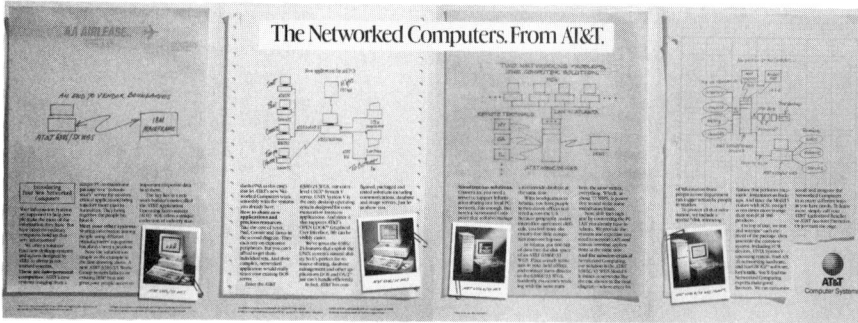

*Page 3*      *Back (page 4)*      *Cover (page 1)*      *Page 2*

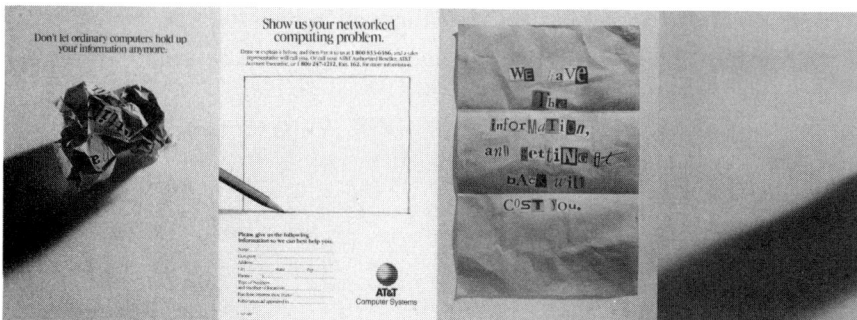

**8.4**

*This AT&T brochure, a business-to-business piece, shows how complicated figuring out the pages can be, though it all looks pretty simple in the actual outcome. The inside four pages are easy to lay out and figure out, but note how the cover and back and fold-in pages don't run in the order you might expect. This could be a direct mail piece if mailed in an envelope, a rack brochure as it is, a hand-out at a convention or a leave-behind after a sales call. Brochures can be put to many uses.*

## OTHER PRINT COLLATERAL

Direct mail, annual reports and brochures will probably dominate your collateral writing. In addition to the range of projects possible listed at the beginning of this chapter, other collateral projects might include how-to brochures, legal flyers, posters, grocery shelf-liners, calendar desk pads, clothing hang-tags, window signs, schoolbook covers, table tents, menus, training kits, labels and recipes, toy assembly instructions, package copy, match books and so much more. Figure 8.5 shows an in-store poster — a collateral project. New forms of collateral writing are always appearing.

When you think about it, there is a world of commercial writing that is needed, good news for all copywriters-to-be. It's not all TV and radio and four-color magazine ads that sustain the large force of copywriters out there. Even highway departments must have someone who writes, "NEXT EXIT: EAT AND GET GAS."

## PRINT COLLATERAL TIPS

- The format is the same as for print media, with one major addition: page numbers for individual pages (or sides, in the case of a table tent) for a piece.
- The second line of the identification needs to be very clear about the nature of the piece.
- Thumbnails need to be done before writing the collateral piece, so you know where you are when writing.
- Copy blocks in collateral are marked "A," "B," "C," etc., on both copy and thumbnails.
- You will use more subheads in collateral advertising than you do in ads.
- If there is a coupon, write it out in its entirety.
- If you need an envelope for your piece, do a thumbnail and write copy for it.
- On direct mail, try to write copy that encourages opening the envelope, near the return address or elsewhere on the piece.
- Take advantage of the newest computer and print production technologies in direct mail, brochures and other collateral efforts.
- Write annual reports when you have the opportunity; such writing is a valuable skill.
- Remember that readers of brochures are voluntary; offer complete information in an interesting way.

## BROADCAST COLLATERAL FORMAT

There are a few rather well-established broadcast collateral projects the copywriter could face in the course of a career. Many of these are written by

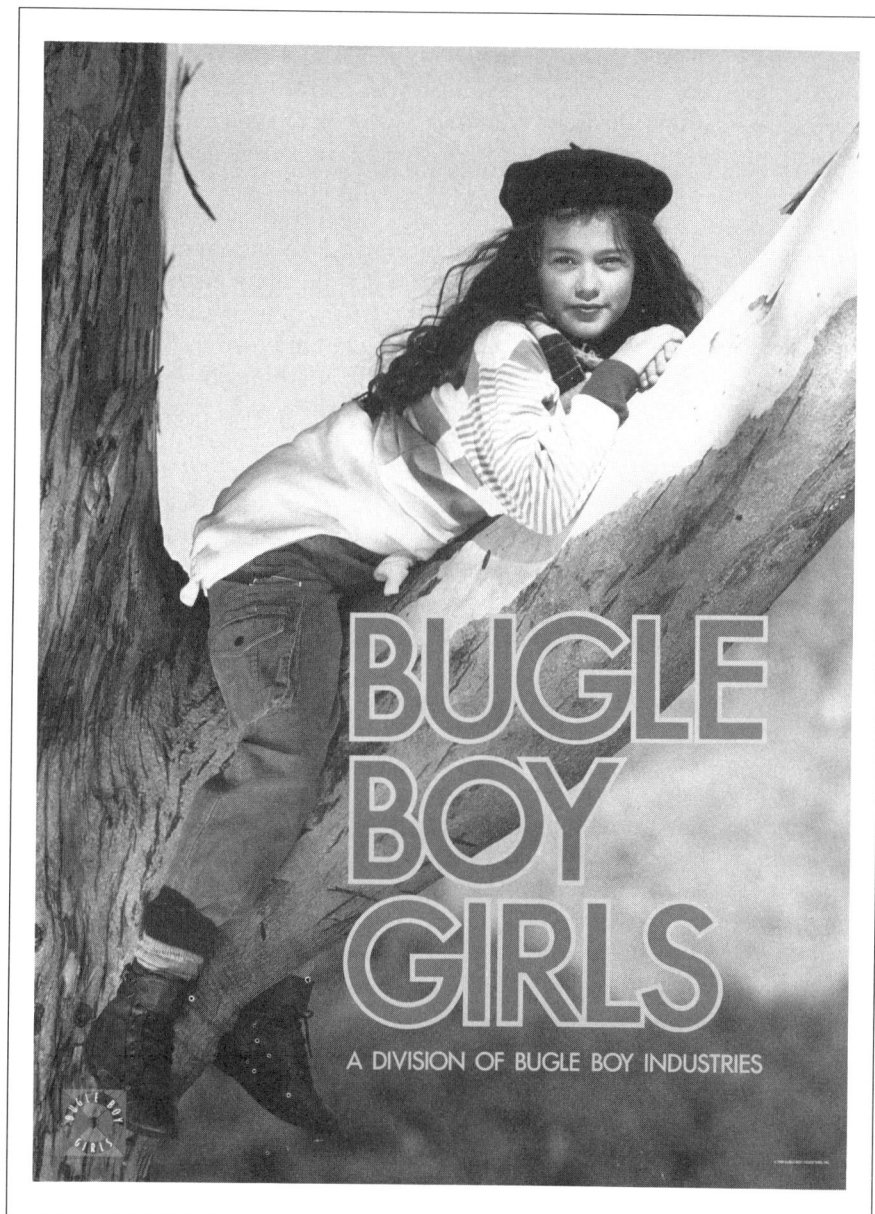

**8.5**

*Here's an in-store poster for Bugle Boy Girls, a new line that certainly challenges the creative people to resolve the apparent contradiction in terms between the parent company (Bugle Boy Industries), another new line (Bugle Boy Boys) and the original campaign for Bugle Boy jeans.*

copywriters with corporations or film/tape production houses or by free-lance copywriters; even so, the advertising agency copywriter may also be called upon for broadcast collateral. Actually, "broadcast" is not exactly correct, because the materials created are not broadcast in the sense of going out over the airways, unless you have created one of those half-hour programs devoted to losing weight or investing in something.

An audiocassette, for example, may be played by the target market in the car and may contain information about a new car or some kind of self-improvement program. Audiocassettes might also be created for supermarkets, pushing various sale items. Audiocassettes are created for caves and zoos and other places a tourist might want to hear about what's being looked at. A 10-minute film or tape about the quality of a certain brand of boots might be played on a TV monitor in a retail store. A film on the accomplishments of a corporation over the past year may be shown at an annual meeting or to a group of salespersons or potential buyers. A slide show, with or without a sound track, might be created to teach employees how to handle customers on the telephone or to update a building project for a board of directors. Or you might write a script for a live presentation, anything from a speech by a corporate executive to a Broadway musical-type show to be presented at state fair auto shows.

With the exception of the speech and the live musical, all of the preceding can be created in the TV or radio format you learned in Chapters 6 and 7. Speeches are usually typed in a format most comfortable to the speaker; however, I have a favorite style of speech format I'll share with you. Live shows are more than likely prepared in the format you've seen in high school plays or in the style of Hollywood movie and TV program scripts, which we shall not explore here.

## The Treatment

A treatment is a working out of the plot of a film, indicating key scenes, how the theme of the film is carried forward, what sound effects or music are anticipated, and so on. If a client is going to pay several thousand dollars for a writer to create a film, it makes sense to see a treatment and approve the direction of the film before the longer work is written.

Let's say the publisher of this textbook wants to create a 10-minute film that will be sent to professors to encourage them to adopt this book for their classes.

CREATING THE AD MESSAGE
10-MINUTE FILM TREATMENT
"THE INTERVIEW"
Jim Albright
9 April 1990

| **SIGHT:** | **SOUND:** |
| --- | --- |
| THE FILM WILL OPEN ON A 22-YEAR-OLD COLLEGE GRADUATE COMING TO AN ADVERTISING AGENCY FOR A JOB INTERVIEW. | (NATURAL SOUNDS, INSTRUMENTAL MUSIC SCORING AND DIALOGUE) |

WE SHALL CAPTURE HER HEIGHTENED SENSE OF ANTICIPATION, AND HER EXCITEMENT, AS SHE IS PUT AT EASE BY THE PEOPLE AT THE AGENCY.

(A SONG WILL BE WRITTEN TO COVER HER INTRODUCTION TO THE LOOK OF AN ADVERTISING AGENCY)

THE TITLE WILL COME ON AS SHE WALKS DOWN THE HIGH-TECH HALLWAYS OF THE AGENCY, AND THE OPENING SEQUENCE WILL CONCLUDE WITH THE WOMAN SEATED AT THE DESK OF THE CREATIVE DIRECTOR, DEEP IN CONVERSATION.

(THE SONG ENDS AS THE WOMAN IS GREETED BY THE CREATIVE DIRECTOR AND THEY START THE INTERVIEW)

THE SCENE WILL THEN SHIFT TO A FLASHBACK AS WE SEE THE GRADUATE IN HER COPYWRITING CLASS.

(REAL CLASSROOM SOUNDS, DIALOGUE, VOICE-OVER AND SOME INSTRUMENTAL MUSIC WILL CARRY THE PLOT AS THE BOOK IS FEATURED)

FOLLOWING SCENES WILL CLEVERLY INTRODUCE THE BOOK, *CREATING THE AD MESSAGE,* AS A NORMAL PART OF THE DIALOGUE BETWEEN THE PROFESSOR AND THE STUDENTS.

THERE WILL BE CLOSE-UPS OF SOME CHAPTER TITLES, DIAGRAMS AND AD EXAMPLES THROUGH THIS MIDDLE PART OF THE FILM.

THE PROFESSOR WILL STEP OUT OF CHARACTER AT THE END OF THE MIDDLE PART OF THE FILM TO MAKE A DIRECT PITCH ABOUT THE BOOK.

(THE PROFESSOR WILL SPEAK ON CAMERA, GIVING A TESTIMONIAL. HE OR SHE IS A REAL PROFESSOR)

THE FILM WILL END WITH THE WOMAN AND CREATIVE DIRECTOR DISCUSSING HER SAMPLE BOOK.

(DIALOGUE BETWEEN THE WOMAN AND CREATIVE DIRECTOR)

HE GIVES HER A FEW SUGGESTIONS AND LEAVES THE DOOR OPEN FOR HER

(CONTINUE DIALOGUE)

RETURN, NOT OFFERING A JOB
BUT INDICATING IT IS A
POSSIBILITY.

WE FOLLOW THE WOMAN OUT
OF THE AGENCY WALKING ON
AIR, FEELING CONFIDENT AND
HAPPY ABOUT THE
EXPERIENCE.

(THE SONG REAPPEARS IN A
LONGER VERSION, PLAYING
THROUGH FINAL TITLES)

END ON BOOK AND FINAL
TITLES AND FINAL PITCH.

(CONTINUE SONG)

## Actual Scenes

You can see that the treatment is only a simple outline of what's going to happen. With this in your hands, its direction approved by the client, it's a lot easier to sit down and write the actual script. So let's take a look at the opening scenes of the film, fleshing out the treatment. The format is the same for a ten-minute videotape or slide show. We'll look at an opening, a scene in the middle of the film and a conclusion.

CREATION OF THE AD MESSAGE
10-MINUTE FILM
"THE INTERVIEW"
Jim Albright
9 April 1990

| SIGHT: | | SOUND: |
|---|---|---|
| OPEN ON ELEVATOR DOORS SLIDING OPEN. | SFX: | (SWOOSH OF DOORS OPENING) |
| DOLLY IN TO 22-YEAR-OLD WOMAN HOLDING SAMPLE BOOK AS SHE EXITS ELEVATOR INTO CAM. | | ("JAWS"-TYPE INST. BUILD-UP) |
| CUT TO REVERSE ANGLE, CAM POV, TO SEE WHAT SHE SEES — HIGH-TECH RECEPTION AREA OF AN ADVERTISING AGENCY. RECEPTIONIST IS LOOKING AT HER WITH PLEASANT CURIOSITY. | | (CONTINUE "JAWS"-TYPE MUSIC) |
| CAM MOVES TO RECEPTIONIST. | SFX: REC: | (INST. STOPS) May I help you? |

| | | |
|---|---|---|
| CUT TO APPREHENSIVE FACE OF WOMAN WITH SAMPLE BOOK. | SFX:<br>WOM: | (INST. STARTS AGAIN)<br>(HESITANTLY)<br>I'm Heather Holiday. I have an appointment with the creative director...Stan Jowalski. |
| CUT TO WAIST SHOT OF RECEPTIONIST, CHECKING HER CALENDAR. | REC: | Ah...yes. Mr. Jowalski is expecting you. |
| RECEPTIONIST SMILES UP AT CAMERA. | SFX: | (INST. STOPS)<br>(STRAINS OF "HALLELUJAH" BREAK OUT) |
| FOLLOW WOMAN AND RECEPTIONIST DOWN HIGH-TECH HALLWAYS. | | (SEGUE TO SONG) |
| SEE WALL DECORATIONS, INSIDE VARIOUS OFFICES AS THEY WALK. | SONG: | NOW YOU'VE GOT IT GIRL, AT LAST, |
| POP ON TITLE FOR FIVE SECONDS: | | YOU GOT THE INTERVIEW, THE INTERVIEW |
| ARRIVE AT ONE PARTICULAR OFFICE. | | STEP OUT PROUDLY, |
| CUT TO CREATIVE DIRECTOR RISING, SHAKES WOMAN'S HAND AND MOTIONS HER TO CHAIR. | | 'CAUSE GIRL IT'S TIME TO SHAKE YA KNOW, |
| SHE SETTLES INTO CHAIR AND HANDS HIM HER SAMPLE BOOK, WHICH HE PLACES BEFORE HIM ON DESK. | | IF ALL YOUR DREAMS COME TRUE. |
| DISS TO COLLEGE CLASSROOM AS CREATIVE DIRECTOR LEANS FORWARD IN DISCUSSION WITH WOMAN. | SFX: | (INST. FADES INTO NATURAL SOUNDS OF CLASSROOM. A PROFESSOR IS SPEAKING) |
| SEE PROFESSOR FROM REAR, TALKING. HEATHER AND OTHER STUDENTS ARE IN FRONT OF HIM. | PROF: | ...so in this copywriting class, the final project will be your sample book. |
| CRAB AROUND TO SEE PROFESSOR FROM BEHIND HEATHER. HE HOLDS UP A SAMPLE BOOK. | | This.<br>This is what you take with you...this and your advertising knowledge... when you go to get a job. |

## Analysis of Film Opening

We'll stop here to note a few things.

- First, don't let that word **segue** (seg-way) bother you. It's an old-fashioned radio term that indicates a slow or fast shifting from one thing to another, as from a song to dialogue, one song to another, dialogue to voice-over, whatever.

- The format is the same as for TV. You can see that once you learn a basic format for audio-visual presentation, it is extendible for all types. Not only would this format work for a slide presentation, but so would the actual words. The SOUND side would work intact on a slide film, and only a couple of changes in the SIGHT side would be necessary.

- Re the last point, note that writing the SIGHT side with a minimum of camera directions and just telling the visual story keeps it general enough to work almost as well in slides.

- One of the nice things about writing a longer film is the luxury of time to set up certain dramatic events. Internally, the writing is as tight as it would be for a 30-second spot. But the additional time allows us to build on the Jaws-type music, the anticipation of the graduate on a first interview, the relief at the receptionist's civility, the Hallelujah chorus, the song sung as the woman goes down the hall.

- As far as introducing the title, some films open on the title, some never show one, and some, as here, tease the viewer a bit, hoping the title will have impact when it comes on after a little build-up.

- POV means camera point-of-view.

## The Same Script for Audiocassette

We'll just re-create a small part of the film's opening to show how you would produce an audiocassette of the same sales pitch. Note that in a longer sound recording of this nature, the word narrator (NARR) is used for the voice talent, rather than ANNC. Why? We don't know, but it's usually the case.

CREATING THE AD MESSAGE
10-MINUTE CASSETTE
"THE INTERVIEW"
Jim Albright
9 April 1990

| | |
|---|---|
| SFX: | ("DING" OF AN ELEVATOR OPENING, SOUNDS OF AN OFFICE. "JAWS"-TYPE MUSIC STARTS LOW AND BUILDS IN INTENSITY) |
| NARR: | A young woman enters an advertising agency with her sample book clutched tightly in her hand. |
| | She wants to be a copywriter, and she is here for an interview with the creative director. |
| | With some hesitation, she approaches the receptionist. |

| SFX: | ("JAWS" SOUNDS STOP) |
| RECEPTIONIST: | Hello. May I help you? |
| WOMAN: | Yes. I . . . I have an appointment with the creative director . . . Stan Jowalski? |
| RECEPTIONIST: | Surely. He's expecting you. Come with me and I'll show you the way. |
| SFX: | ("HALLELUJAH CHORUS" BREAKS OUT, THEN SEGUES INTO . . .) |
| SONG: | NOW YOU'VE GOT IT GIRL, AT LAST |

Again, the format is the same as radio. And, as in radio, more explanation of what is going on is necessary when you are not blessed with a SIGHT side to your commercial presentation.

## The Speech Format

As promised, and briefly, I'll share with you one format that works for me when writing a speech. You might be surprised at how often a copywriter is called upon to do so, particularly if that writer has displayed a broad liberal arts background and comes off as a mature person. As a copywriter, I've written speeches for the Archbishop of Canada, an undersecretary of a government department, several agency presidents, bank presidents and other clients.

The format shown in Figure 8.6 takes into consideration the actual physical problem of reading from a piece of paper. Of course, if a teleprompter or other device is used by the speaker, it's easier to maintain eye contact with the audience and deliver the speech at the same time. This format anticipates a speaker reading from a piece of paper and, in most cases, that's how the speech is delivered.

## Analysis of the Speech

- The physical side of it, the large type, makes sense when you think about it. Try it yourself, looking up at an audience and down to the speech. Now try the same thing reading the smaller typeface that most of this book contains.

- Note the instructions in parentheses. When you write a speech, try to put yourself in the place of the speaker, who is usually under pressure. Whenever you help the speaker out by saying when to point or hold something up, you have functioned as a good speechwriter.

- Also pay attention to the fact that every commercial enterprise has an interesting history. In this case, the age of the bank made going back to pioneering a good way to get into the subject. Even if the client asked you to relate some dry figures somewhere in the speech, you can find a way to make that interesting, as well.

BILL SMITH, PRESIDENT
1ST NATIONAL BANK
"150 YEARS OF PIONEERING"
Jim Albright 27 August 1990

Good evening fellow bankers.

(REFERENCE TO THE MEAL JUST EATEN
AND OTHER LAST MINUTE PERSONAL COM-
MENTS YOU MAY HAVE AT THIS POINT.)

One hundred fifty years ago today, First National was
born to serve the bustling, year-old community of
Springfield, our city.

Our commercial ancestors . . . my great great grandfather
among them . . .

(POINT TO BILL AND HARVEY)

and yours Bill, and yours, Harvey . . .

responded to the call of their fellow citizens for a safe
place to keep the money from farming and ranching that
was beginning to be made.

As we all know by now, our ancestors decided to go
into full-time banking and part-time farming, and 150
years later we are grateful they made that decision.

Ladies and gentlemen, a toast to our commercial ancestors:

(HOLD UP YOUR GLASS AND SIP, WAITING
FOR THE AUDIENCE TO DO THE SAME.)

(speech continues . . .)

**8.6**

*A sample speech format.*

## BROADCAST COLLATERAL TIPS

- On long films and tapes, slide films and cassettes, it helps to write a treatment first, to guide you and to encourage client approval.
- As with radio, the cassette presentation is for the ear; over-explain what is happening.
- Write the speech with the goal of making it easy to deliver and to read.

- Writing broadcast collateral is fun. Volunteer for such projects. If you become good at it, you may carve out another skill you can merchandise if you ever go free-lance.

- The :30 TV commercials contain a story, with a situation, a complication and a conclusion. The same thing is true with long broadcast efforts, but you stretch it out a little so that you have one long story with a situation, a complication and a conclusion.

- Use more visuals against music or sound effects. In the long broadcast collateral piece you have the opportunity to raise the music volume and run interesting visuals — flying over a mountain or watching a sailboat come about.

- In the :30 TV, you have one point to make, and you make it clear with your story; same occurs with the longer broadcast effort, but you have the opportunity to make a lot of other points along the way.

- All commercial writing projects, whether an ad or :30 TV or a longer film, require serious research into product, competition, target market stats and so forth. But in the long run, you will do more research on the longer broadcast collateral efforts than the commercial and probably make more on-site fact-finding visits and study of materials than on the short one.

- You'll have five minutes to an hour to fill rather than :30, so you'll need more information to impart. You'll need to find a natural way to weave in the theme from time to time to remind viewers of the overall message you're trying to convey about this company. To make sure you have a theme for your film, think how you would describe a movie when a friend asks, "What was it about?"

- When the client tells you what the film, tape, slide film or cassette should be about, be careful. Clients may be describing the features they want, rather than what the effort is about. It's up to you the writer to create a theme that will showcase the features the client wants mentioned, a theme that will rise above mere features of the product or company to be written about. (A dog food company may want a film about how nutritious the dog food is. But your theme might be the love affair between a woman and her dog, a story. Once you decide on this theme, then you turn to the task of making the dog food important to the film.)

- One of the great things about writing long films, tapes and slide films is the opportunity to use music the way you always wanted to. In the longer film, you can indulge your predilections for your favorite music, perhaps in the opening as the titles run, as a surprise in the center of the film, or as a big closing — or even all three if the topic can handle it.

- To write the longer films and cassettes, as well as short commercials, you do need to know something about film, tape, slide film or cassette production. You should also have a notion about the effect your writing is going to have on the film's budget. You would not write in a scene to be shot in Hawaii for a low-budget film, for instance; the travel and housing costs for the crew alone could eat up the entire budget.

- Your ability as a screenwriter — to get the details in, to write dialogue and set the scenes in the appropriate format, to control the pacing of the film, tape or slide film — is, unfortunately, taken for granted. But know that the most technically brilliant screenplays will not work if you haven't come up with a good story or a good "angle" or "hook" as it is sometimes described.

## IN CONCLUSION

The format of a print collateral piece takes more figuring out and is a little harder to organize than is that of the normal print advertisement. But writing collateral can be more fun than writing an ad, because of the extended length. The client often has more to say in many collateral pieces than can be said in a one-page ad. Collateral copy for longer pieces should still be concise and punchy, but the feeling of having as much space as you need is reassuring.

When you're a new copywriter on your first job, take every collateral piece you can get and put as much heart into it as you would a network TV spot. When you're an experienced copywriter, keep the collateral for yourself if you have the time, because you will double your value to your employer and reinforce the fact that copywriters are more versatile than any other kind of writer in the variety of media they can write for.

Writing long broadcast collateral pieces is a craft often pursued full time by a number of writers. Copywriting for an advertising agency or a corporation often leads to lifetime jobs not anticipated at the beginning of one's career — jobs as filmwriters, radio and/or TV producers, actors and actresses, business writing specialists PR persons, promotion specialists and so on.

And so don't turn down the opportunity to learn a new craft on somebody else's money, even though you've hired on only for certain activities. You'll find that you're better at certain things and enjoy certain things more than others; and by the age of 30 you may have a clear perspective on what you're good at and want to do and can plan your life accordingly. If that happens by the age of 30, which must seem ancient to you right now, you will truly be hitting your stride early in life and will be extremely fortunate.

—————————— E X E R C I S E S ——————————

1. Write a Creative Work Plan and develop a slogan for a local retail business. Then write a direct mail piece to execute your creative strategy.

2. Write a Creative Work Plan and slogan for a durable goods, packaged goods or service account. Then create a brochure to be handed out at an appropriate place (car dealership, grocery store or rent-a-car agency).

3. Write a five-minute film for a local manufacturing company, using their brochures for information. The purpose of the film will be to attract more visitors to the company, as well as an orientation to what the company does.

# OUTDOOR

An advertising campaign may involve execution of newspaper ads, magazine ads, TV and radio spots, print collateral and broadcast collateral, all with their own format habits and styles. Outdoor advertising has its own format requirements as well. Once you have your creative strategy and are considering what to write to bring that strategy to life, you might start on outdoor first instead of newspaper or the other media that have been determined as best for that campaign. Or in the middle of writing a TV spot, you might realize, "This would be a great outdoor board, too!" If so, here is the format.

## FORMAT

The format for writing down outdoor copy is quite simple. At most you would have:

*Copywriter's thumbnail
for Discount Birds
painted bulletin.*

DISCOUNT BIRDS, INC.
OUTDOOR, 48′ x 14′ PAINTED BULLETIN
"THREE BIRDS"
Jim Albright
28 May 1991

| | |
|---|---|
| PIC: | (3 BIRDS ON TOP OF BOARD) |
| HEAD: | Cheep |
| COPY: | Cheep |
| SLOGAN: | CHEAP BIRDS |
| SIG: | Discount Birds, Inc. |
| ADDRESS: | 1st and Walnut |

The copywriter's thumbnail is shown in Figure 9.1.

## Analysis of Format

The second line of the identification in the upper left-hand corner specifies the medium (outdoor) and type of outdoor (painted bulletin). There are also printed outdoor posters.

With only one word of copy, a one-word head and a two-word slogan strung together, the board is not too busy. But you can see that, with longer copy or a longer head or slogan, you would have room for only one of those most of the time. Remember that the SIG has to be big enough to be readable. That's why you're ahead of the game in this limited-space medium if you have the signature readable on the product, such as Coke, because that way you can combine the PIC and SIG into one graphic element.

Because of limited space, limited copy and limited time available for reading your advertising message on an outdoor board, special effort should be made to create a PIC that is both relevant and startling. The idea in Figure 9.1 was to make the birds look like real birds sitting on a fence, an attempt to be cute with the product (relevance) as hero.

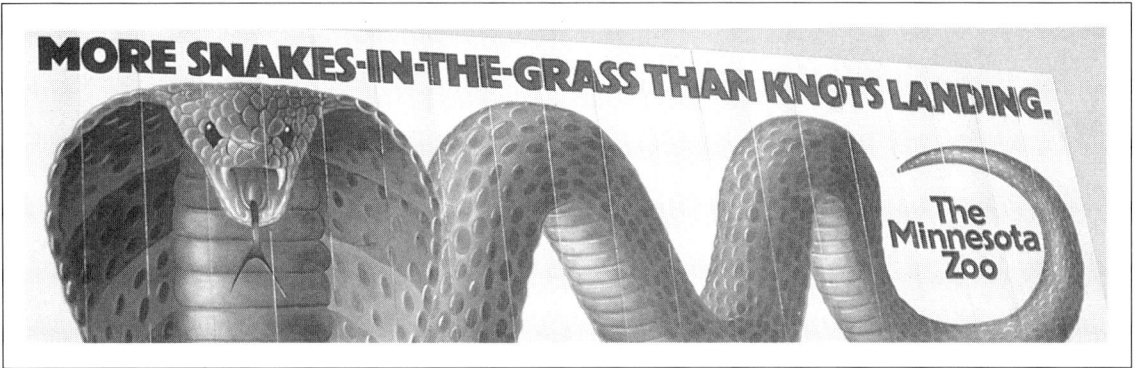

**9.2** *This is a very clever board, in PIC and words. But using "Knots Landing" as the payoff for the joke presupposes general knowledge about the program. It's a bit risky if the copywriter guesses wrong.*

## Examples of Outdoor Copy

(For a local insurance agent)

| | |
|---|---|
| PIC: | (BOARD DESIGNED TO LOOK PARTIALLY BURNED. COPY & SIG PRINTED ON THE TWO REMAINING CHARRED FRAGMENTS) |
| COPY: | Don't just hope you have good insurance. |
| SIG: | (NAME OF AGENT) |

(For an anti-drunk-driving organization)

| | |
|---|---|
| PIC: | (PALLBEARERS CARRYING A COFFIN) |
| COPY: | YOU SHOULD HAVE CALLED FOR A LIFT EARLIER. |
| SIG: | (NAME OF ORGANIZATION) |

These copy samples and Figure 9.2 should give you some idea of how simple the outdoor format is. Before we discuss the outdoor writing format, perhaps you should have some basic understanding of the uses of the medium.

# THE USES OF OUTDOOR

## Outdoor As a Reminder

Used in conjunction with the primary media of radio, TV and print advertising, outdoor is a terrific way, in just a moment, to bring a whole campaign back to the mind of the reader. Much outdoor advertising is of this nature.

## Outdoor for Directions

You have reservations at a Holiday Inn in Nashville, and you've never been to Nashville. After 500 miles of driving you hit the city limits and suddenly realize you don't know where the Holiday Inn is. As if someone anticipated your concern, there's an outdoor board with simple instructions on how to reach your particular Holiday Inn among the several around the city. Earlier that same day, the kids bugged you to go to McDonald's. It couldn't be any other fast food place; that's the one you promised. You found your way to one after seeing an outdoor board announcing a McDonald's at the next exit.

## Outdoor as a Primary Medium

Though usually termed a secondary medium for reminder advertising, outdoor is used by some advertisers as their only medium. Many radio stations, for instance, feel most of their audience is in a car. Obviously they can't advertise on radio because most other radio stations don't air competitors' advertisements. Outdoor provides an immediate pitch to people in cars to change that dial. Outdoor is also a primary medium for many local advertisers with small budgets — restaurants, funeral homes, retail shops and highway businesses catering to travelers. Or outdoor might be a primary medium for a one-time event — a county fair or the like — particularly if the board is near the place where the event will take place.

## TYPES OF OUTDOOR BOARDS

On the one hand, advertisers can choose from a great variety of outdoor boards, based on size and method of reproduction. Many one-of-a-kind boards exist in certain markets — a board with a real waterfall in Dallas, for instance. In New York years ago, a cigarette board blew smoke rings. In Los Angeles, brilliantly painted one-of-a-kind boards advertise a new record album, concert or movie.

On the other hand, outdoor sizes have been standardized for the most part, so a national advertiser can run a certain kind of board in all states without worrying about redesigning the proportions of the board for each advertising area.

## Outdoor Sizes

Painted bulletins are often 48 feet wide by 14 feet high, about a 3.5:1 proportion, a very horizontal board. These are much better for showing a sunbather than a 50-story building. Printed posters are not as wide, a 2.5:1 proportion and so are proportionally higher than painted boards.

## Methods of Reproduction

**Painted bulletins** are just that, hand-painted by remarkable artists who can stand a foot away from something to be read 500 feet away and know what will or will not make sense at that distance. Some painted boards are a series of hanging metal panels that are painted in a shop, then transported to the location to be hung in place side by side.

The paper for posters is printed on giant presses in a few locations in this country. The poster is not printed all at once, but in as many as 10 large sheets for a standard poster. The sheets are pasted up side by side until the board is covered.

## Innovative Boards

Budget permitting, there are many innovations in outdoor, including those with the very expensive interior lighting, sometimes called "backlit" boards. **Extensions** are parts of the visual extended beyond the board, usually above or to the side, seldom down. There is usually a limit of about six feet on how far the extensions can project beyond the board, for structural as well as zoning reasons. Inflatable boards have people and things actually popping off the board. They have a little fan inside to keep them inflated, even if little holes appear in the vinyl fabric that inflates.

Other types of three-dimensional effects are available, even including gluing a car on an outdoor board. The waterfall board in Dallas was specially built for Pearl Beer's "Country of 1100 Springs" campaign. That campaign is long over and so is Pearl's use of the board. But others, including Salem cigarettes, have found ways to adapt the board to their selling message.

Other innovations include reflective disks that make the board sparkle and appear to move, large bows around the entire board at Christmas, and Tri-Vision boards that change every few seconds to one of three scenes. Wild, bold colors may not seem an innovation, but whatever color idea you can come up with can be reproduced by the outdoor people, either in paint or on printed posters.

# WRITING OUTDOOR

## Preliminary Thinking

You could be zipping along at 65, playing a radio loudly, talking with a friend and reaching in the cooler for a soft drink. At the same time you are expected to see, enjoy and absorb the contents of an outdoor board in a few seconds. That's hard enough; what's really tough is being the copywriter who has to create that outdoor board and register an impact when the driver and passenger are both so distracted.

## Writing Reminder Outdoor

As mentioned, outdoor is often characterized as a secondary medium; TV, radio, newspapers and magazines are the primary media. With certain exceptions, also noted, outdoor serves to remind the reader of something seen in the primary media. For example, imagine a Coke TV spot with a scene in which a woman slaps a man in the face (which Coke actually ran), with a good

## 9.3

*Visuals are usually considered vital to an outdoor campaign as an attention-getting device. Visuals usually refer to pictures of things or people. But in the larger sense, anything that goes on the outdoor board, in any ad, is a visual, even if only words, because typography is an art. This all-word campaign from the Richards Group in Dallas makes that point while reminding outdoor readers of the campaign running in other media.*

"With a little momentum, I could've made a name for myself."

—ANONYMOUS

MBank
A Momentum Bank

"With a little momentum, you'd remember me."

—MILLARD FILLMORE

MBank
A Momentum Bank

"With a little momentum we'd have made it in 1491. Tops."

—CHRISTOPHER COLUMBUS

MBank
A Momentum Bank

"With a little momentum, they'd have called me Running Buffalo."

—SITTING BULL

MBank
A Momentum Bank

jingle and the slogan "Coke: Red, White & You." Memorable. If you saw an outdoor board with a woman slapping a man (which Coke did not run) and the slogan, the entire TV spot and maybe the jingle would come to mind. You might even reject the Dr Pepper you were reaching for and opt for a Coke.

One outdoor board could cause you to ruminate for seconds on that Coke TV spot. Reminder advertising has a ping-pong effect, maybe synergistic, in which the combination of the two media has greater impact than either would have alone.

Though it's hard to write concise, yet effective, outdoor copy, reminder advertising is easier because a campaign is already running in other media. In such a case, you have a strategy, a slogan and a graphic look to build upon. There are two schools of thought on how to create reminder outdoor copy when a campaign is running in other media. The first school says it's most effective to reproduce in outdoor the same characters and situations that are currently appearing in print or broadcast. The second school says it's boring for readers who have already seen those other executions to see them again in outdoor. It's better to use the same slogan and graphic look but come up with new situations or characters. In this way, the continuity reflected in the strategy and slogan remains the same, but fresh executions draw even more attention to the campaign.

Figure 9.3 illustrates an MBank campaign that is a good example of the second school. For years the "Momentum" slogan had been executed on TV and in print featuring well-known people who had momentum. This MBank outdoor campaign retains the strategy and slogan of the campaign in other media and the graphic look of typestyles used, but takes a new direction. MBank's slogan permeates the advertising, yet the execution is fresh on every board. This is a good example of how strong writing can always stand on its own without pictures. Of course, Norman Rockwell's art also stood on its own without words. Remember the Nike outdoor with no copy and only the client signature? Note that the copy all starts out the same and serves as a reminder of the strategy and slogan. It also serves to introduce the newest joke. These are one-time jokes, so it was necessary to change the boards often.

When a campaign is this clever, it creates a subtext for the client. A client can't openly advertise and say: "Hey, we're clever people at this bank and we have a sense of humor and so we'd be fun to keep money with." No, the client can't do that. It would be all claim and no proof. But the MBank campaign does make the claim and proves it by being clever.

The debate about whether it's more effective to reproduce the same executions in all media, or vary them in each media, is not restricted to outdoor advertising. The debate pops up in any multimedia campaign. In print and TV, a third point of view has been introduced in Visa advertising. In TV, a career woman takes a new Visa card out of her apartment house mailbox as her male neighbor tries to make her acquaintance. The spot ends when she decides to like him and hints that she'll break in her card by buying him dinner. In a magazine ad that came out later, the same couple is seen at a restaurant table, after dinner, laughing and having a fine time. It's a story—

somebody's dream coming true, though whether his, hers or both is unclear. This advancement of story line under the same creative strategy in the print ad, this reminder of the TV spot, could just as well have been accomplished in outdoor.

## Writing Directional Boards

The use of the board dictates how you write for it, though in no case do you have room for a lot of copy. If the board is designed to give directions, obviously your first job is to write simple, clear instructions on how to get someplace. But if you're writing for a client with an established image and slogan — say, Holiday Inn — you must also be conscious of that fact and make sure the board includes the wording or the look of the established campaign, or both. The art director in this case may have an even harder job, to include all the information you deem important regarding directions while creating a clean layout that reflects the graphic look of the client in broadcast and print.

Lucky is the copywriter creating copy for an outdoor board placed before the NEXT EXIT, where the motel is sitting at the exit itself. This is a lot easier than trying to explain how to get to a downtown hotel 20 blocks from the exit. Many copywriters approach directional board assignments with the attitude that the project holds no opportunity for creativity. Yet there's always a way to add a twist, even if only by saying something like "3 miles to a good night's sleep."

## Writing Outdoor As a Primary Medium

When you're creating a campaign in which outdoor carries the entire message, the pressure's on. When outdoor is the only medium used and more than one board is to be used, the client is often something like a radio station the driver can immediately turn to, a restaurant, a retail outlet or other product or service a driver could reasonably consider purchasing on this car trip. Or the client could be a non-impulse service like a bank. Either way, the copywriter's strategy must be to create an impulse to buy something — whether now or later — in the few seconds an outdoor board is readable, because there will be no other media to ping-pong off of. The copywriter should be concerned with where the boards are to be placed and driving conditions in that place. That means special attention to concise, punchy writing and arresting visuals.

The hardest part of writing the primary outdoor campaign is that you must develop a creative strategy, a slogan if there is room, a visual, just as you would for print or broadcast. But there is little room to present your work. This forces you, more than in the other media, to think of a visual that tells the story on its own. A good place to start would be to think about Gary Larsen's one-panel cartoons in *The Far Side*. He tells a story, more often than not, without words. One of his drawings shows two bears, the one on the right centered in a gunsight. The bear in the gunsight is pointing to the other bear.

That tells a tale. I'm not saying that you should imitate Gary Larsen; he is one of a kind. But it's reassuring to know you can tell a story without words. If you're able to convey part of your advertising story by coming up with a visual first, your copy will be easier to write.

On the other hand, if you come up with a jewel of a slogan or a series of good copy lines, the words might suggest a good visual. It doesn't matter which you think of first, picture or words. The main thing is to execute your strategy with a clear, quickly understood effort.

One beneficial thing about the discipline of creating the primary outdoor campaign is the skill you attain in being concise without losing meaning. In fact, when faced with a multimedia campaign, perhaps you should work on the outdoor first. If you do, it will be easier to create for the print and broadcast parts of the campaign; you may even feel as if you have loads of space and time for the other media, once you've communicated the campaign concisely in outdoor first.

## Slogan or Copy or Both?

You have more flexibility in the limited space of outdoor if there is no slogan in the campaign you're creating or reminding people of. If there is a slogan, you have to decide whether it lends itself to the job at hand. In the original Miller Lite campaign, for instance, the slogan was "Everything You Always Wanted in a Beer. And Less." It was a terrific slogan, but a very important copy point was always made that Miller Lite was less filling and had great taste. Now, by the time you get all that on an outdoor board big enough to read, there's little room left for a picture of the celebrities who inhabit the Miller commercials.

What would you do? You might figure that the celebrities were so well known through the TV spots that featuring one of them in a cute situation might have the most impact. In the all-word MBank spots (Figure 9.3), a picture wasn't necessary. But Bubba Smith tearing the top off a beer can, or 50 Rodney Dangerfields getting off a spaceship, or Joe Piscopo karate-chopping a pizza can be very dramatic when depicted 48 feet wide and 14 feet high. Perhaps all that is necessary is to remind readers of the TV spots with the pictures and merely include the Miller Lite name and logo.

When debating whether or not to use a slogan, or what to say in general, you must think *impact*. Those boards are big, bigger than movie screens. The bigger the picture and the shorter and fewer the words, the greater the impact.

Consider this classic VW outdoor board:

PIC:        (NUNS EXITING A MICROBUS)

HEAD:     Mass Transit

SIG:        (VW LOGO)

If your slogan also happens to have the name of the product in it, you've gone a long way toward solving some of these space problems. Think about "Coke Is It!" Because the name is in the slogan, all you have to write is the slogan and the visual, no signature. Having such a short slogan with the client name in it allows room for a couple more words of copy, if appropriate.

But when you try to write copy, plus a slogan, plus a visual, plus a signature, and — in some cases — an address and a phone number, you're getting into dangerous territory. And the art director will want to do you physical harm if you lay all those elements on him or her to design into a clean graphic presentation.

One good way to start writing outdoor, when there's a good slogan available, is to use your slogan as the only copy. This makes sense, particularly if you come up with a new and unusual visual, because the visual is new while the slogan carries the continuity of whatever the reader has been seeing in print or broadcast. But, as with the Miller Lite example, a long slogan, even if terrific, can create space problems. If you don't use the slogan, you might try to make the visual representative of the slogan (see Figure 9.4).

What it boils down to in reminder advertising is this: first communicate, in a way that has impact, the basic selling message as presented in other media, and then worry about whether you can work in the slogan. In directional outdoor, you should plan to use the slogan if at all possible, because the board will then serve two functions: it will give directions as well as carry the theme of the overall campaign.

If you're using outdoor as the primary medium, you'll have the power to decide whether to have a slogan at all. If you do, you'll either have a short slogan and copy on each board or the slogan alone with a new visual on each board if several different boards are used or when the boards are changed every six months.

## Word and PIC Sizes

It's graphic custom for either the words or the PIC to dominate a design; if they're the same size, the board tends to have a boring look. If the illustrations or photos dominate, they should be very large. If you're selling a pack of gum, perhaps you would make the whole board the pack of gum, instead of showing little people with a little pack of gum, in which case you're not taking advantage of the size of the board. Remember to think about carrying through on the bigger-than-life aspect. If the words dominate the design, they can rule the highway with letters 10 feet high.

## Mandatories

Always be sure whether you must use mandatories on the outdoor, because they certainly muddy the look of the board, even when they're so small you can't read them. And if you can't read them, why put them there? Things like "Member FDIC" and other mandatories are sometimes legally excused from outdoor. It is to your and your art director's benefit to check these things out in order to achieve a cleaner board.

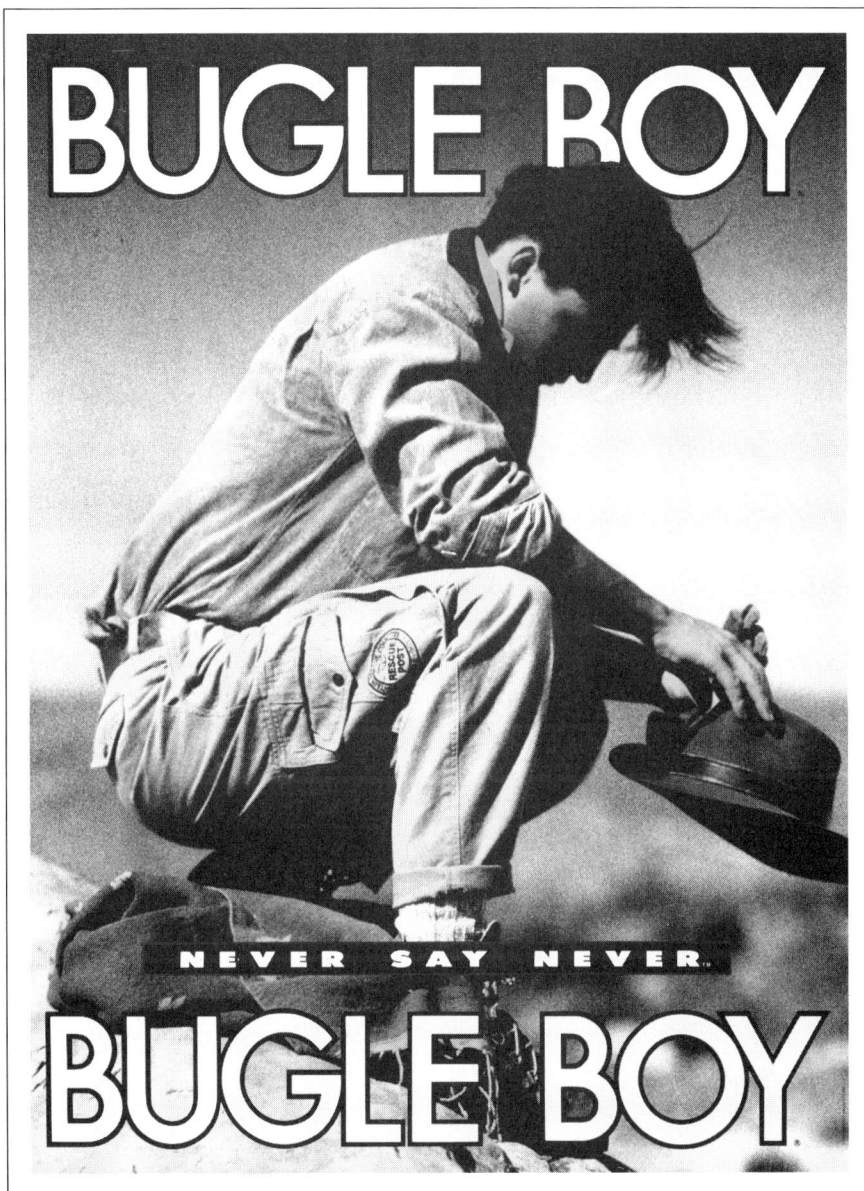

9.4

*Bugle Boy jeans uses NEVER SAY NEVER as the copy, changing only the visuals in this one of a series of outdoor boards. A refusal to say anything about its jeans appears to be the continuity of this campaign. Compare this with the TV spot in Chapter 6.*

## OUTDOOR TIPS

- Be brief — space is limited.
- Be bold — it's a big canvas.
- Be especially attentive to visuals, as they're often more important in outdoor than elsewhere.

- Try to use an ongoing campaign slogan when possible.
- Learn about the various types of boards available.
- If you start a campaign by writing the outdoor first, you might find it easier and less time-consuming to write the other media ads.
- If writing directional outdoor for a client with an ongoing campaign, try to retain the look and sound of the campaign while giving clear directions.

## IN CONCLUSION

Some people, including David Ogilvy, see no reason to clutter the landscape and the cityscape with outdoor boards, except for discreet necessary directional boards. If you hold such a view, and it is a legitimate point of view, you have a moral question to face. If you are willing to risk your job for your convictions, or risk your client if you are free-lance or own your own advertising agency, that's your decision.

But whatever your decision, as with anything else, if you decide to take somebody's money for doing something like writing for outdoor, do it with all your heart. Outdoor, whether considered a good or bad idea, is a unique art form, and offers you an opportunity to do a very good job of selling your client's products or services.

## EXERCISES

1. Create three reminder outdoor boards that continue a local retail campaign, using that campaign's slogan and strategy.
2. Do the same for a national durable goods, packaged goods or service account.

# CHAPTER 10

# ART DIRECTORS, THUMBNAILS AND PRINT PRODUCTION

In this chapter we shall follow an art director/copywriter team through the checklist of steps to an advertising message. On the Koder Bread account, they will follow familiar steps: They will analyze the situation, research the problem, come up with a CWP, execute their creative strategy and, finally, go into production. On the way, you'll meet this mysterious creature, the art director, who has been mentioned so often up to this point. If art directors (ADs) develop creative strategies, write slogans, headlines and sometimes copy, then it makes sense that copywriters (CWs) become familiar with the art director's duties.

Though it's unlikely the copywriter will do more than suggest visuals and make thumbnail designs to illustrate the thinking behind the visuals, any copywriter will find an understanding of art directors and their **graphic** concerns helpful in creating copy. Nothing is more embarrassing for a copywriter than to be told that a visual can't be done or that, because of the peculiarities of print production, a deadline can't be met; the copywriter should have known these things.

## THE ART DIRECTOR (AD)

Art directors and copywriters have been working as teams for a long time. When creatives are gathered for bull sessions, over and over you'll hear "my writer" and "my art director." In truth, many ADs and CWs spend more time with each other than with their spouses. Not only do they work together all day, five days a week, often longer than eight hours a day, but they also work together at night and on weekends when a crisis is happening. And crises have a way of happening one after another in advertising. In many situations, however, CWs and ADs also work with several other partners. Even so, there is usually a favorite partnership, in which a certain AD and CW team hit it off better than with others. It's like marriage.

## Creating in Comfort

The AD and CW have two levels of functioning: strategic and executional. In just about every creative assignment, including radio in many cases, the partners work together to develop a creative strategy and agree on the broad outlines of the creative execution — what the actual copy and art will be like. They like to be comfortable while creating, especially when developing the CWP and creative strategy.

The creative strategy sessions can happen at a Saturday night backyard barbecue, during a long lunch, on a fishing trip and very often in the office. Many agencies encourage their creative teams to get out of the office when it's time to come up with ideas for a new campaign. But when it's time for the execution of the specific copy and graphic materials, the AD and CW will return to the agency or corporate office or perhaps go to a home studio or office to work alone. It's not as common for corporate ad departments to encourage creatives to leave the office to create; and even many agencies are, in the view of the creatives, a bit stodgy about this and insist that their employees be on the premises most of the time.

Stodgy or not, many agencies and maybe some corporations create "think tanks" for their creatives to retire to in times of creative need, comfortable rooms with no phones and pillows everywhere. In addition, the creatives are often allowed exceptional freedom in the decoration of their offices.

It's odd for writers and artists to be on a payroll in the first place. Advertising agencies are unusual in having creative types on staff, because artists and writers traditionally work for themselves or at least not in sterile office situations. Companies recognize that creative people are different; and many are the account executives (AEs) who, taking clients or others on a tour of the offices, enter the creative department (after leaving the bank-like account services department) with some reference to "Now let's take a look at the zoo" or other such witticisms.

If you think about it, most of the creative suppliers to the advertising business don't work at the agency or corporation — including photographers, acting and modeling talent, illustrators, and many others. These outside suppliers work at home or in offices that may be lofts or warehouses; this is not to say they aren't businesslike — they just need to create in a comfortable environment.

## Where Do Art Directors Come From?

Some art directors come from art schools to corporate ad departments and advertising agencies. Some learn the advertising business on the job; there are still art directors who break into the business that way. A few art directors have no advertising training and no art training but great talent; they are people who have willed their way into the business. And through hard work and raw intelligence they have made it into the ranks of art directors. Many of these started out in the "bullpen," where they were trained in the skills of paste-up and layout and other aspects of print production. Many art directors come out of commercial art schools that teach advertising thinking and design. In the best of these schools students are also taking photography, art, broadcast and sometimes copywriting so that the art school experience brings together the main players in the art director's future life.

More and more these days you find an AD who went to college, majored in advertising and discovered during that time that he or she had a talent for and an interest in art direction. That AD was trained to think as an advertising person; but upon graduation with a journalism or advertising or communications degree realized she or he had to go on to one of the commercial art schools to learn a variety of hand skills and achieve the graphics knowledge an AD needs to do the job. Some ADs then go on to become creative directors, who supervise writers and art directors.

## WHAT DOES THE ART DIRECTOR *DO*?

To appreciate the multifaceted life of an AD, follow Arlene the AD and Connie the CW through a mythical advertising campaign from beginning to end. As the story begins, Arlene and Connie are drinking coffee in Connie's office and racing to see who can finish a crossword puzzle first. They've just finished an assignment and are taking a break before the next one. They don't have to wait long.

## The Job Order

An account executive (AE) comes in with a **job order** for the Koder Bread account. Arlene and Connie listen attentively as the AE explains that Koder wants a whole new campaign. Past advertising has been fine, and Koder has the largest market share in Gotham City; but the new president of Koder Bread, the grandson of the founder, wants to do his own thing and the agency cannot convince him to stick with the old campaign.

In addition, Koder's lawyers have persuaded the new president that Koder's long-time slogan — "Freshest Bread in Town" — may be false advertising or at least hard to prove. The president concurs and decides a whole new campaign should be launched if Koder has to change its slogan anyway. Because Koder is Arlene and Connie's account, they're already familiar with the AE's analysis of the situation and constantly keep up with research on the account. The AE has prepared a CWP lacking only a creative strategy, so Arlene and Connie will start by coming up with a creative strategy.

## Getting to Work

The creative team gets to work. They go to a long lunch in a restaurant with a fireplace, taking their legal pads and pens. During lunch and afterward, while having herbal tea, they have a breakthrough. They know they must stick with the freshness theme, because freshness is essential with bread and essential to continuity with the old campaign; but the new slogan would have to pass the lawyer. Both women make suggestions, but it's the AD, Arlene, who says "Fresh As Ever."

"That's it!" cries Connie, with only a slight twinge of jealousy — not because the AD thought of it, since ADs write headlines and slogans all the time, but because it was such a good idea. "It'll go by the lawyer," she says. "All it says is that Koder's as fresh as it's ever been, and that's a true statement. It's perfect."

## The First Approval

Back at the office the team exposes "Fresh As Ever" to the creative director (CD). He likes it, pending their creative execution, and together they agree on the creative strategy that led to the slogan: to reassure present customers and persuade potential customers that Koder Bread stands for freshness. The CD tells them he's sure he can get approval for the strategy and slogan from the AE and other agency management types and urges them to develop a creative execution for a TV spot, a radio spot, a newspaper ad and an outdoor board.

## Starting the Creative Execution

At Arlene's condo that night, they toss ideas back and forth. Will they have a continuing character? Do they have a serious sit and pitch person? Humor? Physical fitness approach? Koder family tradition? The two have worked together long enough to be honest, and when one says, "No, that stinks," it's taken as intended — it's not a good idea. Nothing personal.

Finally it's Connie who suggests the bread be featured as a "carrier." She says, "What is bread but a carrier?" They come up with a campaign that covers all Koder products — wheat and white bread, hot dog and hamburger buns — with every conceivable food that might be "carried," burgers and hot dogs, sloppy joes, peanut butter, cream cheese, on and on. The copy will always end with "Koder Bread. Fresh As Ever."

They decide to show vignettes (short visual situations) on TV, of people in normal eating situations using Koder Bread products. They decide on what those vignettes will be, mom and kids at lunch, backyard barbecue, breakfast and so on. The same theme will be carried out in newspaper, with photography. The campaign will be carried out on radio with humorous dialogue and music, and in outdoor with adaptations of the vignettes used on TV to remind people of the TV spots. Connie believes she should write a jingle for the TV and radio, and Arlene agrees.

This all sounds very neat. In fact, and more naturally, Arlene and Connie may spend several weeks accomplishing what they have to this point, though it's not rare for things to come together in one day. But it's unlikely. Either way, this is a true accounting of what many AD/CW teams do.

Up to now, they've worked together on strategy and have outlined the creative execution far enough so that Arlene can begin to work on the TV storyboard and newspaper and outdoor layouts. If headlines remain to be written, Arlene will either wait for Connie to write them, or they will write them together. After the headlines for newspaper and outdoor, Connie will want to write down the TV for Arlene so that she can make an accurate storyboard. "Write down" is the way to see it here, because they have collaborated on the TV spot; and it's a matter of wordsmithing for Connie, not creating the idea. When Connie writes the TV, she will also create a thumbnail storyboard to show Arlene how she sees the commercial and thumbnails for the print and outdoor as well.

And so the two retire to their own places to work on their second level of expertise — the creative execution. The thumbnails Connie creates for Arlene are shown in Figure 10.1, and the revisions are shown in Figure 10.2.

## After the Writing

Using Arlene's revision of the thumbnails, the team meets with the creative director for approval to proceed. He agrees with the direction they are taking, makes a few minor copy and visual suggestions, and they return to their offices. This creative director has the power to approve this team's campaign and permits them to go ahead with preparation of materials for a client presentation. But many times at this point the creative director will have to sell their idea, alone or along with the team, to the account executives and other agency personnel — or, in a corporate situation, to the marketing or advertising director.

(Note: This process sounds very smooth. Sometimes it works this way. Sometimes the creative director turns it all down and they have to start over again.)

While Connie takes her time with the radio copy and the jingle, Arlene is very busy. She can draw well enough to illustrate the storyboard, newspaper

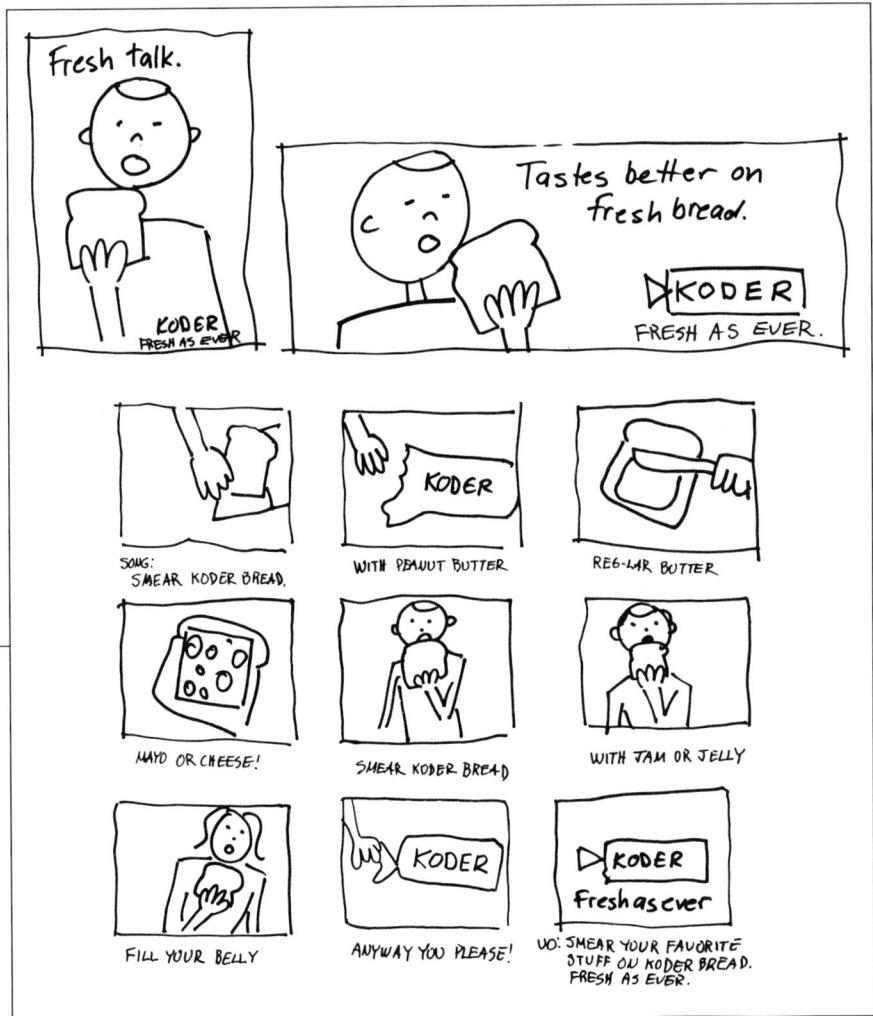

10.1

*Copywriter's thumbs for newspaper, outdoor and TV. These crude drawings are better than the author can do, but they are not as good as some copywriters can do. The main thing is to give the art director some visual idea of what the copywriter is thinking.*

ad and outdoor board, but she prefers to only direct the preparation of that presentation art. (Other art directors do not draw well enough to do this and must turn the work over to others who do draw well.) In some agencies or corporate situations, she could even turn the design of those three pieces over to someone else. But most art directors like to be responsible for designing print and outdoor and for figuring out the TV panels for presentation.

## Design

The design of an ad is the rewarding aspect of getting an ad put together for an AD. It gives the same satisfaction that a well-turned phrase or a great jingle does for a copywriter. The thumbnails may well have been the final design, but Arlene goes home thinking she can improve on the thumbnail designs.

*These art director
thumbs pretty much
follow the copywriter's
ideas, because the
copywriter and art
director discussed the
project before the
copywriter did her
thumbs. If a copywriter
were working inde-
pendently of the art
director, chances are the
AD thumbs would be
much different. As it
is, you can sense the
"tightening" the AD
did on these visuals.*

When playing the role of designer, the art director starts out with many
elements that must be in the ad, such as the visual, the headline, the copy, the
slogan, the signature of the client, maybe a separate logo to go with the
signature, mandatory information, a map or a special 800 phone number.
This is the tight little box that all ad people — ADs, CWs and producers — are
stuffed into when trying to create something original even though loaded
down with restrictions. You can see how stressful such a task might be.

The designer's job is to make clear the point of the ad — in this case that
Koder Bread is fresh as ever and that it is a good product to smear stuff onto.
But over and above that, the designer's job is to create a presentation of those
main points and include all the other elements in a way that will attract the

**10.3**

*Rough layouts for newspaper, outdoor and TV. Notice how the AD has subtly focused on facial expressions and actions, thinking more and more of the photographer who lies at the end of this road.*

reader's attention and lend the client an image that is exciting and reassuring to the buying public.

It's not unusual for an AD who wants to handle the design and direct other folks in the rest of the project to scratch out a design on the back of an envelope, if she's working with a layout person who knows the way the designer thinks. In this case, Arlene had a better idea for the newspaper design than the thumbnail done earlier, while in the car on the way to the office. When she got there, she called in a layout person, explained her idea, then asked for a **rough layout** (Figure 10.3). She also gave the layout person her ideas for outdoor and the TV storyboard.

## How Rough Is a Rough Layout?

The layout person can be an assistant art director who hopes to design and direct art some day, but right now is learning all the jobs in the art department. He or she is probably already pretty good at paste-up and other facets of production art and has also been entrusted to do rough layouts and **comprehensive layouts.**

The layout person starts with a rough pencil or black marker layout, or a colored rough layout, trying to represent the designer's idea in the exact size for an ad or in the exact proportion in the case of outdoor. The rough layout may be exactly what the designer had in mind. Even if it is, the AD might not like her own idea upon seeing it in rough layout form and will try a new design.

In this case, Arlene liked the rough layout and instructed the layout person to go on to a comprehensive layout, after informing the layout person of the typeface she prefers for the ad and outdoor, and how the photo or illustration should be represented. She also approves the rough layout of the panels for the storyboard.

## The Comprehensive Layout

Depending on the amount of money a client is willing to spend, the comprehensive layout may look almost like the finished ad. Type could be set for the headline and body copy; actual photos could be taken. In most cases, the body copy is "greeked," set in nonsense letters that occupy the space where the actual copy will go. Figuring out how to take typewritten or computer-written copy and change it into a typeface set in shorter or longer lines is called copyfitting. Arlene could copyfit the copy, or the paste-up or layout person might be assigned to the job. In this case, she asks the layout person to figure out the size of the copy blocks, because Arlene has other fish to fry.

## Pre-Production Planning

While the layout person is assembling the comprehensive layouts, Arlene arranges for a typesetter to set type for the newspaper and outdoor ads after, and if, they are approved by the client, as well as to set any type needed on the TV spot. She also chooses a separator to make negatives for the newspaper ad.

Then Arlene and Connie look through talent books for actors for the TV spot, send for tapes to look at the actors, and in the end call in some of the actors to read for the parts. This is called casting. Arlene and Connie also work together in choosing a production house to shoot the TV commercial, by first looking at sample reels of other commercials those houses have shot and then by chatting with representatives or directors of those houses.

Connie has written a jingle that Arlene likes, and they go about the process of choosing a music production house to set those lyrics to music and produce the sound track. They listen to sample reels containing advertising music created for other customers of the music production house. Arlene and Connie

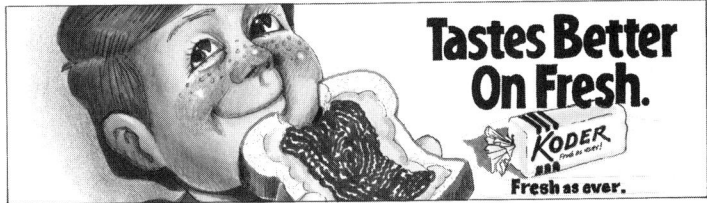

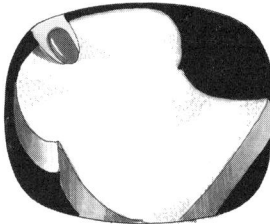

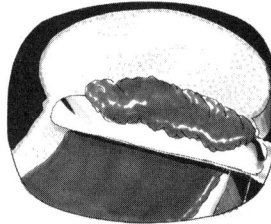

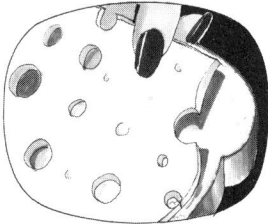

*Presentation materials or "comps" ( for comprehensive art) on the Koder project. For these materials, the roughs are usually sent out to a free-lance artist or art studio. On occasion there will be a talented art director who can do this kind of finished art, but that person would be foolish to do this kind of art on salary, when he or she could do it for money as a free-lance or studio artist.*

both enjoy chatting with the music person and sipping coffee in the musician's office while listening to his suggestions for a melody to go with the lyrics. It's up to them to say yes or no to the melody suggested. If they hear something they like, the music person may record a piano track of the music for Arlene and Connie to take back to the creative director. If the creative director approves of the melody and the lyrics, he may have the power to approve a "demo track" (demonstration tape) in which several instruments and singers may be used to give a close approximation of what the jingle will sound like.

During this time Arlene has also secured approval to use the typesetter and separator she has chosen. And both Arlene and Connie have to convince the creative director that their choice of a TV production house and talent is appropriate to the project.

In some cases Arlene and Connie could be spending all their time on the Koder Bread project alone, as it appears here. But more likely they have other accounts to service, and the Koder activities are spaced between those other projects.

## Presentation Materials

Arlene and Connie get together to review the presentation materials (Figure 10.4). Chances are that Arlene has been supervising the preparation of the materials, so there should be no surprises, although some improvements may occur to either one of them after seeing the materials.

With the demo of the jingle and the storyboard, newspaper and outdoor comprehensive layouts in hand, Arlene and Connie retire to the conference room to rehearse their **pitch** and then give it, first to the creative director, then to the AE and other interested account and management persons. If all like the materials, even with some changes or suggestions, the materials are finalized and the presentation is scheduled to take place one last time before the public sees the campaign — to the client.

## The Client Pitch

The presentation will take place in the agency's offices, although often a presentation may be made at the client's headquarters. Arlene and Connie have taken no great pains to dress any differently, since the client is accustomed to seeing them in their jeans and sweaters.

They feel nervous about the presentation, but not because they're going to have to speak in front of people. They just don't want to be rejected and have to go through the creative process all over again. Worse, they don't want to be rejected and have the agency assign the next try at creative execution to another team. This is another example of the stress built into the advertising business, agency or corporate, for corporate creatives would feel the same tensions.

Connie, according to Arlene, is "better on her feet" than the art director, so Arlene's role in the pitch is to hold up the materials and explain the graphics; Connie explains the creative strategy, reads the copy and plays the jingle.

Connie presents the materials sitting down, trying to avoid an overly formal situation. She is low-key in her delivery, explaining every step of the creation from the beginning, as if explaining the process to her husband and children, dropping in amusing tidbits of interest as she goes along. When Arlene says Connie is better on her feet, she means Connie is good at ad-libbing and fielding client questions without getting flustered, whether sitting or standing.

## The Finale

The client loves the "Fresh As Ever" campaign, gives the go-ahead to the agency to proceed with preparation of the finished materials, and Arlene and Connie are taken to a long celebratory lunch by the AEs, where they modestly give credit to the CD for his guidance and the AE for his marketing help.

One would think the work would really start now, with TV production, final music production, illustrations for the newspaper, photos for the outdoor, type ordering and paste-up, and all the other details to be completed. And indeed production of the advertising materials starts now. But the real work took place the first time Arlene and Connie sat down to work on a creative strategy and a slogan. That was the heart of the campaign; all the tasks that followed, though important, were but building blocks on a structure that was clearly envisioned and needed only to be completed.

Now that you have some idea what an art director does in a team effort with the copywriter in story form, we'll take a more structured look at the print production elements with which a copywriter should be familiar.

# PRINT PRODUCTION AND THE COPYWRITER

## Remember the AD When You Write

You should know that, compared to TV and radio, **print production** is tough and time-consuming; and for you to suggest three blackbirds flapping in the air while they peck at a king's nose, in a photo, is a horrible thing to sell to the client and then leave up to the art director to produce. (It's a horrible thing for the copywriter to sell anything to the client without the AD's agreement.)

Don't indicate typefaces, printing techniques or other uniquely graphic aspects to the AD no matter how much you know about the subject. The AD is an expert on the subject and will do just fine without your suggestions. Much acrimony arises when ADs question a CW's choice of words in body copy. Sometimes the AD is right, but it irritates a writer. The same thing happens the other way.

It's okay to indicate a visual as "Boy and girl on picnic blanket"; don't describe the boy and girl's appearance except as necessary, or the color of the blanket, or the state of the sky, or the angle the picture is to be shot at. Give the AD credit for knowing the craft.

movable type, Gutenberg, in the fifteenth century. Many type styles are named after the people who invented them; other names of typefaces were chosen for various commercial reasons.

An AD watching TV with you might say things like, "That's Souvenir. That's Times Roman" as commercials run and words pop onto the screen. ADs use books published by type houses that are full of various styles and sizes of type. The two basic styles of type are "Roman" and "Gothic," also known respectively as serif and sans serif type. The serif type has little graceful extensions on the letters; sans serif does not. This book is printed in a serif type called Janson. The chapter titles and headings are printed in a sans serif type called Futura Condensed.

There are arguments in advertising about whether one type style reads better than another, whether one has more class than another, and even whether type set in reverse (white on black) reads as well as black on white. These are arguments based on the knowledge of the AD that a certain style of type can have as much influence on the impact of an ad as the picture or the copy. Figure 10.6 shows some basic examples of typefaces, only a fraction of what is actually available.

You may not see it in a thumbnail design, but by the time the ad design reaches the rough layout stage, the AD will have chosen at least to feature a serif or sans serif typeface and may even have chosen the exact style to be used.

## After Approval of an Ad

Whether the client approves a thumbnail design or a finished comp, the ad is now ready to be produced for publication. The last step is to actually mail a proof of the ad and/or a negative of the ad for the publication to print from, depending on the publication. Let's take a look at some of the parts of the print production department. Many elements come together in the "production art" process, to be combined by various specialists.

## The Picture

After client approval, the AD takes a copy of the approved layout to a photographer or illustrator, whichever is to be used.

If it's an illustrator, the AD spends considerable time telling the artist, usually free-lance or with an art studio, what is wanted. A deadline is agreed upon, and by that date the illustrator shows up with the drawing, in black and white or color or whatever was needed. The artist delivers the art only; the rest of the ad is being handled by other people.

In the case of the photographer, the AD arranges a time for the shoot, makes known his or her preferences for a specific model or model type, and then goes to the studio to direct the photographer in the shoot. Again, the finished picture is delivered as a picture and not as part of a layout, though the photographer had a copy of the layout to follow in order to see the relationship of the picture to the rest of the ad.

Amelia

American Greeting Script

Antique Shaded Roman

Arnold Bocklin

Avant Garde Book

Bodoni

Benguiat Medium

Broadway Engraved

Caslon Antique

Cheltenham Book

Cooper Black

Frutiger #75 Black

Futura Medium Condensed

Helvetica Light

Palatino

Parisian

Peignot Bold

Playbill

QUARTZ LIGHT

Rainbow Bass

Reporter

Revue

Souvenir Bold Outline

Times Roman

UMBRA

**10.6**

*Here is a small sample of the latest typefaces and the traditional look as well. There are hundreds of typefaces — maybe thousands — some dating back to the fifteenth century. The design and/or selection of typefaces is an art form in itself, and in some art schools may be a two-semester course.*

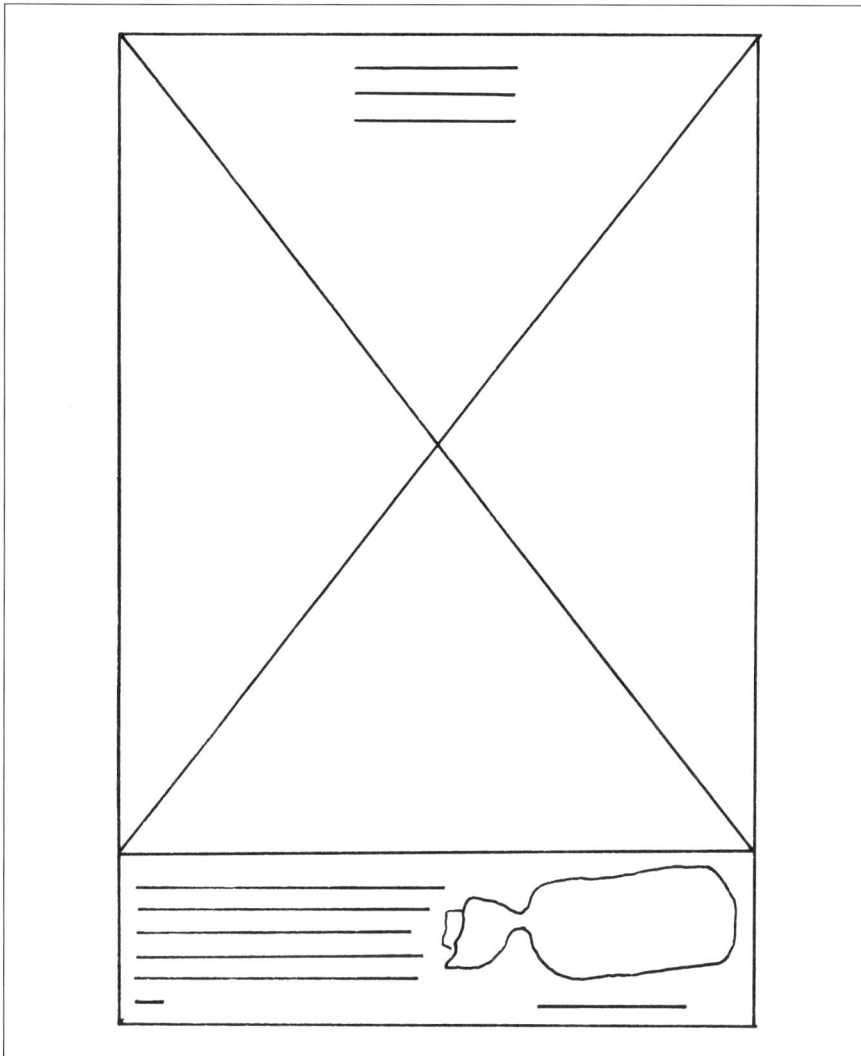

**10.7**

*A fairly simple type layout. They can be much more complicated than this, but you can see how the typesetter is only interested in where the type goes in relation to other parts of the ad. The big PIC means nothing to the type-setter, but the bread to the right of and above the type tells the type-setter what area there is to work in. This layout will be exactly to the scale of the actual ad.*

## Paste-Up

Whether the paste-up person translates the typewritten copy into instructions to the type house or the AD or someone else does, the type finally comes to the paste-up person to be put down on a **mechanical,** which is the official name for what most people call a **paste-up** or "camera-ready art." The AD or layout person will prepare a "type layout" that the paste-up person follows in pasting down the type into position on the ad (Figure 10.7).

Some paste-up people do nothing but paste down type, but most learn to handle other aspects of production art, including drawing (or pasting) lines

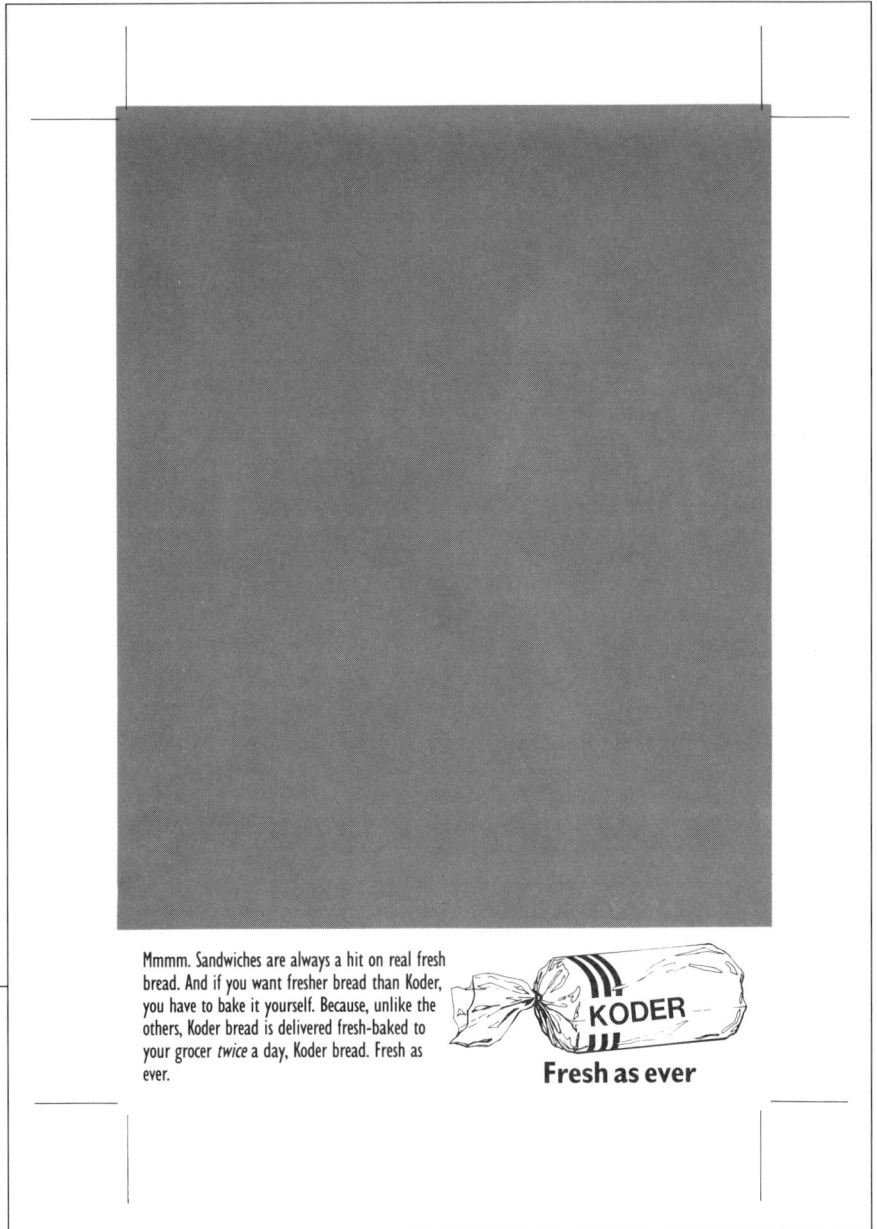

**10.8**

*A simple mechanical,
the material from which
the final ad is printed. It
is also called a paste-up.
Notice the overlay,
where the picture
will go.*

Mmmm. Sandwiches are always a hit on real fresh bread. And if you want fresher bread than Koder, you have to bake it yourself. Because, unlike the others, Koder bread is delivered fresh-baked to your grocer *twice* a day, Koder bread. Fresh as ever.

**KODER**

**Fresh as ever**

onto the ad where needed, creating "overlays" to indicate where a picture will fit in, exactly sizing the ad to the publication's required dimensions for bleed or non-bleed ads, and writing directions regarding colors to the publisher on a tissue overlay.

When the art or photograph comes in, the art director will check it to be sure it's right and indicate to the paste-up person how that picture is to be cropped. The paste-up person will usually make a photostat or "stat" (or PMT, photo mechanical transfer) for his or her own use in assembling the mechanical. Though the black and white stat will be pasted on the layout to indicate to a separator (negative maker) how the picture fits in, it will usually have words written over the stat like "For position only" to tell the separator that this is not to be reproduced. On the mechanical that includes a picture, the overlay will feature a colored acetate, usually red, that will allow the separator to photograph the mechanical as it is, the overlay blocking out the area for the art or photo to be stripped into later (Figure 10.8).

Before it goes to the separator, the mechanical goes to the art director for approval, then to various agency people and the client for their initials, because this is their last chance to make corrections.

## The Separator

The mechanical goes to the separator, who used to be called the "engraver" when pictures were etched onto metal for letterpress (hot-type) printing, as opposed to the current method of cold-type (or offset) printing. The separator shoots a negative of the mechanical, or four negatives if it's a four-color job, or any number in between. Then the separator usually shoots the art or photography on another negative or negatives and combines the two into one combination negative that contains all the elements of the ad.

From that negative the separator can print a proof for approval by the art director and others. If the ad is a newspaper job in one color, the proof (called a velox) can be used for printing. Most magazines require the negative to print from (Figure 10.9). Other kinds of materials are furnished if the job is for rotogravure (the Sunday supplement) or silk screen printing, etc.

In a collateral piece, this operation is the same, except the negative goes not to a publication, but to a printer. In many cases the separations can also be done by a printer; in other cases the separator is a company that only does separations, then sends them on to the publication or the printer. In the case of a painted outdoor board, a tight (finished) layout is enough to give to the painter. If printed posters are to be used in outdoor, proofs and negatives will be sent to the outdoor poster printer.

## Other Production Matters

The complete copywriter will pick up many other useful bits of information about print production over the years or can learn more about the process through some excellent textbooks and handbooks written for students, including Roy Paul Nelson's excellent textbook, *The Design of Advertising* (Wm. C. Brown Publishers).

You will want to know about subjects not covered here, such as half-tone and line art, four-color separation, copyfitting, the variety of type styles, printing processes, and other knowledge representing the day-to-day tools of the AD. If you're an advertising student, you're probably required to take a graphics class, where all of this information, including basic design techniques, will be covered.

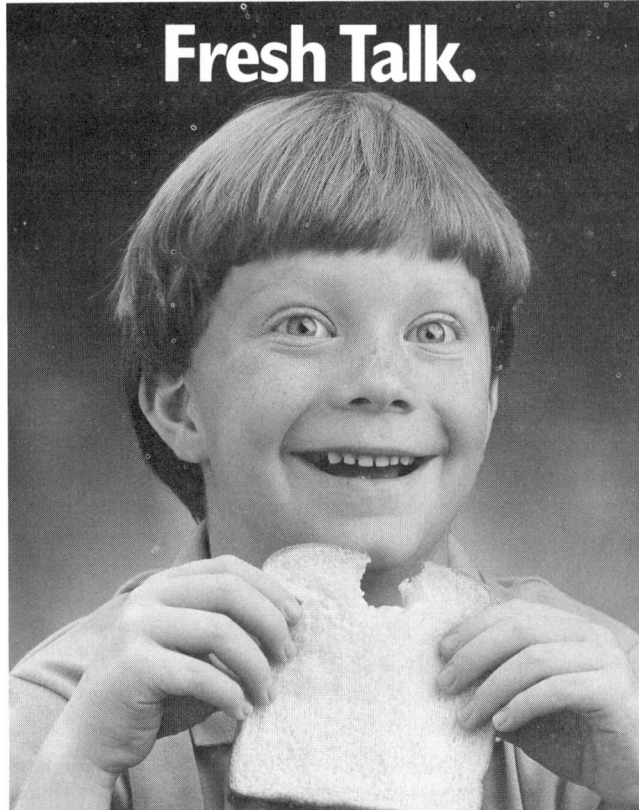

# Fresh Talk.

Mmmm. Sandwiches are always a hit on real fresh bread. And if you want fresher bread than Koder, you have to bake it yourself. Because, unlike the others, Koder bread is delivered fresh-baked to your grocer *twice* a day, Koder bread. Fresh as ever.

**KODER**

**Fresh as ever**

**10.9**

*This is what it was all about, the final Koder print ad.*

But it might be instructive, and serve as a recap in this chapter, to give you a (not-exhaustive) list of suppliers the AD works with, names you'll hear your partner refer to once in a while.

## Checklist of Advertising Suppliers

- Photographers.
- Talent—models and actors.
- Paper suppliers. You won't *believe* how complicated the choice of paper can be.
- Separators (also known as engravers). They take the art and/or photos and enlarge them or reduce them and shoot them onto something that can be printed from. Separators also shoot the pasted-up copy and strip

the copy and art/photos together on negatives or plates, just as the layout indicates.

- Printers. Always at the end of the advertising chain, they tend to be cynical when you say it's a rush job. All their jobs are rush. (If not, they make it that way.) The main thing to realize is that your AD is responsible for the printer and may be at the print shop at 3 A.M. supervising a run.

- Illustrators.

- Typesetters.

- Layout artists (in larger agencies, usually, or sophisticated corporate set-ups. Otherwise, the AD may be the one who prepares preliminary and comprehensive layouts).

- Designers (again, usually in larger agencies; otherwise, the AD will conceive and design the print ad).

- Paste-up artists (production artists), who prepare mechanicals (also known as paste-ups). In a very small agency or corporate situation, the AD might also perform this function; some ADs prefer to paste up their own work, just as some writers prefer to type their own copy.

- Air-brush artists, the people who cloud windows on car ads and make cigarettes look perfect and punch up the look of ice cubes in whiskey ads.

- You, the copywriter. The AD must create the overall concept with you and put up with your silly or great ideas on how printed material should look.

- Neon sign makers. There aren't many of these people, but they're vital when you need neon for a trade show booth or an outdoor board.

- Booth makers. A combination of creative people and carpenters, who can translate the AD's design into a booth that can be easily broken down for shipping and easily assembled in trade shows anywhere in or out of the country.

- Advertising specialty representatives. These "reps" are aware of the very latest developments in advertising giveaways from pens to ashtrays to hats and T-shirts. The number of advertising specialties is enormous, and a client may often request such items. The AEs usually handle this; but ADs and CWs may suggest such items, and the AD may be involved in supervising the way the client name and logo are printed on these items.

- Pop-up and other printing specialties in ads, like 3-D pictures and musical ads. These people are apart from the publications that run the ads and must be dealt with before the ad goes to the publication.

## IN CONCLUSION

Regardless of the genius of your words, print advertising is a look. Cast your eyes around any display of print advertising at an awards show, and you're struck by the power and beauty of the displayed material long before you can get close enough to read that lazy copywriter's words.

You must respect that look and the effort and stress it takes for your AD to achieve it. Graphics is the business of excessive neatness, and consistently being neat can take its toll on your AD and his or her people. Take them to lunch sometime.

You can be helpful as a copywriter if you know something about print production. But it won't do you much good to get books on the subject; like swimming, you can read all you want, but only by getting in the water can you learn anything useful. What you can do, while in college, is to get involved in some of the print production processes by working on the college newspaper or on free-lance brochures. After you graduate, hang out with your AD. Go with your AD on some shoots and trips to suppliers. After a few years, you'll learn enough not to make life miserable for ADs when you're writing a piece, and you won't try to use difficult or impossible visuals.

### EXERCISES

1. Take one of the previous TV spots you have written and create a thumbnail storyboard to illustrate each scene in the TV spot.

2. Take a previously written print ad and create a thumbnail illustrating that ad.

3. Create a thumbnail for a previously written direct mail piece.

# CHAPTER 11

# PRESENTATIONS

If there is an extra step in the process of creating an advertising message, it would be *presentation*. Because it doesn't matter how well you've analyzed the situation, researched the problem, developed a CWP and executed the creative strategy, you'll never get to production of the materials unless you sell all the preceding work to the agency management and the client first. That means a presentation.

It's possible (shiver, you shy people) that no matter what job you take in the advertising business, you'll make more presentations in a week than you will have made in all of your college career. Ours is a business of communication; and before the public can hear your pitch, you'll have to make your pitch in person.

To whom? If you're a copywriter, you make the pitch to your art director and then to your creative director and/or copy chief. Then you make the pitch to the AEs and the account supervisors, to others in agency management and then to the client. And then, if you're really unlucky, but really good at presentation, you may be asked to give the pitch to the employees of the client, assembled in a huge auditorium and probably not eager to hear you talk about advertising. (But they'll be glad to get the time off from work.)

The AEs and the media and research people aren't excluded from making presentations, nor is anybody else in the agency or corporate scene. Presentations are a way of life in business, and especially so in the advertising business.

Meetings are one thing; you can sit and volunteer your opinions or not. But when you're the person who must stand before all those eyes and especially if you have a sensitive bone in you, it's quite a challenge.

Keep in mind that the following suggestions for presentation techniques are specifically for creative people, as opposed to the more formal offerings of those who wear suits. That's not a joke, since many ADs, CWs and production people don't wear suits. In many situations, it would be out of character for a laid-back copywriter to suddenly appear in a three-piece pinstripe suit to sell a campaign to the client, who is accustomed to seeing that person in less formal garb. Such costuming may seem insincere, and it could follow that the presentation might be seen as insincere by your audience. With all that, there are still many copywriters and art directors and creative directors who do dress impeccably, who are as skilled as their less sartorially spiffy colleagues, and for them the more formal presentation may be in order.

In the long run, presentation skills can vary widely and all approaches can be effective. The goal in any presentation, basically, is to persuade the audience to your way of thinking. In advertising, that means persuading the client to part with his or her money for your idea or, within the agency, persuading the agency management to let you make such a presentation to the client.

A last introductory point: Any college speech course will teach you the historically accepted ways to make a presentation. The suggestions in this chapter describe actions that have contributed to successful creative presentations in the past.

## KNOWLEDGE IS POWER

Nothing is more important than knowing what you're going to say and having supporting facts or arguments to back up your points. The biggest fear-inducing aspect of presentation is ignorance of what you have to say.

As with your advertising campaign, have one clear point to make. Let everything you say bolster that one point. You don't have to search for that one point in most creative presentations, because you have a creative strategy. If the strategy has been exposed to the client and approved by the client prior to the meeting, then your one clear point is that this creative material you are about to expose supports that creative strategy in the best way possible. If the client has not seen the creative strategy prior to your presentation, then your one point is that this is a super strategy, and here's how the creative materials bring it to life.

If you've written the campaign and sweated over it with the AD and CD for weeks, you should be familiar with the materials you are to present. If the creative strategy is clear and understandable to you, the only thing left to be nervous about is your own innate fear of presentation, the cotton mouth, the shaking hands, the sweating. By knowing your materials as well as any human on earth could know them, you go a long way toward reducing these outward indicators of inward panic. If you fear presentations anyway, as you read this, it should be some consolation to know that the more presentations you give, the less nervous you will act in them, over time. Note the "you will act" phrase; you'll probably retain your dislike for presentations all your life—some research has indicated shy children grow up to be shy adults no matter what—but thorough knowledge of your subject should ease 90 percent of your problems.

## WRITING THE PRESENTATION

Rather than referring to "writing" presentations, a better term would be "preparing the presentation," because writing implies complete sentences and paragraphs. The worst thing you can do is to go into a presentation with a prepared script. It doesn't hurt to write a complete script for yourself just to see what you have to say. But by the time you get to the presentation, the script should not accompany you.

The main problems with a script, no matter how well written, are (1) you might lose your place and have a very awkward moment, or you might read the same thing twice and (2) you will have to read it, and regardless of how good a reader you might be, a group of five to ten people will rightfully think it odd you're reading to them. They'll wonder why you just don't hand the writing to them and let them read it at their own speed. Your impact on your audience is lessened considerably by reading, because it looks as if you know nothing about the subject other than what's on paper. After all, you created this campaign, with others, but reading a script makes the audience think it's all new to you.

### Prepare an Outline

Whether you're preparing the presentation for yourself or someone else—and as a copywriter you will be asked to write speeches and presentations for others—the final draft should be in outline form. This is nothing new. Since the eighth grade teachers have been telling you that. But why? The Roman numeral outline keeps you on track while allowing your own brand of improvisation to come through, your own personality and persuasive powers to come through, your humor to come through. You can leave the road of continuity from time to time with relevant asides and still come back to the track. You can be interrupted by questions and then pick up where you were.

It's amazing how well you can give the presentation to a spouse or colleague and then in the big meeting, through fear of presentation, forget most of the main points you wanted to cover. Even the most experienced speakers know they can forget important points when caught up in the give-and-take of presentation. And it is give-and-take. This is not a unilateral speech you're giving. Your opening remarks could be interrupted by questions, because if the audience doesn't buy your basic premise, the materials you show will mean nothing.

## Start with a Brief Marketing Recap

The client and agency people already know what information they gave you and what they asked you to do. So you don't have to linger on the assignment. But a short statement of the problem to be solved will start the presentation off with the familiar and let the audience know that you understand the problem, that you are on all fours with them. A good place to get the material for this brief introductory marketing statement is the Creative Work Plan — which, if done correctly, should contain more than enough material for your recap of the problem.

# BEFORE THE PRESENTATION

After you prepare your outline, rehearse it alone and with your AD and maybe your spouse or roommate. Even after you feel as if you have it down, attending to some other details will add to your feeling of comfort in making the presentation.

## Check Out the Room

Go in early — maybe a day or more before the presentation — and check it out. Know where you'll sit, where the audience will sit. Get comfy with the environment in which you must present. It's you under the gun. You should have the right to dictate the circumstances under which you could possibly make a fool of yourself. Feeling comfortable is easier if you're presenting in your own agency or corporate headquarters. But it would be well worth your effort to take a half hour to look at the room if you've never been there before.

A case in point is the Bozell advertising agency pitch to American Airlines. The myth has it that the agency took photos of the client's presentation room long before the pitch for the business and constructed a duplicate room in which to rehearse, at a cost of $25,000. This may seem extreme. However, they got the account. As some AEs like to say, "It ain't creative unless it sells." Looking back, you can see that such attention to detail was creative.

If you need VCR or film or sound equipment, don't just ask if it's available. Test it. Make sure it's what you want. If it isn't, bring what you need, even if you have to rent it. Very few agency or corporate bosses will object to the cost of this kind of professionalism.

## Materials

Don't let your materials let you down. Have backups, extra projection bulbs, slides and so on. Why penalize yourself with potential breakdowns and the resulting embarrassment and interruption of the rhythm of your pitch when you can control your materials? And when you're checking out the room beforehand, plan where your materials will go. Are there cork walls for push-pins? Are there shelves for displaying storyboards? Easels?

## Know Costs

If you're pitching creative, for goodness sake don't neglect finding out what your creations will cost. Somebody's sure to ask you, and the little time it takes for you to call production houses for "ballpark" prices or to check with your print production and broadcast departments for equally general prices will make you look buttoned down and organized. And it will give you yet another point or two on the path to selling your ideas.

## Make Sure You Can Deliver

If you propose Madonna as the spokesperson, check and make sure she'll do it. If you propose a comedy team, make sure they're still together, will do it, and find out what the price will be. If you propose buying a piece of established music, find out who the publisher is and how much it will cost to use that music, whether it's available for use in advertising, or whether you can rewrite the lyrics.

What could be worse than bringing the house down with your wonderful campaign, to have them carry you out on their shoulders, only to find out in the cold dawn of the next day that what you proposed can't possibly be done? Nothing, that's what. Make sure you can deliver not only people and music, but also props, locations, costumes, photography and any other detail necessary to the campaign, ad or spot you're so desperately trying to sell. Make sure you can deliver.

## Get Materials Presentation-Ready

There are other things you can do to add to your comfort and make the presentation more effective. One is to paste the copy for print materials on the back of the layouts. That way you won't have to turn your back to the audience to read copy from the print or look down at a podium. You can hold the piece up, maintain eye contact and read copy all at the same time.

You can prepare your outline in 14- or 18-point type, if you're using a computer. Or you can type it out and ask your AD to blow up your outline on the photostat machine. This makes it easier to keep your place, because even with an outline you can lose your place.

If a person in another room is to run the tape or start a machine, provide a copy of your outline, so he or she will know when to be ready. Smooth executions of such things add to the aura of the rightness of the campaign.

## DURING THE PRESENTATION

These hints on how to act and what to do during the presentation will have to be learned, of course, before the presentation. You can't refer to a handbook while you're in the act of pitching. You can decide on and practice some of the following before the actual presentation.

### Sit or Stand?

Sit if possible. Most good presenters stand up; it seems to be a tradition. But often, more often than you might think, it pays to sit and pitch. In some cases, particularly with small audiences, standing up could be considered a sign of arrogance; it might be intimidating to the audience, particularly if you're a 24-year-old and they're middle-aged. When you sit, you put yourself on the same level; an audience should appreciate that. If you're more comfortable standing, however, you should do that, because the main thing is that you be comfortable.

### Get the Audience on Your Side

Tell the audience how you got the assignment, how you felt when you got it, and the research you did. Then tell them about all your false starts. Two things will happen.

1.  They'll get a kick out of your trials and tribulations and sorry efforts. And you'll be a human, not a robot presenter with a mouth full of "should" and a heart full of "give me your money."
2.  They might like one of your rejects.

Take them through the creative process with you. If this sounds a lot like telling a story, as you do in the actual materials, it's not a coincidence! This is the key to good presenting, this storytelling. First you start out with the marketing recap. But immediately, you switch to telling about your reaction to the marketing plan, where your head was at. You tell this the way you would tell your spouse or date over dinner, in conversational tones, with humorous asides, if you're capable of that.

### Get Your Concept Up Next

When you've finished giving them insights into how the creation proceeded and reveal your creative strategy, have a concept board that also shows your slogan and the signature and logo, new or old. Point to it. Talk about it. And leave it up the entire presentation, so the audience is always reminded of the overall theme you're pitching.

In fact, as you show your materials, leave them all up. Piece by piece you're building a feast for the eyes, almost like stocking the Christmas tree for kids. Color is everywhere, on materials that fill up the peripheral vision of the audience. It builds and it builds until the amount of work that went into your campaign is evident, and impressive.

## Don't Get Ahead of Yourself

Don't let the audience walk in and see your materials spread around the room. Reveal them one by one as you talk about each, so you have total focus on the job at hand. If you have the stuff all around when they walk in, they'll be reading other stuff ahead of you and not listening to you persuade them.

## Pitching Layouts and Storyboards

You and the AD have created, and lived with, the visuals for a long time. They're self-explanatory to you, as they should be to the ultimate reader when the materials are produced. But it's new to the client. You shouldn't hurry your presentation at any point, but particularly when explaining visuals. Whether you explain them, or the AD does, you should patiently and slowly point out each aspect of the visual, down to what people are wearing, if necessary.

On the print ads or outdoor or collateral materials, walk through all the visuals first, explain what they are, explain why they're there, what they do for the sell. Then read the copy, which will make a lot more sense when the audience has the visual firmly in mind.

On the storyboards, same thing. First explain the intent of the TV spot, and then panel by panel explain how the spot progresses and tell that visual story. Only when this is crystal clear do you go back and read the copy, with as much expression as you can. Normally, it helps to have the AD hold the storyboard and point to the panels as you read the copy.

## The Radio Pitch

Radio is tough to pitch from a script. If you have a flamboyant personality and don't mind taking a little kidding about the way you imitate voices or sing, then a straight pitch right from the copy can work well, because again you become a human doing his or her thing.

If the radio (or TV) has a jingle, you have another problem. It's hard to sell a jingle by reading lyrics, no matter how well you read. The best situation is to have a good demo tape of the music; but unless your agency or corporate bosses are willing to finance the jingle (and some agencies *do* finance a jingle, gambling on the client's later approval and payment), the client will have to pay for a pig in a poke. Some want to know all about the jingle before they pay for it. This could take the edge off your presentation.

If you have a demo tape of the jingle, play it every chance you have. Play a long version before the TV presentation or radio presentation, whichever comes first. And plan on several versions of radio and TV spots, so you have the excuse to play the jingle often. It takes a lot of listening to fall in love with a piece of music, and you can't expect anyone to make a judgment on music on one listening.

If you have a jingle, an effective way to pitch radio without paying demo rates for announcers or actors is for you to read the voice parts timed in between the lyrics. This can make for quite a dramatic presentation, because you're live and the music adds to the aura of show business.

## HINTS FOR HANDLING QUESTIONS AND CRITICISMS

### Know What's Important

Any copy that stops a reader's eye or brain and keeps him or her from listening to you is bad copy, no matter what argument you can come up with to the contrary. Know that. And tell the client you'll make a change, because you don't want any mental questions to keep people from reading, liking and wanting your copy.

This is not necessarily a presentation technique, though you're under more pressure in a presentation than across from the client in his or her office. As a copywriter, no matter how much you're in love with your own words — and you should have that kind of confidence — you must admit it when the copy isn't clear to the reader. You may say it's the audience's problem if they don't understand you; but if it gets in the way of selling, it's your problem. It's only smart to be open-minded about whether your copy communicates or whether the visuals communicate what you intended.

### Practice Diplomacy

If the clients don't like something, don't blow up and don't be defensive. Tell them, in your most appealing way, that "that might be a good idea. Let us go back and take a look at it." Then you can do what must be done. But don't be a wimp, either. If you disagree with a particularly stupid remark, but you know the agency doesn't want dissension, again, "take it under advisement."

Some things you just can't give in on if you know they're right and if they're essential to your basic pitch — things like the creative strategy, a great slogan, a particular slogan. If you and the agency management have agreed on these things, chances are you're right. But if you've sold the creative strategy and slogan and your creative execution, it doesn't hurt to give in on costuming, hair color, certain actors and so on. The client likes to feel creative, too. These are little things to give in on. The main thing is to sell the overall concept of your campaign.

## Protocol

It's best to address the client by his or her first name if you've been introduced that way. And most of the time you will be. Whether you're 25 or 50, you sound subservient if you call people "Mister" or "Miz" or whatever. Clients are paying full price for your talent, and for you to act humble will shake their confidence in you. You must be an equal in their eyes, or it will be hard to sell them anything.

Eye contact has a lot to do with this. Look them straight in the eye when you pitch. Stand or sit up straight and exude confidence, even if you're scared to death. It makes an audience nervous when you're nervous. Eye contact makes you look confident and makes you look honest, because it's an American feeling that people who can't look you in the eye aren't trustworthy.

On the other hand, don't maintain eye contact with and zero in on the authority at the meeting. That makes him or her feel uncomfortable, and it makes the aides (who hold a lot of power) angry.

## Ask for the Business

Don't give your pitch and stop without telling the client (or the consumer) what you want. Have in mind a specific request, a specific something you want the client to do at the end of your pitch, even if it's as simple as saying "Yes" to your campaign and authorizing the next steps on the way to production.

## PRESENTATION HINTS

- Know your subject so well you need only an outline.
- Start with a brief marketing recap.
- Check out the room before presentation.
- Make sure your materials are ready and that you have extra bulbs and other supplies.
- Know costs of production and availabilities of talent pitched.
- Sit if you can.
- Don't reveal materials ahead of time; leave them up as you pitch.
- Take criticisms seriously; learn to say you'll "take it under advisement."
- Ask for the business.

## IN CONCLUSION

Presentation is a nonmanipulative art. You don't have to feel like a snake-oil salesperson because you are making a presentation or are successful at it. In the long run, it's what you show that will sell. But the way you show it can get you over the hump. Nobody will be standing next to the ultimate consumer explaining the advertising, but you have to stand next to the client and explain the advertising if it's ever to see the light of day with the consumer. It's sad that it has to be that way, but it is. So the presentation is what will do the job. You're a guide to the materials, that's all. Remember that. It should make things easier. The important thing is to be enthusiastic and knowledgeable. There is no more powerful presentation than one that contains those two elements.

# SELECTED SHORT SUBJECTS

Inclusion in this chapter does not mean a subject is unimportant in advertising, but only that it has been touched upon briefly and needs some further explanation.

## PUBLIC RELATIONS

Public Relations (PR) is a professional field of communications that is often lumped in with the advertising business. In the general view that both disciplines are concerned with presenting the best face for commercial clients or causes, the lumping may be accurate.

But there is a real difference between PR and advertising. Advertising is out front about its aim: to sell. When ads run in print or broadcast, the space and time is reserved ahead of time and the advertising, good or bad, will run. Advertising's writing style is openly persuasive, with no apologies.

PR, on the other hand, is actually commercial journalism. The writing style for press releases and feature stories, print or broadcast, is supposed to reflect the journalistic style of the medium for which the PR writing is intended: newspaper style, magazine feature style, medical journal style and so on. And PR practitioners are never really sure their work will be printed or broadcast, which can cause stress in trying to collect fees for writings and events that may be ignored.

Although advertising can address issues of heavy import — environmental impact or product recall — PR is normally the craft that deals with all aspects of public policy, meeting with the press, staging events, announcing internal management subjects, and more.

PR uses the tools of advertising, because certain events must be advertised in print and broadcast, causing a gray area in which one is never sure whether one is involved in advertising or PR at the moment. But obviously, if the copywriter is creating a TV spot to promote a charity marathon run sponsored by a company, the copywriter employs the copywriting skills for a persuasive spot that has as its goal the communication of a PR activity.

It's not rare for an advertising copywriter to be asked in the course of his or her career to write a PR release on a variety of matters or even to sit in on plans for a PR campaign. The complete copywriter should be able to adjust to the more journalistic aspect of PR, and it would be good to take at least a basic PR course that will expose you to the drill of PR writing and conceptualizing. If you study PR in one or two courses, you'll be better educated in the field of commercial communication, and you'll have a better understanding of what your goal is when you're asked to participate in PR functions.

PR today has distinguished itself far beyond press releases and other writings; many corporations depend on PR experts in formulating policy at the highest level and in serving as the voice of the corporation to the world.

## RETAIL ADVERTISING

The philosophy of this book is that if you can write effective advertising copy for one medium, you can do it for any medium. The same philosophy holds true for different areas of advertising. In this book we have used retail advertising examples, but we haven't really examined what retail is as opposed to other forms of advertising.

In its most basic form, retail advertising is concerned with selling a product today, at a certain price, and usually in a certain local area, though a national chain like Sears or Wal-Mart could prepare an ad to run nationally. In such a case, the ad will still have to be localized as to address, specific prices in that area, and perhaps changing of inappropriate merchandise (heavy coats in Miami, for instance).

In most cases you'll be concerned with newspaper as the retail advertising medium. If you look at your newspaper, you'll see that most of the advertising is concerned with retail — department stores, car dealers, restaurants and the like. Retail also includes movies, a unique and segmented form of retail advertising, sometimes created by the movie makers themselves and sometimes by agencies that specialize in theater advertising. Retailers have been branching into radio, TV and other media, but newspaper is the main medium for retail at this time.

One of the biggest problems for a copywriter engaged in retail advertising is the fact that the ad runs today, and tomorrow you're judged on your copy by how many actual sales were made. This is tough stuff, as opposed to a Pepsi campaign that may have to run a year before it's known whether your idea was any good.

So far we've focused on agencies and corporate marketing and advertising departments as the environment in which the copywriter works. But the fact is that many, many great copywriters have begun their careers in department stores or retail advertising departments, or even as catalog writers for Sears and others. The discipline of daily writing and the pressure of selling immediately are good experience for the writer who wishes to move into the flashier and comparatively stress-free positions in agencies and corporations.

Don't blow off retail positions when you're a beginning copywriter. A year or two in a department store advertising department will not only make you a crisp, dependable writer, but will also give you valuable samples of your writing when you're ready to merchandise yourself to agencies and corporations later on.

Besides price listings, the main difference between writing retail advertising and advertising concerned with the long haul or image will be the diversity of items you'll be selling. Your goal will be, in many cases, to combine many items and their prices as well as the persuasive sell for each item under one umbrella theme for the retail outlet selling those items. But on the whole, the principles of strategy and writing enunciated in prior chapters should serve you as well for retail advertising as for a campaign to prevent forest fires.

Probably the most interesting aspect of retail is how you the copywriter become intimately involved in the production process of the newspaper. You'll find yourself checking out deadlines and space requirements with more attention than you might spend on a national magazine ad or radio. Your preoccupation with the newspaper process will stand you in good stead if you ever move on to an agency situation, because you'll know more about what you're doing if the agency is creating newspaper ads, and you'll ask sharper questions about production when you're faced with other media. Most regular advertising agencies usually don't handle much retail advertising, because the turn-around time is too fast and unprofitable for the normal agency environment.

Retail advertising is a big subject, so big that full-semester retail advertising courses are available in college advertising programs. That's why there's not much copy on the subject here.

## NEWSPAPER ADVERTISING

Though it's a massive medium controlling billions of dollars in advertising expenditures, we haven't really addressed newspaper advertising in detail in the same way we have radio, TV and magazines. The reasons for that are (1) it is mainly a retail medium (and except for the tighter, more hard sell style of copy required for retail, the principles of writing espoused in this book hold true for retail) and (2) except for certain production problems, you write an effective non-retail ad for newspapers in essentially the same way you do for magazines, and the magazine writing hints will work for newspapers.

The production problem is the biggest one for copywriters working on a newspaper ad. You still want startling graphics and great copy of the kind you would write for local, regional and national non-retail accounts. But a four-color visual you might suggest for a magazine ad would not only be incredibly expensive if used in the newspaper, but also not as effective. The reason for that ineffectiveness is rather pragmatic and requires a short explanation of *screening*. When a photograph is shot through a screen by a separator to reduce the picture to dots, black and white or color, the kind of paper the photograph is to be reproduced upon has a bearing on how many dots can be reproduced in a square inch. The more dots per inch, the sharper the photograph is when reproduced on that paper.

Newspaper paper stock is rather crude compared to what is used in magazines. The ink disperses faster on newspaper stock, because it's more porous, so the screen is normally 65 or 75 dots to the inch. On the slicker paper of magazines, the screen can be raised to 120 dots per inch, which means a more concentrated, sharper picture. And in some of the more elegant magazines, there may be 150 dots to the inch, accounting for amazingly clear reproduction of pictures.

Therefore, many art directors employ what is called *line art*, which does not have to be screened and which reproduces very well on the pulpier newspaper stock. So as the copywriter for newspaper ads, even though you're writing an ad that may appear in both magazines and newspapers with essentially the same copy, you'll frequently be concerned with a very different visual for each medium. This won't keep you out of awards shows, where the examples of creativity in newspaper are noteworthy every year — perhaps indicating how the visual limitations of the medium bring out the creative best in writers and art directors.

Newspapers have smarted from these limitations for many years and have introduced many innovative ways to reproduce color in an effective way. Most prevalent of these techniques is the Sunday magazine in color (the rotogravure), a printing process that is a bit different from other printing processes and allows for retail and other advertising to be displayed in the newspaper in effective four-color. But even there, you'll note that the paper stock is of a slicker quality than the rest of the newspaper.

Though newspapers have also introduced color printing in recent years, on the whole it has not been as satisfying to art directors as other forms of color print advertising. One of the best ways for an advertiser to run color advertising in the newspaper is to create inserts of all kinds that ride along inside the newspaper. Color quality can be controlled; they can be fun to write; and good design is possible. On the whole, writers and art directors content themselves with creating newspaper ads in competition with other black and white ads and turn their attention to the strategy, the copy, and effective graphics suitable to the medium.

# TRANSPORTATION ADVERTISING

These media include bus advertising, inside and out; **bus benches;** ads on cabs inside and out; subway advertising; bus station, airport and train station advertising; and where appropriate, trolley and cablecar advertising. Also called *transit advertising*, the discipline is similar to that of creating outdoor boards. Some jokesters like to comment on the fact that bus bench advertising is a weird idea if people are sitting on the benches, obscuring the messages. But any medium that has held up for years must have some staying power, and evidently the benches aren't always occupied.

As a copywriter, you'll be concerned with exactly what kind of transit you're creating for. Even though you might be relying on stereotypes, it still seems reasonable to assume that your audience for transit advertising will be different for an airport pylon than for the outside of a bus. This is not a sociological comment, but merely an observation based on experience with both media over the years. Transit advertising gets very specialized. The ads you write for the inside of the bus will be very different from those on the outside of the bus, because all kinds of people see the outside, but a more definable group sees the inside.

When you're writing for these media, think about exactly where your message will appear from the point of view of the viewer. You can have a rather involved message on the back of a bus, for the drivers sitting at a light with nothing else to do but read (and listen to the radio), whereas the side panels on the bus are more like moving outdoor boards, which have to communicate immediately, usually with a reminder message, perhaps mainly to pedestrians.

# PROMOTION

Another full-semester course in many college advertising curricula is called "Sales Promotion." As a copywriter you might be called upon to create advertising for this area of advertising, not realizing it is an important and specific field. You might be called upon, for instance, to create a point-of-purchase (POP) display for your soft drink account, even though you normally concentrate on radio and TV for that product. In many cases, particularly in large agencies, you will find a promotion department with its own stable of writers and art directors and production people, print and broadcast. Even in that case, because of deadlines or other problems, you might be asked to create a point-of-purchase display.

In such a case, you'll find your art director invaluable, because POPs depend most of all on how they look for their effectiveness. Research, for instance, indicates that grocery store buyers are more attracted by an open barrel of goods than they are by the same goods, at the same price, neatly shelved. So your starting point for a POP display may be based on that, or similar, psychological insight into the impulsive buying habits of shoppers. From there on it's up to you and the art director to create some arresting words and very arresting graphics that work to empty the barrel, or whatever you've chosen.

But promotion is a much bigger subject than POP. Promotions may include contests, price-off sales, giveaways, charity events, merchandise at a discount, introduction of new products (which could involve hanging a sample of a product on doorknobs), and anything else relating to a short-term, finite advertising campaign for a very specific purpose. If there is a hallmark of promotion, it's that the term of the campaign is short and comes to a definite end at some point in time.

The promotion people will normally be up on what's happening in advertising and PR for the account being serviced, and the promotion copywriter should try to incorporate the general campaign strategy and themes of the media campaigns into the promotional campaigns.

One promotion that plays off a separate client (California raisins) has been successful with Hardees. For four weeks in 1987 and six weeks in 1988, Hardees offered the popular singing raisin figures for 99 cents each, if certain food items were purchased. The fact that the promotion ran two weeks longer in 1988 than in 1987 is pretty good shirttail research telling you that the 1987 promotion was a success.

The Budweiser "Pick A Pair" of six-packs promotion began many years ago. Interestingly, it offered nothing in the way of incentive to the consumer, though it did offer an attractive display to stores selling the beer and consequent excitement. Using Johnny Carson sidekick Ed McMahon as spokesperson on radio and TV as well as in print and life-size cutouts, the promotion was a full-scale national campaign for a few weeks every year. That the idea comes back year after year is evidence that the promotion works, though some people might question the morality of urging people to buy twice as much alcohol.

## BUSINESS-TO-BUSINESS ADVERTISING

An enormous amount of advertising money is spent each year in business-to-business advertising, which used to be called "industrial advertising," a somewhat pejorative term and rather limited. "Business-to-business" is really a very good definition of the entire field. The target market is not the general public, but a business to whom the advertiser wants to sell products. That sell could be as general as Apple Computers selling to companies or as specific as a steel company selling to General Motors.

The vehicles for business-to-business advertising, for the most part, are called *trade books*, magazines devoted to a specific industry, from *Iron Age* to *Advertising Age*, from *Air Brush Monthly* to *Commercial Grocer*. Though you might think that reading one of these—outside of *Ad Age* or *ADWEEK*—would be a boring proposition, these books are read in great numbers by people in the business covered by the book.

The main medium for business-to-business advertising, magazines, has an eager and interested reader. Your advertising in that book is hitting interested eyes. If you're advertising a non-corrosive glass pipe instead of metal pipe in something called *Plant Piping*, you'd certainly catch the eye of those in the company who are charged with buying and replacing pipe that corrodes.

The Empire State Building Rose 5 Times Faster Than The World Trade Center.

☐ True
☐ False

Programmers Using C++ Can Be 5 Times Faster Than C Programmers.

☐ True
☐ False

Believe it or not, both statements are true. The Empire State Building soared to completion in just a year (1931); the World Trade Center opened in 1973, five years after groundbreaking.

And, AT&T's new C++ Release 2.0 boosts programmer productivity up to five times, compared to C programming. Its cornerstone is a set of advanced, object-oriented features found in C++. Among other things, C++ objects can inherit or share attributes from other objects, to help you bypass days of low-level coding and debugging.

To top it off, your favorite C tools and training are still useful, since C++ is a superset of the C language. C++ works best under UNIX® System V, the UNIX system standard, but also runs under DOS or OS/2,® for those who haven't made the switch yet. Any way you use it, C++ can put you at the pinnacle of productivity.

For source code licensing information and a technical prospectus on C++ Release 2.0, call 1 (800) 828-UNIX, extension 433.

Software For The Open-Minded.

Photo: World Trade Center reaching the 104th floor (taller than the Empire State Building).
© 1989 AT&T. UNIX is a registered trademark of AT&T.
DOS is a registered trademark of Microsoft Corporation.
OS/2 is a registered trademark of International Business Machines Corporation.

AT&T
The right choice.

**12.1**

*This announcement of a new computer programming language is aimed at a business audience.*

Business-to-business advertising may also be found on TV, in newspapers — in every medium, in fact. You don't find it as often as you find the mass appeal advertising, but you find it. You also find a large amount of business-to-business advertising in all kinds of collateral material, including films for companies. John Deere, for instance, produces dozens of films every year, in good times, for its line of tractors, harvesters and other equipment, to be shown to farmers in meetings or in feed store video displays.

It has been fashionable for the TV copywriter with the broad public awareness account to look down at business-to-business writers, which is ironic in many ways. First, the business-to-business writer must do more research and be more engineering or scientifically acute than his or her mass appeal colleagues. There is a more serious and scholarly approach to business-to-business advertising than is found in other advertising. Second, business-to-business writers, despite their more scholarly discipline, don't get paid as much or have as much status as their colleagues in mass appeal advertising. That doesn't seem fair, because in the last 10–20 years, maybe even longer, the advertising techniques for business-to-business writing have been exactly the same as for mass media. It took the business-to-business writers a long time to figure out that the purchasing agent who reads *Purchasing Weekly* during the day also reads *Time* at night and watches TV. Once that thought took hold, business-to-business advertising took its place as a creative area of advertising that looks up to no one (Figures 12.1 and 12.2).

## SPECIALTY ADVERTISING

A truly unique field, specialty advertising has come on in recent years as another surprisingly major part of advertising. There's not really a lot of copy that can go on pencils, ashtrays, "gimme" hats, notebooks and thousands of other giveaways or low-cost products carrying brand names. The success of the specialty advertising industry indicates the importance of specialty advertising as a part of the marketing mix for many companies. The people in the agency most concerned with this area can include the creative people and the account service people, but often you'll find that the promotion people are very knowledgeable on the subject.

## ALTERNATIVE MEDIA

You should be aware of some traditional alternative media, such as the sides of barns, sky-writing or banner-pulling airplanes, or Beetleboards (VW Beetles or other cars covered with advertising). Some new, and fascinating, alternative media are appearing; these include parking meter advertising and rest room advertising. It will be interesting to see if they catch on and add to the estimate of 1,500–5,000 advertising impressions a day in America.

## YELLOW PAGES

Yellow Pages account for over 6 billion dollars a year in advertising revenue, an astonishing amount that ranks the medium as one of the biggest. Yet it's not talked about much in creative courses on advertising, either graphics or copywriting. Part of the reason may be that Yellow Pages are little ads; and once you know how to write and lay out an ad, you can do it for this medium.

# Small World.

If you're doing business in today's global market, you already know how easily AT&T can bring Tokyo to Toledo or Rome to Nome. Millions of businesses, large and small, use AT&T to make doing business across the country or the ocean more like doing business across the street. Our long distance network is the world's largest and most sophisticated computer network.

That technology has enabled us to make advances that change the way business operates...from telemarketing to FAX transmission to making communication by computer as easy as a phone call.

Making everything about communication easy for your business is the reason we're here in Miami. So make AT&T your choice. We can make a world of difference for your business.

**AT&T**
The right choice.

© AT&T 1989

**12.2**

*Though this long-distance ad is aimed at a business audience, note that the copy is simple and straightforward. It's only the subject matter that might not be interesting to someone not meant to be reached by these ads.*

Another reason may be that the Yellow Pages have more stringent rules on what can be said and shown, because the Yellow Pages have established themselves as credible; they don't want to lose that credibility with actual creative selling. There is, in fact, a debate among Yellow Pages publishers these days as to whether it is a creative medium or a listing. And indeed, with the proliferation of more and more Yellow Pages because of deregulation of AT&T, some publishers have gone to color and, in some cases, little ads.

Yellow Pages are used by national advertisers, but they're mostly filled with small advertisers in a certain area — they're sometimes the only form of advertising used by small retailers and service companies. If you're ever in the position of decision making for such a small account, you'll be doing your account a favor by suggesting a look at Yellow Pages as a substantial part of its advertising, even though, like most creative people, you might want to do more media-oriented and splashy advertising.

The future of Yellow Pages promises an expansion into electronic publishing, whereby your computer will be hooked to an external database, enabling you to call up electronic Yellow Pages. This is a very exciting development, because it will only be a step from there to moving Yellow Pages, and so you will be back into the splashy creative advertising again. Yellow Pages should be studied in advertising curricula, probably more in the media and campaigns courses than in creative ones. But you should know Yellow Pages exist as a viable advertising medium.

## NAMING THINGS

Naming things is hard . . . whether it's the name of a company, product, service, cause or whatever. Strangely enough, it's not coming up with the name that's so difficult, but selling it to the client that's hard. Maybe it's because most everybody you deal with speaks English, and deep down they feel as if they could have found a name just as well as you, if they had taken the time. This is generally true of all copy, in fact, but copy (as opposed to naming) involves a unique idea and execution that may intimidate the client a lot more than a simple name. The truth is, as a creative director, Kevin Begos, once said, you can name something "Ralph" and it will work if the advertising of the name is done right. "If it doesn't work that way," he would say, "who would name a car Chevrolet these days?"

### The Strategy of Selling a Name

- Don't submit more than five names at a time. AEs or clients can reject 50 names without reason just as easily as five. So slow down the process and focus more on the quality of each name.

- Love each one you submit, or you may get stuck with a name you don't like.

- Point up your favorites by writing a slogan and a few lines of copy for them, to illustrate usage. If you have an art director involved, talk him or her into a rough logo.

- Pitch names on separate pieces of paper with a little rationale for each. This showcasing will demonstrate the respect you have (and the client should have) for each of your creations. Names in a list tend to look unimportant.

## Strategy of Creation

The very best name is the one that describes the function of the company or product. Weedeater is a good example. Gutbuster is another, for a stomach-reducing appliance. Another approach is a name with a built-in sales point, such as Janitor In A Drum, for a cleaning product. A third way to go involves historical or family values, such as Wells Fargo Bank, Boatman's Bank, McDonald's, etc. History is not too difficult, but family names don't necessarily suggest anything. They're in the "Ralph" category. Fourth, there is a tendency to place more reliance on computer-generated names than on those that are human-generated; Exxon is an example. Xerox and Unisys sound as if they have the same pedigree. These are pretty good names; but again like "Ralph," the advertising (human-generated) will have to set the tone for what they mean.

Then there are nonsense names that work pretty well if the product is good — such as Screaming Yellow Zonkers. Unfortunately, in that case, the consumers liked the name more than the product, a snack food. So there was high initial trial, but low repeat business.

Generally, naming things is fun if you work for an agency or a company and you're assigned that project. If you're a free-lancer, get a lot of money up front, because you'll have to sit through a lot of soul-searching and mind-changing, particularly if a group is making the decision.

The bad part of naming, again, is that everybody's an expert. The good part is that you are one of the everybodies.

# NEWS NOTES

A big part of advertising is the news. Yes, your eyes glaze over at the thought. You feel that way because of two factors. First, *news* is sort of a godly word in the journalism schools, kind of like *bishop*. "We need stuff like that, but keep me away from it . . . too serious," you might say. Second, it just seems sort of boring, all that stuff about elections, taxes and trade barriers. But it's only the word *news* that's stopping you, just as the word *yogurt* stops a lot of people from trying it.

Think about what news really is. Like history, it is made up of tales of great and not-so-great men and women. It's commercial gossip, when you realize the level it's been raised to. It's truly what's happening, if you'd but follow it.

## How to Be News Literate

Watch the first ten minutes of the *Today* or other morning show, at either 7 A.M. or 8 A.M. Tune in the network news on radio at 8 A.M. or 9 A.M. Read the paper for the local hot stories. Read *Time* or the *Wall Street Journal* (The Daily Diary of the American Dream). You're supposed to be interested in this; we're talking capitalism, which supports the advertising industry. At night, watch the network news and/or the news hour on PBS or CNN.

## Benefits of Being Up on the News

1. You can add to any conversation at any level of society. Being up on the news gives you an in.

2. You know more about what's going on than most people. Advertising people are supposed to be this way.

3. If you look at the favorite comedians of any era, you will find that most of the time they comment on current events, and they get laughs. Don't you want that mystique?

4. It's fun. You find a real swell little morsel on page 7 one night, and then it moves steadily toward the front of the paper, and finally it's the main story. Watergate happened that way. Copywriters, art directors and their friends would throw parties centered on a Watergate hearing or a Nixon speech.

5. News knowledge is great for elevator talk.

The news is about crazy dictators and, when it's important, rock stars. It's about evangelists gone mad, men and women doing their thing.

Copywriters have to know the news. Knowing the news is the starting point on any job. Only when you're aware of where the world is today can you start on a project that runs tomorrow. To too many people taking a course like "Radio News," the news is just something to deal with as an academic subject. No wonder all the stuff on the wire copy looks like Greek to students who have no contact with news unless actually working on it.

## News Sense

Many students have their antennae out for campus and fraternity news or any hot gossip that concerns people between the ages of 18 and 22. But the outside world, that's for old people. They seem to enjoy that stuff. "Give me the comics or the crossword puzzle . . . you want the front page? Here, I don't need it," you might say.

If you hope to be a copywriter, news interest will come to you, because it's in the nature of a copywriter to be curious about everything, including the news. In fact, the news is candy for the eyes of a copywriter, something to relax with and enjoy. And it's a source of ideas, maybe because life teaches over and over that truth is indeed stranger than fiction.

And the truth is that in a year or two you will be a copywriter, if that is your ambition. And you will naturally be dragged into obsession with the news because of the interests of those with whom you work. Why not get a head start on a big part of the copywriting life? Or get a head start on life in general, should you end up somewhere else, because those comedians who make a living making people laugh about the news are talking to an audience that knows news or else wouldn't be laughing at the comedian. That's the same audience you want to buy your products and services.

Current events. Ych! What horrible words. But again, what is news but the daily stories of men and women up to all their old (and new) tricks? Stay up with it. How can you expect to write satire about America if you don't know what's happening here?

How can you be tuned into America without knowing as much as your audience about what's going on? There's not much anyone can do at this point — unless it's your adviser — to make a learned person out of you, a person who knows history and editing and art, etc., but you can get started on a lifetime of fascination with the news — if you want to be a copywriter or ad person. Otherwise, do what you want about the news.

## IN CONCLUSION

This is the conclusion of not only this chapter, but also the strictly copywriting aspects of the book. The next chapter deals with getting a job, giving some general hints that may accelerate your search for that first job — that is, if you want to be a copywriter. This textbook has been written for what is often a required course, and if you intend to be in advertising, but not in the creative department, this book should at least give you insights into the creatives you will be dealing with.

But if you want to be a copywriter, know how hard it is to break into the field. As are all worthwhile occupations, copywriting is most rewarding in fun and money, but very difficult to get into in the first place. The three most important attributes you can bring to your intention to be a copywriter are (1) a passion to write, (2) a passion for capitalism, (3) a passion for advertising. With those assets, you can't miss, if a monstrous capacity for hard work is also part of your makeup.

I'd like to say that copywriting has been the most satisfying of several careers I've had. Though nothing compares to the rewards of teaching, teaching wouldn't be so much fun if it weren't copywriting and advertising that I teach. I've been a banker, a PR person and a practicing lawyer. Copywriting offered a unique experience, daily. Never were two days the same. You cannot get bored in this business. You can be paid well as an artist. You travel, meet great people in many areas of business, including show business, and you can enjoy star status.

There are more people who want to be copywriters than there are jobs for copywriters. But the same is true of acting and other wonderful careers. And every year new actors and new copywriters find themselves at work. If you're good, and if you care enough, there is no doubt that you can go anywhere in advertising that you desire, including what I consider to be the most intellectually stimulating craft a modern writer could want — copywriting.

# CHAPTER 13

# JOB TALK

## SHOULD YOU TRY COPYWRITING?

The good news is that although the advertising agency represents the major leagues for an advertising copywriter, and so is the hardest to get into, there are plenty of other very enjoyable copywriting jobs: for media, for corporations, for large retail stores, for broadcast production houses and for other places that will give you good samples that will enable you to get into an advertising agency eventually, if that's your goal. *Samples* is a key word, as we shall see.

The bad news is that there are too many college graduates who want entry-level copywriting positions, agency or otherwise. Though the competition is tough, any job that is worthwhile is tough to land. Tough or not, college graduates get copywriting jobs every year in agencies and corporations. Those jobs are out there.

## Is It Worth It?

In a corporation, life is usually less stressful for a writer than for people with the more traditional jobs, perhaps because most corporations are less familiar with the duties of a writer than with those of a salesperson. This is as it should be, because a writer in the broad scheme of life doesn't usually work well within the corporate structure and appreciates the freedom.

Though there is higher income and more status in being an advertising agency copywriter, the agency executives have higher expectations of a writer. It's more stressful in an agency because of those high expectations. But there's a reward for that stress: If you can make it through a few years in an agency, you'll have enough samples and experience to start your own business, go free-lance or go to another agency at a much higher salary.

You must, of course, be obsessed with copywriting to master it, to gain experience and hone your skills. But, having mastered the craft of copywriting and then tiring of it as some writers do, you won't have wasted your time. You will have been a working writer and can build on your experience in another area of commercial writing — doing anything from films to instruction manuals to magazine journalism. This is an advantage the writer has over, say, an account executive, whose skills are in managing within a structure and who has not necessarily honed a skill as easily marketable as the copywriter's.

So, is it worth it? Yes, if you're obsessed by writing in general and copywriting in particular. No, if you are anything less than obsessed, because obsession is what will give you the persistence to finally make it as a writer.

## How Do You Get In?

Ask a hundred copywriters how they got started. In most cases, it's not your typical tale of "Company comes to college, interviews for writer, hires writer." That does happen, by the way, and appears to be happening more and more when there are good times in the advertising business.

Most of the time there is a more bizarre and torturous route into copywriting, especially copywriting for an advertising agency, because breaking into agency copywriting is akin to breaking into acting. It takes a lot of determination and rejection before you land the job.

Does this mean you should start out with a bank ad department or a department store or a TV station? Maybe, as long as you're writing for a living. But if your goal is the agency, you might not be happy with any other place.

At any rate, there are some job-hunting methods that have proved to be helpful for potential entry-level copywriters, agency or otherwise.

## WHERE TO LOOK

If you want to be a copywriter in an advertising agency, get a list of agencies in the area where you want to live. The larger markets, of course, have more agencies and so more opportunity. But if you yearn to live in New Mexico, you'll find a small, excellent ad community in Santa Fe. And they exist in many other charming small markets.

You can find most American advertising agencies listed in the *Standard Directory of Advertising Agencies* (Agency Red Book). *ADWEEK* magazine publishes regional directories of agencies. In both, most information listed will give you some information about the agencies, their accounts, their billings, addresses, phone numbers and the names of people to contact in the area of creative. There is also a *Standard Directory of Advertisers* (Advertiser Red Book), which lists most American corporations who advertise and the names of the marketing and advertising people to contact. In addition, you can often get the names of agencies and corporations who might be interested in you from advertising professors, from people in the business the professors know, and from your own observations of local businesses and agencies.

It's a good idea to have a subscription to the *ADWEEK* in your area and also *Advertising Age* and to read them faithfully for a year before you start job hunting. At the end of a year you'll know the names of many agencies, who is getting a new account or losing one, and have a good idea of where you want to interview because you'll have your finger on the pulse of the market.

And, of course, you'll also respond to the corporations and agencies who come to your school to interview. Even then, you'll want to research the agency or corporation so that you'll sound intelligent in an interview.

## YOUR SAMPLE BOOK

With more than 20,000 advertising students in college today, competition is a bit more fierce than in 1965, when there were about 700. **Sample books** have been getting fancier as the competition has increased. There are now "portfolio" schools that teach college ad graduates more copywriting skills and help them, in conjunction with art director students, to put together quite impressive sample books. If you're a college ad grad and want to be a copywriter, the very best thing you can do is to attend the portfolio school. But, if you're like many college graduates who are impatient to get started or can't afford the portfolio school, you may have to do the best you can to assemble a sample book while in college.

Either way, you must have writing samples before you can interview as a copywriter. Many ad schools have a course that helps students put together a sample book. Many students work on college publications and get real samples that way. Many even do free-lance copywriting while in college and make a little money and get samples. Many do all three. But one way or the other, you must have samples to show when the agency creative director or copy chief or head writer agrees to see you.

### The Book Itself

The following is a minimum recommendation for a sample book that can expose your skills to a potential employer; it's a book that the author knows has worked for many of his students over the years. But again, the increased competition for entry-level copywriting jobs and the new portfolio schools are evidence that this sample business is getting harder every year.

Your sample book will be fine if it's a three-ring, hardcover plastic binder, which usually sells for $8–$10. If it's cheaper and flimsier than that, it looks cheap. If it's an expensive hand-tooled leather affair, it will look as if you don't need a job or are overly concerned with impression rather than substance.

## The Contents of Your Book

In my experience it's impossible to recommend a sample book that will appeal to all copy chiefs and creative directors. Some feel a copywriter should have an art director create page-size color layouts and storyboards; this is an excellent thing to do if you have the money and time. Others feel the actual writing is the most important thing, along with thumbnails for print ads, outdoor boards, collateral material and storyboards. It's this book with thumbnails that the following advice is based upon.

Whether you write all-new original advertising for your sample book or use assignments (cleaned up) on which you received "A's for original work," or a combination thereof, the contents of the book, at a minimum, should include:

- Your **resume**
- Three different newspaper ads, each with a creative strategy and slogan
- Three different magazine ads, each with a creative strategy and slogan
- Three different radio spots, each with a creative strategy and slogan
- Three different TV spots with a different creative strategy and slogan
- One campaign containing at least one each of newspaper, magazine, TV, radio, outdoor and direct mail, with a complete Creative Work Plan and slogan

Your writing samples will be most representative if you try to cover four advertising areas:

1. *Durable goods.* A campaign for cars, appliances, stereos, TVs, computers and other items costing over $300 and meant to last at least three years.
2. *Retail.* A campaign for a typical retail account — a department store, clothing store, restaurant, supermarket or other typical local newspaper advertisers.
3. *Service.* A campaign for a service such as banks, car rentals, stockbrokers, hotels — anything you can't hold in your hand or haul in a truck.
4. *Packaged goods.* A campaign for coffee, detergent, snack food — anything that comes in a package, usually in a grocery store.

If you're ambitious, there are two more areas you might include in your book:

5. *Business-to-business.* A trade campaign, mostly print, though some trade advertisers use broadcast and other media.

6. *Cause.* A campaign for the American Heart Association, the Society for Abused Children, the state's anti-littering campaign or the like.

## The Presentation of the Contents

- The cover of the sample book is best left blank; if you do write something on the cover, be sure it is neat and attractive.

- The first inside page should contain your resume.

- The order of the materials after that could start with the newspaper ads and end with the campaign.

- The creative strategy for each of the 12 ads and spots could come on an introductory page or on the copy itself; the CWP should precede the campaign.

- The thumbnails are placed at the end of the copy on print ads and outdoor ads, on a separate page for collateral materials and TV storyboards. If you can have your thumbnails drawn by someone with good drawing skills and an advertising design sense, so much the better. Be consistent with thumbnails — have them all hand-drawn or all computer-created.

- Though not necessary, many students find it attractive to use section dividers between newspaper and magazine, magazine and radio, etc.

For the vast majority of creative people who will review your sample book, the suggested format should give a true picture of your writing ability. Some of those reviewing your book — maybe the ones you most want to work for — will want ad-size layouts. To satisfy these people, you'll have to employ an art director to help you or go to a portfolio school.

An appendix at the end of this book contains examples of each type of ad and of an ad campaign from one student's sample book. These examples are typical of the sample book just summarized.

## YOUR RESUME

There's no one way to write a resume, at least for a creative person. Some resumes are wild and zany and covered with pictures; others look like a banker's application. Both can work. Following is a resume for Collette Grad in a format some people use. Be warned that there are many formats, many differences of opinion on what should be in the resume. This resume follows the school of thought that bare bones information is best, because you should save something to talk about in the interview. Those of differing opinions say write it all down and go to two pages if necessary. This resume is also of a school that says employers may seem interested in your education and talent, but that deep down they figure they can teach you copywriting, and what they really want to know is whether you're a dependable worker who could hold a job, show up on Mondays and get along with the other employees.

If you use a computer, centering your resume is easy and gives you a slightly different look without going overboard. If you type it, it's harder to center things, but worth the trouble.

# Example of a Resume

Collette Grad
1234 Main Street
Sunset, California 90045
555-500-5000

## EDUCATION

Sunset State University
BA, advertising, May 1990

*Related courses:*
Copy, graphics, media, PR, campaigns,
advertising management, retail, promotion,
bank internship, 90 hours liberal arts.

## WORK EXPERIENCE

*1987–1990*
Ski instructor, Indian Lodge, Cloudcroft, NM
(Christmas and spring breaks)

Sales rep, KLUB radio
(during school, 20 hours a week)

*1986*
Waitress, Kampus Klub

*1980–1985*
Created baby-sitting service with 2 partners,
car washing and lawn care service, drug store
soda fountain, paper route for two years

## HONORS/ACTIVITIES

High school & college paper ad manager
Dean's list, four years California Ad Club
scholarship, two years

## REFERENCES

From a professor, a banker and an advertising agency
creative director upon request

# Breaking Down the Resume

Let's investigate the parts of the resume (remember, this is only one way to go).

**Name and Address**    It's confusing and temporary looking to have both your school and home address. Most people only have one address. Don't you want to look settled rather than desperate? If in school, use the school address. If living at home, use that address. Everybody's got to be someplace, one place, at a time.

**Objective**    Because you may interview for a variety of different jobs as a writer — from a department store to a TV station to an agency — why use an objective? If you do, keep it simple: JOB OBJECTIVE: Copywriter. They all know what that means.

   Above all, don't write senseless blather that goes something like "Looking for an entry-level position that will enhance my abilities and sick sick sick . . ."

**Education**    When you have been in the business a little while, this part will go down near the bottom, with your job experience in advertising up at the top. But at this point, your education should probably come next. Keep it short and factual. If you have a high GPA, it's okay to list it, though many creative people don't care as much about that as about your samples.

**Activities and Honors**    Honors are honors and list them, but make sure they're true honors. Activities are tricky. You say a lot about yourself by what you list here. Any activity relevant to writing or advertising makes sense, even PR officer of a social organization. But beware the plain listing of Greek organizations; most of the people you interview with were not in such organizations and may resent you for this. Still, if your position in the Greek organization was as president or relevant to advertising, consider mentioning it. Consider carefully whether to list activities that were good for points in your fraternity or sorority, but really don't mean anything to the interviewer, such as campus tour guide.

**Work Experience**    This is a hot area. List all your work experience, down to your own babysitting or lawn service when you were 12 years old. Create a history of a hard-working individual, with a variety of jobs, no matter how insignificant to you. It's very significant to your interviewer that you're not a couch potato, in terms of work, that you understand the importance of working and being on time and all that important stuff. A long list of your jobs will be quite valuable and will spark conversation in an interview.

**Health**    Forget it. Who's going to say on a resume: "Well, frankly, I haven't been feeling too good lately . . ."?

**Interests**    If it's bee-keeping or advertising research or playing center field for the Yankees part of the year — fine. But it's hard to see how reading and skiing and surfing add much that interviewers don't see all the time.

**References** It might be arrogant and jumping-the-gun to list names and addresses. And it could be dumb, because the interview may require a different kind of reference from what you thought. Some people say, "References available on request," and that's okay, if uncreative. There's another way, such as, "References from a presidential candidate, a billionaire and a professor on request." You get the point. It's a detail, but you're doing something a little different in a minor part of your resume that says you will be a careful person down to the last dotted "i" on an ad.

## Selling Yourself

Please be careful about slavishly following the suggestions just made. Advertising is the craft of being original for a living. That originality extends to cover letters and resumes as well, and as a creative person you might be able to come up with something much better. Here you are, trying to sell yourself. If you can't sell yourself in an original way, how can you expect people to hire you to sell products you know even less about than yourself?

What has just been suggested is safe, simple and a bit different from the run-of-the-mill resume. That's all you can say about it. As with anything else, it's the substance and not the form that matters. Your substance lies inside you and is expressed through your sample book.

## BEFORE YOU WRITE A COVER LETTER

With a resume and a sample book, you have all you need for a job interview. Some students are taught to send out resumes with **cover letters** to everybody in the world, long before graduation, like throwing a hundred baited hooks into the water when fishing. And truthfully, sometimes it works. Sometimes you catch an interview.

But on the whole, you have a better shot at a job when you can get an interview without a cover letter and can show your samples in person, rather than when yours is one of the hundreds of resumes and cover letters that come unsolicited through the mail to creative directors every spring and end up in the wastebasket.

## Getting an Interview without a Cover Letter

How do you get in to see the interviewers without going through the resume and cover letter ritual? If you're a copywriter, you're creative, so be innovative about making contacts. There are certain basic approaches you can try:

- Get the name of the person you want to see. It will probably be the creative director or copy chief or a creative group head of some kind. Call the agency or corporation and make sure that person still works there, because advertising people in both agencies and corporations move around a lot.

- A few days later, call that person. And call and call and call until that day when the secretary is out and you get the person directly. Most creative people have a soft spot for you, though there are some who've forgotten what it's like for you. Forget them; they'd be lousy bosses anyway.

- Tell the person you want to "show your samples." If she or he says, "Well, we don't have any openings," ask the person to see you anyway, because you want some advice. The people who do remember what the job-hunting procedure is like normally welcome the opportunity to play mentor and critique your work.

## What Can Happen

- One, there actually may be a job—they just didn't want to admit it. And if your samples are good and you come through the interview without doing something appalling, you might get that job. It's happened.

- More often, and always assuming your work has promise, the person you talk with may recommend you call one of his or her friends in the business, and this is invaluable. When you call that recommended person and say, "Bill Bigshot over at XYZ agency said to call you," you can get through the secretary and into an interview.

- Maybe you'll repeat the process there.

- For some people, this goes on for a year or two, and in the meantime they make money to live on by waiting tables, etc. This contradicts the natural progression of life after college as espoused by parents and friends; but if you're obsessive about being a copywriter, you can't get off on some other career track without diluting your passion to achieve your goal.

- For others, a job pops up when they least expect it.

## YOUR COVER LETTER

There are times, however, when a cover letter enters the picture. Perhaps one of those phone calls resulted in "I'm interested in seeing you, but send me your resume first." That requires a cover letter. Perhaps you called a company recommended by a professor or a parent or friend, or you saw a company job listing on the bulletin board, so you know there is interest in hiring a writer. That requires a cover letter to go with your resume.

Perhaps the perfect agency or corporation exists in a town you want to live in; and though you have no invitation from them or knowledge of a job opening, you want to try to get into that specific company. To let the company know that you've picked them out of all the others, that you did research about them, send an unsolicited cover letter and resume; they might be flattered by your attention.

These are legitimate reasons to write a cover letter. But there's no good reason to send out resumes and cover letters months in advance to every advertising agency there is, because agencies often do not know in advance what their needs are going to be. Agencies have interviewed a good writer on a Monday, but had no job to offer, and then by Tuesday had a job and hired the next good writer who walked in. It's dumb luck. On Monday night the agency got a new account and needed a writer right away. Some writers have been hired on Monday and fired on Tuesday, because on Monday night the agency lost the account.

## The Thrust of a Cover Letter

Your cover letter should be the best piece of copy you ever wrote. It's about you, so no research is necessary. And it describes how you can be of benefit to the agency or corporation, not how you're looking for a place to start and begin a career on their money. It's about how they'll help themselves by hiring you to do this and that . . . for not very much money. To paraphrase President Kennedy, tell not what the company can do for you, but what you can do for the company.

Some writers and a lot of art directors go hog-wild with cover letters and resumes, coming up with all sorts of direct mail or other wild pieces that set them apart from the competition. These are not the resumes and cover letters you find coming out of college placement offices, but they work for those who are truly creative.

At the least, your cover letter, with resume attached, should knock them over with your writing. The point you're trying to make is how good you are at the job you want—as a writer—so why not illustrate exactly how good you are? The cover letter should never be one form letter that you duplicate, but should be tailored to the specific company you're sending it to.

## Sample Cover Letter

Let's assume that Ace Advertising of Denver is a place you have your eye on, and you decide to send them a resume and a cover letter without being asked, with the goal of getting them to grant you an interview. You've done your research and find that Ace has several good accounts, including Stormy Airlines, First Denver Bank and the Denver Broncos football team. You've also determined that the person to talk to is the copy chief, Mr. Kop E. Chief.

It is a small agency, 10 million dollars in total billings, which is a very respectable size. Following is a sample of how your cover letter to them might sound, assuming you fit the background of the person writing the letter. Obviously, your own background will be the key to the letter. Keep in mind that this is a cover letter sent without request. Had you contacted them and had they invited you in for an interview, you would not need a cover letter, because you would be there in person.

Sure, that letter has a lot of coincidences in it, apparently, and maybe it is an exaggeration in some respects, given her skiing ability and the experience in banking. But the point is, you must find some sort of similar linkage in your letter so that you'll stand out among the prosaic majority of letters that every company receives every spring. It doesn't take a great deal to stand out compared to the other people. All you need is an edge.

Collette Grad
1234 Main Street
Sunset, California 90045
555-500-5000


4/11/91


Mr. Kop E. Chief
Ace Advertising
5678 Elm Street
Denver, Colorado 34567


Dear Mr. Chief:

Would you hire a water baby as a copywriter? I look out the window and what do I see? Miles and miles of nothing but the Pacific Ocean. This is Sunset, home of Sunset State U, where I have majored in advertising. Sunset, Oceanville, U.S.A.

But east of here is New Mexico, where I've taught skiing the past three years in Cloudcroft. How did a surfer learn to ski? With persistence, Mr. Chief, raw persistence.

With the kind of dedication and hard work I can bring to your shop, I believe. And I bring some experience in banking, airlines and football. I was an intern in a local bank's ad department, I've flown over the mountains and I've been a football cheerleader.

I'm eager to show you my book, and I'll fly to Denver on my own dime for the opportunity. From what I've read about your agency it's a busy place. So I'll call you next week to see if you'll meet with me. Even if you don't have a slot open right now, I'd appreciate your advice on breaking into the Denver market.

I hear there's some skiing there.


Sincerely,


Collette Grad

---

Many — too many — cover letters start out with something like "I want to locate in a growing agency that will help me develop my career goals." What poppycock! The company is not a charity. It isn't waiting around for you to graduate. They will hire graduates, however; they must to stay vigorous. But it is the graduate who writes the strong cover letter, like a piece of well-smithed copy, who will get the nod, if anybody gets a nod from unsolicited letters.

Note that the letter is short. There's no need to tell a life story here. Besides, your intent is to write a punchy piece of copy that results in an interview. Don't start philosophizing in a cover letter.

Why should Collette spend her own money to go up there? One, she wants to show how passionate she is about that city. It has to be flattering to them. Two, there are several universities near Denver sending students to interview, and their travel doesn't cost the agency a cent.

The very best way to accomplish Collette's goal would be for her to graduate, create a sample book at a portfolio school, move to Denver, find a place to live, temporary or permanent, wait tables if necessary, bug Chief on the phone, then go see him with book in hand. No cover letter, no blind solicitation. And Collette would receive more attention for indicating her preference for living in Denver, and moving in, than would somebody stopping by to visit who is "willing to relocate." Those people seem to be fishing, and impermanent.

If you've been encouraged to write a cover letter to a company, you should do the same research about the company ahead of time and craft a letter much like the one above. The only difference will be that you don't have to talk about getting advice in case there is no job open, because in this letter you were encouraged to write about a job that is available to someone.

## JOB-HUNTING HINTS

- Be obsessed with a career of writing in general and copywriting in particular.
- While working on your big break, either wait tables or at the least take a job that requires writing.
- Create a good sample book; go to a portfolio school if you can afford it.
- Create a resume.
- Try to get personal interviews instead of writing and sending cover letters willy-nilly.
- If a cover letter is called for, think of it as the best piece of copy you will ever have to write.
- If sending an unsolicited cover letter, ask for advice if there is no job open.
- As for what to wear and what to say in an interview — be yourself. That's what you're selling. If they don't like what you are and how you act, there will be no job regardless of your pure talent.

## IN CONCLUSION

Job hunting is a necessary evil. After all the work you've done to get your degree, it doesn't seem fair that you now have to knock yourself out to get a chance to prove what you can do. But life isn't fair. Know that the graduates who really want jobs get them eventually.

It's important that you hold out for what you want. I'm not kidding about waiting tables. If you take a job that isn't what you want, then you run the risk of being unhappy in a couple years, a couple of years in which you haven't gained experience in what you want to do.

That means you will start over again at the bottom in experience, even though you're older and have a family and a mortgage by then. It's better to take temporary jobs to keep you alive until the right opportunity comes along. It will, if you're the right sort and if you concentrate on the perfect job, not on a lot of money. Once you get a perfect job for you, at any pay scale, and master that job, the money will come. (If money is the main thing to you, that's fine. But get out of advertising and into real estate, or at least get out of the creative side of advertising. It takes four or five years of creative experience to start pulling in the big bucks. And they are big, with experience and talent.)

Good luck.

## EXERCISES

1.  Prepare a resume for yourself.
2.  Find an agency or corporation in a city where you want to live and create an unsolicited cover letter to go with your resume.

ACCOUNT EXECUTIVE:   (1) In an advertising agency, the person most concerned with a specific client liaison, budgeting, media, coordinating members of the account team and initiating job orders or changes on behalf of the client; (2) in media sales, a salesperson or sales representative.

ACCOUNT SUPERVISOR:   Supervisor of account executives, with responsibility for more than one advertising account.

AD MANAGER:   Client-side person responsible for coordinating with the advertising agency and/or directing activities of the advertising department.

AGENCY:   As used in this book, refers to an advertising agency.

ANNC:   Announcer, usual indication on a radio spot for a person not playing a character role.

ART DIRECTOR:   The strategic equivalent of a copywriter in conceptualizing, with specific art skills in the execution phase.


BASHING:   Denotes creating conflict in an ad or spot by making sport of an ethnic, sexual, racial, geriatric or other recognizable group.

BROADCAST PRODUCTION:   The process by which radio and TV spots are taken from script form to finished production.

BUS BENCH:   As used in this book, advertising on bus benches.


CAMPAIGN:   A series of ads and/or commercials with a common strategy, slogan and graphic look, meant to run over a short or indefinite period of time.

CLIENT:   The company or person paying an advertising agency to create and place advertising; often refers to an employee such as the ad manager or director of marketing.

COLLATERAL MATERIALS:   Non-commissionable advertising such as direct mail, annual reports, give-aways, point-of-purchase displays, business films, etc.

COMPETITOR RESEARCH:   Research on what the competitors of your client are doing in their advertising, and/or research on all products and services and social trends that may impede sales of your product or service.

COMPREHENSIVE LAYOUT:   A newspaper, magazine or other print layout depicting as closely as possible how the final effort will look.

CONSUMER RESEARCH:   Research on the target market to determine the demographics and psychographics and other lifestyle factors necessary to pinpoint the ultimate consumer.

COPY POINTS:   Things the client thinks make his or her product or service worth buying. Could be anything from a sale to a unique ingredient. Usually support a strategy as a reason why.

COPYWRITING:   The act of creating ads and spots and collateral materials that satisfy a creative strategy, whether through writing or thinking or both.

COVER LETTER:   An intense piece of copy about yourself and the potential employer that accompanies a resume when mailing it to a prospective employer.

CREATIVE:   As used in this book: (1) an art director or copywriter; (2) the ability to be an art director or copywriter.

CREATIVE DIRECTOR:   The person in charge of art directors, copywriters, print and broadcast producers. Usually a former copywriter or art director. Occasionally the agency owner or former print or broadcast producer.

CREATIVE EXECUTION:   As opposed to creative strategy, the actual print and broadcast materials that bring the creative strategy to life.

CREATIVE STRATEGY:   The "big idea" behind an advertising campaign; the unique advantage to the ultimate consumer of buying this product or service; the answer to "Buy this product or service because . . ."

CREATIVE WORK PLAN (CWP):   A formal list of informational items that guide the advertising agency in creating an ad or advertising campaign.

CU:   In television tape or film, a close-up.

CUT:   In television tape or film, the instantaneous movement from one scene to another or one viewpoint to another.

DIALOGUE:   Words spoken by a character or characters in some sort of plot.

DISS:   In television tape and film, a slow transition of one scene or viewpoint to another, one picture slowly fading as another slowly comes on.

DOLLY:   In television tape and film, the movement of the entire camera toward or back from an object, scene or person.

DOWN-SHOT:   In film or television, refers to a camera angle shooting downward from overhead.

DURABLE GOODS:   As traditionally explained, goods costing more than $300 and expected to last more than three years, from stereos to cars to appliances and more.

ECU:   Extreme close-up of a person's face; a camera shot.

EXTENDIBILITY:   The potential for an advertising campaign to continue with new and different executions under the same creative strategy.

EXTENSION:   Something added to an outdoor board, usually on top, that extends the graphics contained on the board proper.

FLASH FORWARD SOUND CUT:   The sound from the next scene comes on before the present scene is over.

FORMAT:   As used in this book, the normally acceptable form for copy on a print ad, broadcast script or collateral material.

GRAPHICS:   Loosely, anything in a print ad outside of the words; and in the case of unusual typographical approaches, includes the words themselves. Can refer to anything from design to print production. In television, art or words that show up on the screen.

INST.:   Abbreviation for instrumental music in a broadcast spot.

JOB ORDER:   What the account executive writes to the research, media and creative departments when asking for work to be done for a client.

LOGO:   Originally, a "logotype" was a unique signing of the client name; now it refers to a graphic integrated into the client name or a separate graphic accompanying a signature.

LS:   In television tape or film, a long shot, whether full figure of a person or shot of a mountain.

MARKETING DIRECTOR:   Often the chief person in a corporation responsible for all communication and sales, and normally the boss of the advertising director.

MCU:   In television tape or film, a medium close-up, between a medium shot and a close-up.

MECHANICAL:   The pasted-down type and pictures on print advertising, in a form ready to be made into a negative or engraving. Also called a paste-up.

MEDIA PERSON:   Someone involved in planning and buying media on a specific advertising account.

MS:   In television tape or film, a medium shot, from the waist up.

MUSIC PERSON:   Normally the music producer who conceives the melody line for the lyrics a copywriter writes and conducts the musicians in the recording session.

OUTDOOR:   A billboard, in popular terminology.

PACKAGED GOODS:   A category of advertising referring to products that come in a package, usually grocery items.

PAINTED BULLETIN:   An outdoor board that is painted rather than printed.

PAN:   In television tape or film, the movement of the camera itself from left to right or right to left.

PANEL:   One of the scenes on a storyboard.

PASTE-UP:   A mechanical.

PITCH:   Any presentation asking someone to buy something.

POINT-OF-PURCHASE:   Advertising created to influence consumers where the products or services are available, most noticeable in grocery stores, hardware stores, etc.

PRE-PRODUCTION:   The activities that take place before a radio or TV production.

PRIMARY RESEARCH:   Research that starts at zero and proceeds in the directions dictated by the project.

PRINT PRODUCTION:   Rendering print materials into printable form.

PRODUCTION ARTIST:   One who gets print materials ready for the printing process.

PRODUCT RESEARCH:   Researching the assets and liabilities of the product or service you are charged with selling.

QUICK CUTS:   In television tape and film, a series of scenes in one- or two-second bursts, usually to a music track.

RESEARCH PERSON:   A person in the agency, corporation or independent research house who is concerned with your account and conducts whatever activities are necessary to get you the information you need.

RESUME:   A clean and quick detailing of your work experience, education and life, used as a basis of discussion for a potential employer.

RETAIL:   The common name used for local newspaper advertising; also means a business that sells a service or a product to be carried off by the purchaser. Also used to denote local business advertising in media other than newspaper.

ROUGH LAYOUT:   A print advertisement rendered in actual size but with economy of effort.

SAMPLE BOOK:   That which an art director or copywriter takes with him or her to get a job, a book which shows the creative abilities of that individual.

SECONDARY RESEARCH:   Research on information already in existence, whether encyclopedia or trade magazines or whatever.

SEGUE:   A radio term meaning to move from dialogue or music or sound effects into some other sound.

SERVICE ADVERTISING:   Advertising that is non-product, such as banking or car rentals.

SFX:   Sound effects.

SHELF LINERS:   Ads on grocery shelves that promote a product below or above.

SHILL:   As used in this book, a person supposed to be a character who is actually acting as an announcer.

SIGHT:   The designation in a TV script above the visuals, called "Video" by most of the world.

SIGNATURE:   The client's name and logo, if there is a logo.

SLOGAN:   A snappy distillation of the creative strategy, affixed to all ads and spots.

SNAPPER:   The ending to the body copy, print or broadcast, that is humorous, moving, philosophical or otherwise a twist.

SNAP ZOOM:   In television tape or film, a zoom in or out that gives the sensation of a violent change.

SNORKLE LENS:   A camera lens on the end of a flexible cable used in television and film to get in among small objects.

SOUND:   The designation in a TV script above all the sounds that will be heard in the spot.

SPOT:   The correct way to refer to a TV or radio commercial.

STORYBOARD:   A series of visuals (called panels) showing the high points of a TV spot, with copy, SFX and music described beneath each panel, to show a client what a TV spot will look like.

SUPER:   (1) a verb meaning to flash words on the screen in a TV spot; (2) a noun meaning the words that are shown on the screen over another scene or by themselves.


TARGET MARKET:   The specific people a specific piece of advertising is trying to sell.

THUMBNAIL:   Small little drawings, crudely done, that illustrate what print or broadcast advertising might look like.

TRANSITION LINE:   In print advertising, the line of copy that comes after the headline and before the earnest sell in an ad. It attempts to explain the picture and headline and introduce the copy that is to come.
up in sections, like wallpaper.

TRUCK:   The movement of a TV camera or film camera from left to right and right to left without moving the lens.

24, 30-SHEET POSTER:   Outdoor boards that are pre-printed and pasted up in sections, like wallpaper.


UP-SHOT:   In film or television, refers to a camera angle shooting upward from the ground.


VOICE-OVER (VO):   The equivalent of an announcer on TV.


ZOOM:   In television tape or film, the movement of the camera *lens*, not the camera, as in a dolly, into or out from the subject of the shoot.

# A P P E N D I X

This appendix presents representative selections from the contents of one student's sample book. In addition to a resume, the following pages contain examples of each type of ad (newspaper, magazine, radio, and TV) and of an ad campaign. A complete sample book should contain at least three examples of each type of ad in addition to the ad campaign. See pages 241–243 for a complete discussion of the sample book and its contents.

**CHERYL GAULT**

P.O. Box 13841 UNT
Denton, Texas 76203
(817) 566-6608

## EDUCATION

University of North Texas
Denton, Texas
BA  R/TV/F, Advertising
May 1991

Related Courses:
Copy, commercial production, campaigns,
media, advertising sales, corporate video,
free lance script writing,
internship with ABC Films, Volcanic Films.

## WORK EXPERIENCE

Advertising Sales Rep, North Texas Daily- 1991
Copywriter/Production Assistant,
Sammons Communications, INC.- 1990
Waitress, Chili's Restaurant- 1989
Dining Director, Matthew's Restaurant- 1988
Activity Instructor, Child's Play Day Care- 1988
Dining Director, Luna's Restaurant- 1987-1988
Product Scanner, Jamail's Grocery- 1984-1986

## HONORS/ACTIVITIES

Gamma Beta Phi National Honor Society- 1986-1988
Dean's List
Chi Omega Scholarship recipient- 1988 & 1990
Alpha Epsilon Rho (R/TV/F society)  1987-1990
Member of North Texas Ad Club- 1990-1991

## REFERENCES

From a professor, a producer/director,
and an advertising manager upon request.

NORDSTROM CLASSIC TIES
MAG., 4 COLOR, BLEED
"KNOT BAD"
CREATIVE STRATEGY: To promote status and self worth,
by wearing a Nordstrom Classic Tie.

Cheryl Gault

HEAD:                             TIE ONE ON FOR SIZE.

PIC:                              (FOUR DIFFERENT TIES ARE
LAID OUT ON A PLATFORM. A
WOMAN'S HAND REACHES OUT
TO TOUCH THE TIE ON THE FAR
RIGHT SIDE)

COPY:                            When you visit Nordstrom's
Men's Department, you'll find yourself
doing a lot of oohing and ahhing over our
ties.
                 With the newest in floral and
paisley silk prints, you simply will knot
know which to choose.
                 But no matter what style
you become tied-down to, you'll certainly
look impressive in one of Nordstrom's
Classic Ties.
                 They're sure to leave her
breathless.

SIG:                              Nordstrom Classic Ties.
SLOGAN:                      Ties to satisfy.

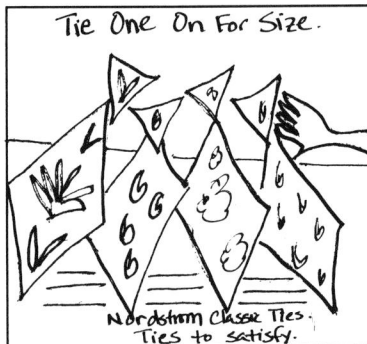

HOLIDAY INN
NWSP., HALF PAGE, B&W
"SWEET DREAMS"
CREATIVE STRATEGY: To show that Holiday Inn is striving
to make hotel stays as comfortable
as possible.

Cheryl Gault

HEAD:                          ROOM, SWEET ROOM.

PIC:                           (A LARGE SIGN, HANGING ON
                               A NICELY WALLPAPERED WALL)

COPY:                                  Whenever you stop for the night
                               at a Holiday Inn, you'll probably be
                               surprised at how "at home" you'll feel.
                                       There's a reason for that.
                                       Holiday Inn has redecorated,
                               and we think you'll be impressed. You
                               see, we want you to be as comfortable
                               in your hotel room as you would in your
                               own. Even if it *is* for just one night.
                                       And everything is picked up in
                               our rooms!
                                       So check in to a Holiday Inn. You might
                               come to think of us as your second home.

SIG:                           HOLIDAY INN
SLOGAN:                        Your <u>new</u> home, away from home.

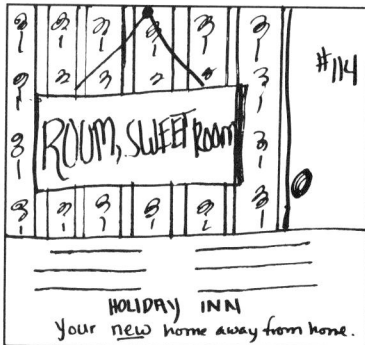

HOUSTON NETWORK
:30 RADIO
"TIME IS MONEY"
CREATIVE STRATEGY: To promote Houston Network's
lower long distance rates.

Cheryl Gault

| | |
|---|---|
| ANNC: | Do your long distance calls sound like this? |
| SFX: | (PHONE RINGS) |
| SUE: | Hello? |
| LARRY: | Sue! |
| SUE: | Larry, it's so good to hear from you. I was just thinking ... |
| LARRY: | Oh, sorry Sue. Gotta go. This call is costing me a <u>fortune</u>. Bye! |
| SFX: | (CLICK) |
| ANNC: | Don't be cut short by high rates, put your money where your mouth is, at Houston Network. Our rates are 25% lower than the other guys. And we do everything we can to make your dollar stretch from here to there. So your calls can sound more like this. |
| SFX: | (RING) |
| SUE: | Hello? |
| LARRY: | Sue, it's Larry again. Listen, I have <u>so</u> much to tell you, I... |
| SUE: | But Larry, I have to eat dinner. |
| LARRY: | Oh, that's okay. I'LL WAIT. |
| ANNC: | Houston Network. We'll put <u>less</u> money where your mouth is. |

Chezee's Ice Cream Parlor
Self Mailer, 4 pg, 2C
"It's Big"
CREATIVE STRATEGY:  To convince consumers that by coming to
Chezee's for ice cream, you will receive a
larger amount of ice cream, as well as
everything else (more helpings of candy bars
and bigger cones) than you would by going
to any other parlor.

Cheryl Gault


(Page One)
CHEZEE'S ICE CREAM PARLOR
SELF MAILER, 4pg, 2C
Cheryl Gault


COVER   (page one)

HEAD:                              THE ICE CREAM THAT ATE EL PASO.

PIC:                               (A BIG TRIPLE SCOOP OF ICE CREAM
                                   WITH A FAINT DRAWING OF A CITY
                                   IN THE BACKGROUND. FLAVORS AND
                                   CONE ARE SCRATCH -N-SNIFF.
                                   FLAVORS:   BANANA PUDDING SWIRL
                                              WHITE CHOCOLATE MOUSSE
                                              HONEY DIPPED CONE)

PAGE TWO: (upper column)

HEAD:                              WHAT IS BIG?

PIC:                               (LARGE CONTAINERS OF ICE CREAM
                                   AND A SCOOPER DRIPPING WITH ICE
                                   CREAM TO THE SIDE)

COPY BLOCK "A":                        Texas is a big state, with a lot of
                                   big things in it:
                                       Big Tex.
                                       Big steaks.
                                   And big ice cream, at Chezee's Ice
                                   Cream Parlor.
                                       We'd be dern tickled to give
                                   you a huge helping of our homemade,
                                   sinfully sweet-tasting ice cream that
                                   comes in 10 (please don't drool on
                                   the card) flavors.

Chezee's will be sure to fill
you up, Texas style. And we'll
keep you coming back for more!

PAGE TWO: (lower column)

HEAD:                                   GIVE US THE GOODS!

PIC:                                    (AN ARRAY OF BRAND
                                        NAME CANDY BARS)

COPY BLOCK "B":                          Because big appetites have
                                        big imaginations, Chezee's has lots
                                        of goodies for you to help create a
                                        monster of an ice cream!
                                        We've got whole candy bars
                                        waiting to be cut up and mixed into
                                        big chunks, to give your ice cream
                                        shape.
                                          Boy, will it have shape!

PAGE THREE:

HEAD:                                   ICE CREAM-WARE.

PIC:                                    (BIG WAFFLE CONES LINED UP)

COPY BLOCK "C":                          And how else are you going to hold
                                        all that ice cream together except in one
                                        of Chezee's dee-licious honey dipped
                                        cones!
                                          You may have to hold one of these
                                        wranglers with two hands, because of
                                        their incredibly LARGE size... or even
                                        to balance your ice cream!

COPY BLOCK "D":                          So come in to Chezee's Ice Cream
                                        Parlor with this coupon, for some heel-
                                        kicking, foot-stomping good ice cream.
                                        And don't worry, we will fill you up.
                                             Because at Chezee's,
                                        we don't want you to go away hungry.

SLOGAN:

COUPON:

----------------------------------------------------------------------------------------------

(COPY BLOCK "E")                    For a whoppping big scoop,
                                    and a heck of a deal, bring in this
                                    coupon to Chezee's Ice Cream Parlor
                                    to get a monstrous scoop of ice cream,
                                    any flavor, for only 12 cents.
                                    Chezee's Ice Cream Parlor.

----------------------------------------------------------------------------------------------

PAGE FOUR:

UPPER LEFT:                         A Big Deal At:
                                    CHEZEE'S ICE CREAM PARLOR
                                    1212 Kings Drive
                                    El Paso, Texas   79912
                                    (915) 584-4295

ADDRESS:                            (MAILING LABELS FROM
                                    MAILING LIST)

UPPER RIGHT:                        (FIRST CLASS POSTAGE)

266

Appendix

Page Four

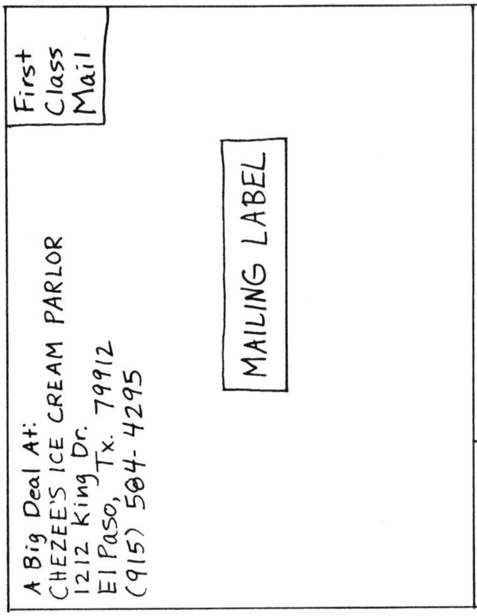

First Class Mail

A Big Deal At:
CHEZEE'S ICE CREAM PARLOR
1212 King Dr.
El Paso, Tx. 79912
(915) 504-4295

MAILING LABEL

Page One

Banana Pudding Swirl

White Chocolate Mousse

Chocolate Suicide

THE ICE CREAM
THAT ATE EL PASO.

Page Two

"A"

"B"

Page Three

"C"

"D"

We don't want you to go away hungry!

"E"

CHEZEE'S ICE CREAM PARLOR.

FIRST ALERT RECHARGEABLE FLASHLIGHT
:30 TV
"WATCH OUT"
CREATIVE STRATEGY: To show consumers how easy it is to
use the First Alert Flashlight when you
don't have to worry about batteries.

Cheryl Gault

| SIGHT | SOUND | |
|---|---|---|
| 1. OPEN ON NIGHT SCENE, MS WOMAN IN KITCHEN WASHING FRUIT. LIGHTS GO OUT. CAN STILL SEE HER SHADOW. | WOMAN: | Honey, grab the flashlight, will you? We blew another fuse. |
| 2. WOMAN REACHES FOR MATCHES AND A CANDLE. LIGHTS IT. | MAN: | Okay, just a sec. I've gotta find some batteries. |
| 3. CUT TO CU WOMAN'S FACE. | WOMAN: SFX: MAN: | (SIGH) (THUD) Ouch! |
| 4.WOMAN ACTS CONCERNED | WOMAN: | Honey? |
| 5. CUT TO WIDE ANGLE, SUBJECTIVE SHOT OF MAN FUMBLING AROUND IN THE DARK. THE OBJECTS IN THE HOUSE ARE VISIBLE, BUT VERY DIMLY LIT. | MAN: SFX: MAN: | No problem, just stubbed my toe. (REOW!!!!) Stupid cat! |
| 6. CUT TO MS WOMAN, WHO SEES THE FLASHLIGHT NEARBY, AND GRABS IT. | WOMAN: | Uh, honey? |
| 7. MLS WOMAN WALKING THROUGH THE HOUSE, WITH THE FIRST ALERT FLASHLIGHT. | SFX: | (PIANO CLANKING, SOUND OF CRASHING BOXES) |

| SIGHT | SOUND | |
|---|---|---|
| 8. CUT TO MCU, OVER-THE-SHOULDER SHOT OF WOMAN ENTERING A ROOM, TO FIND HUBBIE ON GROUND, SURROUNDED BY BOXES. | | |
| 9. CUT TO CU MAN ON THE GROUND. | MAN: | Found the batteries? |
| 10. CUT TO CU WOMAN. | WOMAN: | Nope. Found our handy First Alert Rechargeable Flashlight instead. No batteries, remember? |
| 11. CUT TO CU MAN. | MAN: | Oops. |
| 12. LIGHTS TURN ON AGAIN. | MAN & WOMAN: | Ugh! |
| 13. CUT TO MLS BOTH. | | (LAUGHTER) |
| 14. DISSOLVE TO SUPER: | | |
| The First Alert Rechargeable Flashlight Batteries Not Included. | VO: | The First Alert Rechargeable Flashlight. Batteries not included. |

1)

1a.)
WOMAN: Honey, grab the flashlight, will you? We blew another fuse.

2)
MAN: Okay, just a sec. I've gotta find some batteries.

3)
WOMAN: (SIGH)
SFX: (THUD)
MAN: Ouch!

4)
WOMAN: Honey?

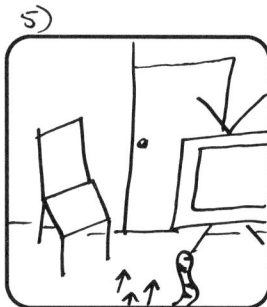

5)
MAN: No problem, just stubbed my toe.
SFX: (REOW!!!)
MAN: Stupid cat!

6)
WOMAN: Uh, honey?

7)
SFX: (PIANO CLANKING, SOUND OF CRASH-

8)
ING BOXES)

9)

MAN: Found the batteries?

10)

WOMAN: Nope. Found our handy First Alert Rechargeable Flashlight instead. No batteries, remember?

11)

MAN: Oops.

12)

MAN & WOMAN: Ugh!

13)

14)

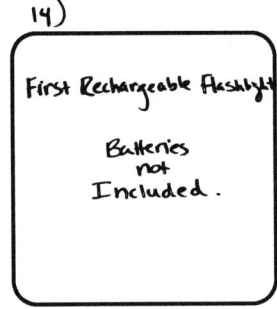

First Rechargeable Flashlight

Batteries not Included.

VO: The First Alert Rechargeable Flashlight. Batteries not included.

CREATIVE WORK PLAN
Cheryl Gault
23 November 1990


1). CLIENT: Global Recycling Inc.

2). KEY FACT:  People don't realize the full extent of what plastic
              can be recycled into.

3). CONSUMER PROBLEM:  Apathy. People don't seem to care
                       about recycling plastic in addition
                       to paper, aluminum, etc. People don't
                       recycle at all, due to lack of time,
                       energy, or unfamiliarity.

4). ADVERTISING GOAL:  To increase awareness of the importance
                       and benefits of recycling plastic.

5). PRINCIPAL COMPETITION:  Other forms of recycling: paper,
                            cans, clothes, etc.

6). TARGET MARKET:  All ages, classes, and life styles. Anyone who
                    is concerned about conservation and the depletion
                    of our land.

7). CREATIVE STRATEGY:  To use an unlikely object (plastic bottle)
                        as a character that will portray the benefits
                        of recycling plastic, in hopes of motivating
                        people  to take part in this cause.

8). REASON WHY:  Recycling is basically a boring subject. By using what
                 is to be recycled as a character, it will try to liven up
                 this worthy act of conservation.

GLOBAL RECYCLING INC.
MAG., FULL PAGE
"FFFFFT!!"
Cheryl Gault
23 November 1990

| | |
|---|---|
| HEAD: | THEY SAY CATS HAVE NINE LIVES? |
| PIC: | (A CAT WALKING BEHIND AN EMPTY PLASTIC BOTTLE) |
| HEAD: | I CAN BEAT THAT. |
| COPY: | Because when recycled, I can be used over and over. In so many interesting ways: flower pots, toys, carpets, and the list goes on.<br><br>As long as I'm recycled, my life is virtually **endless.** Much longer than, say, a cat's.<br><br>However, sometimes my life is shortened by someone who doesn't care if I live on. They don't understand how really **important** I am. Some think I'm nothing but plastic!<br><br>Sigh.<br><br>The truth is, there's more to me than meets the eye. So please. Let me live; again and again. |
| SLOGAN: | Give a bottle a break, recycle plastic. |
| SIG: | GLOBAL RECYCLING INC. |

GLOBAL RECYCLING INC.
NWSP., HALF PAGE B&W
"FUNNY FACE"
Cheryl Gault
23 November 1990

| | |
|---|---|
| HEAD: | NO RESPECT! |
| PIC: | (AN EMPTY PLASTIC MILK BOTTLE, WITH RODNEY DANGERFIELD'S FACE ON IT) |

COPY:

 I'm tellin' ya!
 Us plastic bottles get no respect. Everyone just uses us, then throws us away. Just like you would an old sock-YUK.
 But hey, we're not plastic! I mean, okay we're *plastic*, but we've got a real purpose here.
 Not like mother-in-laws. HA!
 **Recycle us**. Why? So we can be used as safety products, like helmets. So we can make kids smile, by becoming their toys.
 There's so much we can do, if given the chance. Show some respect.

SLOGAN:     Give a bottle a break, recycle plastic.

SIG:       GLOBAL RECYCLING INC.

GLOBAL RECYCLING INC.
OUTDOOR, 48' × 14' PAINTED
BULLETIN
"BRANCH OUT"
Cheryl Gault
23 November 1990

| | |
|---|---|
| HEAD: | THE BOTTLE WITH A MILLION FACES. |
| PIC: | (LARGE, EMPTY PLASTIC BOTTLE. TO THE LEFT OF THE BOTTLE IN A SMALLER DRAWING IS A PARK BENCH, AND A FLOWER POT. TO THE RIGHT OF THE BOTTLE IS A CAR, AND A MOTORCYCLE HELMET.) |
| SIG: | GLOBAL RECYCLING INC. |
| SLOGAN: | Give a bottle a break, recycle plastic. |

THE BOTTLE WITH A MILLION FACES

Give a bottle a break, recycle plastic.
GLOBAL RECYCLING INC.

GLOBAL RECYCLING INC.
:60 JINGLE
Cheryl Gault
23 November 1990
(tune of Yankee Doodle Dandee)


SONG:
(15 seconds)

I'M A LONELY PLASTIC BOTTLE,
WHO NEVER EVER GETS TO BE
RECYCLED WITH THE OTHER BAGS
AND CANS,
EVERYONE JUST IGNORES ME!
TOYS AND HELMETS, FLOWER POTS,
ARE ALL A LITTLE PART OF ME;


CHORUS:
(10 seconds)

R-E-C-Y-C-L-E, RECYCLE ME TODAY,
PLASTIC WILL GO A LONG, LONG WAY.


ANNC:
(15 seconds)

Hi, I'm your little plastic bottle, and I've got
something here to say.
I know I don't look like much, and although
I'm just plastic on the outside, there's
imagination and durability all over me!
And plenty to go around.
Auto parts, toys, tools, I could go on
forever! So take another look at me and
think about this:


TOYS AND HELMETS, FLOWER POTS,
ARE ALL A LITTLE PART OF ME;


CHORUS:
(10 seconds)

R-E-C-Y-C-L-E, RECYCLE ME TODAY,
PLASTIC WILL GO A LONG, LONG WAY!

GLOBAL RECYCLING INC.
:30 RADIO
"THE GINZU BOTTLE"
Cheryl Gault
23 November 1990

ANNC:                                    INTRODUCING!
                                         The remarkable, the incredible.
                                         The amazing, PLASTIC BOTTLE!
                                         Yes, the plastic bottle.
                                         It melts, it swelts, it changes form! It's cut up,
                                         it's sput up, but wait,
                                         there's more!
                                         If you recycle now, your plastic
                                         bottle will become a pipe, a toy,
                                         a fence post.
                                         SOMETHING USEFUL!
                                         Don't let this remarkable hunk of
                                         plastic go to waste.
                                         RECYCLE.
                                         Your kids will thank you for it, the
                                         world will love you for it, and
                                         now you can work on the house
                                         KNOWING your plastic has been
                                         put to good use. Over and over and
                                         over!
                                         Act now. Get in your car and deee-rive!
                                         It's not drastic, spastic, OR elastic.
                                         It's plastic!
                                         So give your bottle a break, and recycle
                                         plastic today.
                                         A message from Global Recycling, Inc.

Production Note: This spot is
to be read fast, and exaggerated.
Some words may have no actual
significance, but neither do the
Ginzu Knife commercials.

GLOBAL RECYCLING INC.
:30 TV
"PROMOTION"
Cheryl Gault
23 November 1990

<u>SIGHT</u>

<u>SOUND</u>

SFX: (MUSIC UP, UNDER THROUGHOUT)

1). OPEN ON LS
INTERIOR OF A
REFRIGERATOR.
ZOOM IN SLOWLY
TO MLS OF 1/2
EMPTY PLASTIC
BOTTLE OF MILK.

MB:  This is just a temporary job, you know.
I'm going places. I mean, I don't want
to be a milk bottle forever!

2). SLOW DISSOLVE
TO MS BIG WHEEL TOY.

If I'm lucky, I'll be recycled. Then I could
get a great job as a child's toy. Maybe
even a Big Wheel.

3). SLOW DISSOLVE TO
MS PARK BENCH.

Or I'll find work outdoors, in the open
air. I'll get to hear <u>all</u> the gossip as a
park bench.

4). SLOW DISSOLVE TO
MLS INTERIOR REFRIG.
ZOOM IN TO MCU PLASTIC
BOTTLE.

I <u>could</u> just keep this job and get a
transfer, but I want to travel. Oh, the
possibilities are endless. If only
humans knew all that I can do.

5). MCU HAND REACHING
FOR BOTTLE.

I hope I'm recycled!

6). DISSOLVE TO SUPER:

VO:  Give a bottle a break, and
recycle plastic.

<u>Give a bottle a break,
recycle plastic.</u>

SFX:  (MUSIC OUT)

Production note: MB represents Milk Bottle.

\* MB: – Milk Bottle

1)

MB. This is just a temporary job, you know. I'm going places. I mean, I don't want to be a milk bottle forever!

2)

If I'm lucky, I'll be recycled. Then I could get a great job as a child's toy. maybe even a Big Wheel.

3)

Or I'll find work outdoors, in the open air. I'll get to hear all the gossip as a park bench.

4)

I could just keep this job and get a transfer, but I want to travel. Oh, the possibilities are endless. If only humans knew all that I can do.

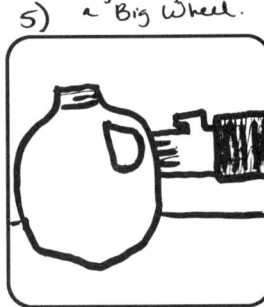

5)

I hope I'm recycled!

6)

Give a bottle a break, recycle plastic.

GLOBAL RECYCLING INC

VO: Give a bottle a break, recycle plastic.

SFX: (MUSIC OUT)